Shareholders' Agreements:
A Tax and Legal Guide
2nd Edition, 2004

Aird & Berlis LLP

Contributing Tax Partners:
Jack Bernstein, Stuart Bollefer, Henry Chong and Robert Martini

Contributing Corporate Partners:
Steven Kelman and Dennis Miller

CCH CANADIAN LIMITED
90 Sheppard Avenue East, Suite 300
Toronto, ON M2N 6X1
Telephone: (416) 224-2248 Toll Free: 1-800-268-4522
Fax: (416) 224-2243 Toll Free: 1-800-461-4131
www.cch.ca

A WoltersKluwer Company

"TaxWorks" is a registered trademark of CCH Canadian Limited.
The CCH Design is a registered trademark of CCH Incorporated.
"Linking professionals with knowledge" is a trademark owned by CCH Canadian Limited.

Published by CCH Canadian Limited

Important Disclaimer: This publication is sold with the understanding that (1) the authors and editors are not responsible for the results of any actions taken on the basis of information in this work, nor for any errors or omissions; and (2) the publisher is not engaged in rendering legal, accounting or other professional services. The publisher, and the authors and editors, expressly disclaim all and any liability to any person, whether a purchaser of this publication or not, in respect of anything and of the consequences of anything done or omitted to be done by any such person in reliance, whether whole or partial, upon the whole or any part of the contents of this publication. If legal advice or other expert assistance is required, the services of a competent professional person should be sought.

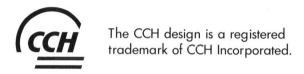

The CCH design is a registered trademark of CCH Incorporated.

Library and Archives Canada Cataloguing in Publication

Bernstein, Jack, 1952–
    Shareholder agreements : a tax and legal guide / Aird & Berlis LLP. — 2nd ed., 2004.

First ed. written by Jack Bernstein ; with legal precedents by Lawrence Chernin
Includes bibliographical references and index.
ISBN 1-55367-379-4

    1. Stock ownership — Law and legislation — Canada. 2 Taxation of bonds, securities, etc. — Canada. 3. Contracts — Canada. I. Aird & Berlis (Firm) II. Bernstein, Jack, 1952– . Shareholder agreements. III. Title.

KE1432.S43   2004   346.71'0666   C2004-903223-2
KF1448.S43   2004

© **2004, CCH Canadian Limited**

All rights reserved. No part of this work covered by the publisher's copyright may be reproduced or copied in any form or by any means (graphic, electronic or mechanical, including photocopying, recording, taping, or information and retrieval systems) without the written permission of the publisher.

A licence, however, is hereby given by the publisher:
  (a) to a lawyer to make a copy of any part of this publication to give to a judge or other presiding officer or to other parties in making legal submissions in judicial proceedings;
  (b) to a judge or other presiding officer to reproduce any part of this publication in any decision in judicial proceedings; or
  (c) to anyone to reproduce any part of this publication for the purposes of parliamentary proceedings.
"Judicial proceedings" includes proceedings before any court, tribunal or person having authority to decide any matter affecting a person's legal rights or liabilities.

Typeset by CCH Canadian Limited.
Printed in Canada.

PREFACE

One of the most common legal documents is a shareholders' agreement. Any corporation having more than one shareholder should have a shareholders' agreement which sets out the rights and responsibilities of the shareholders. It would provide for the manner in which corporate decisions are to be made, the protection of minority shareholders, operational and financial issues and the situations in which a shareholder may sell his shares. These agreements involve a host of commercial, legal and fiscal issues.

Changing tax laws have significantly affected the structuring of life insured buy-sell arrangements over the last few years. This book provides a practical, easy-to-read and comprehensive text on the business and tax considerations involved in structuring shareholders' agreements. It reviews the commercial issues in detail. The most recent tax changes and jurisprudence are considered and several innovative arrangements for the buy-out of a shareholder during his lifetime or on his death are discussed.

The book also includes a legal precedent for shareholders' agreements prepared by Aird & Berlis LLP.

The book should be a valuable tool for lawyers who draft agreements, accountants and other advisors who are asked to comment on agreements and for insurance agents who structure life insured buy/sell agreements.

Toronto   Jack Bernstein

TABLE OF CONTENTS

	Page
Preface	iii

		Paragraph
1	*General Contents of Shareholders' Agreements*	
	Introduction	105
	Contents of a Shareholders' Agreement	110
	Title	115
	Date	120
	Parties	125
	Recitals	130
	Consideration Clause	135
	Business of the Corporation	140
	Interpretive Provisions	145
	Organization and Management of the Company	150
	Financing	155
	Use of Surplus	160
	Share Capital	165
	Exit Provisions	170
	General Sale Provisions — *Inter Vivos* and *Post-Mortem* Buy-Outs	175
	Income Tax Implications of Buy-Sell Provisions	178
	Funding *Inter Vivos* and *Post-Mortem* Buy-Outs — Alternatives	180
2	*Tax Considerations — Inter Vivos Buy-outs*	
	Sale of Shares by Individual Shareholders	200
	Overview	205
	Qualified Small Business Corporation	210

	Paragraph
Tax Implications for Vendor	215
Sale of Shares by Holding Company	220
Tax Implications for Purchaser of Shares	225
Purchase for Cancellation or Redemption by Corporation	230
Shares Owned by an Individual	235
Shares Owned by Holding Company	240
Tax Implications for Remaining Shareholder	245
Staggered Redemption	250
Change of Control	255
Non-Compete Payment, Retiring Allowance or Consulting Fee	260
Non-Resident Vendor	265

3 Buy-Sell Agreements and Life Insurance

	Paragraph
Overview	300
Buy-Sell Agreements and Business Continuation Planning	305
Funding *Inter Vivos* and *Post-Mortem* Buy-Outs — Alternatives	310
Funding from Outside the Corporation	315
Funding from Within the Corporation	320
Insurance Funding	325
Types of Life Insurance	330
How Life Insurance Policies are Taxed	335
Insurance Planning Issues	340
The Exempt Test and Life Insurance	345
Transfers of Life Insurance Policies	350
Life Insurance and Share Valuation	355
Life Insurance as Collateral, Capital Dividend Account Planning, and Quebec Concerns	360
Non-Insurance Planning Issues	365
The Sole Shareholder	370
What about Partnerships?	375
Issues for Non-Resident Shareholders	380
Summary	385

4 Buy-Outs on Death

	Paragraph
Overview	400
Criss-Cross Insurance	405
Criss-Cross Insurance — Individual Shareholders	407
Criss-Cross Insurance — Holding Companies	409

	Paragraph
Deferred Sale Method	415
Deferred Sale — Individuals	420
Deferred Sale — Holding Companies	425
Corporate Share Repurchase	430
Corporate Share Repurchase — Individuals	435
Illustration	440
Stop Loss Rules	442
Tax Implications for the Survivor	444
Corporate Share Repurchase — Holding Companies	445
Combination Method	450
Corporate Partnerships	455
Conclusion	460

Appendices

1 *Shareholders' Agreement* 1000

2

Overview	2000
Classification of Corporations for Tax Purposes	2005
Arm's Length, Related Persons, Affiliated Persons and Associated Corporations Rules	2010

	Page
Index	185

ONE

GENERAL CONTENTS OF SHAREHOLDERS' AGREEMENTS

¶105
Introduction

In the absence of a shareholders' agreement, the relationship between shareholders of a corporation will generally be governed by the applicable corporate legislation under which the subject corporation was incorporated. For example, corporate legislation provides that the board of directors of a corporation is elected by a simple majority of the votes attaching to its issued and outstanding voting shares. These default rules will apply unless shareholders have entered into a contract that provides otherwise. It follows that, in the absence of a shareholders' agreement, minority shareholders are not entitled to representation on the board of directors. The importance of this is that directors are generally responsible for managing, or supervising the management of, the business and affairs of a corporation and, subject to certain statutory exceptions relating to minority shareholders' rights, minority shareholders may not be in a position to exert any meaningful influence on the management and direction of the corporation in which they hold a stake. The exercise of statutory minority shareholder rights generally requires litigation by the minority shareholder(s) (in respect of which outcomes are uncertain), significant expense and frequently involves or will result in acrimony between the shareholders.

Furthermore, because the articles of incorporation of most non-public corporations contain liquidity restrictions, a minority shareholder may not be in a position to sell his or her shares of the corporation to anyone, regardless of changing circumstances, without the consent of a majority of the directors or shareholders of the corporation.

Shareholders are therefore encouraged to enter into a shareholders' agreement — a contract by and between them which serves to alter their statutorily prescribed relationship in accordance with their expectations. A shareholders' agreement can thus serve to minimize disputes between shareholders with respect to, among other things, the management and administration of a corporation and provide for liquidity rights, by creating contractual rights, responsibilities and remedies which do not exist in corporate statutes.

This Chapter outlines the salient provisions that are normally dealt with in shareholders' agreements. A form of shareholders' agreement is included in this book as Appendix I and contains a number of the provisions discussed in this Chapter. However, it is important to note that there is no standard shareholders' agreement appropriate for all cases. While it is fair to say that the themes and concepts of shareholders' agreements tend to be somewhat consistent from case to case, the manner in which such contractual rights, responsibilities and remedies are combined, interact, and are drafted, will vary widely, depending upon the needs of the shareholders, the legislative context and a lawyer's drafting style.

Readers should be aware that the structure and content of a shareholders' agreement may be modified from what is discussed in this Chapter to reflect the chosen buy-sell structure agreed upon by the shareholders. Chapter 4 — Buy-Outs on Death — contains a detailed review of various buy-sell structures, and the impact of the chosen structure should be considered when the shareholders' agreement is being drafted.

In addition, this Chapter provides an introduction to the key income tax issues that affect shareholders' agreements when a shareholder's interest in a corporation is purchased by another shareholder. The tax planning issues are different for buy-outs during a shareholder's lifetime (*inter vivos* buy-outs) and those that occur after a shareholder's death (*post-mortem* buy-outs).

The closing sub-section of this Chapter reviews some of the principal funding options that may be used by shareholders on a buy-out.

¶110
Contents of a Shareholders' Agreement

The discussion set forth below deals with the contents of a shareholders' agreement in the order in which they might typically appear and provides references to the relevant legislative provisions applicable to the operation of corporations and shareholdings. This Chapter concludes with a brief discussion of the tax implications of various buy-sell provisions and the applicability of general anti-avoidance tax rules.

¶115 Title

The title of an agreement has no legal importance. It merely denotes formality and can serve as a quick way to identify whether the subject shareholders' agreement is a unanimous shareholders' agreement. As discussed in the section "Organization and Management of the Company" below, unanimous shareholders' agreements are different from other shareholders' agreements in that all of the shareholders of the corporation are parties, and because such agreements may circumscribe, in whole or in part, the powers of the board of directors of the corporation.

¶120 Date

The execution and delivery of a shareholders' agreement can have an impact on the tax status of a corporation. For example, entering into a shareholders' agreement can provide a shareholder with *de facto* control or, depending on the nature of the rights or options contained in the shareholders' agreement, *de jure* control over the corporation effective as of the date of execution of the agreement, despite the fact that such shareholder does not own a majority of the issued and outstanding voting securities of the corporation and, if such controlling shareholder is not a Canadian resident, a corporation's status as a Canadian Controlled Private Corporation (CCPC) may be lost, together with certain tax advantages enjoyed by CCPCs. Shareholders should thus consider the relevance of this to their decision to enter into a shareholders' agreement.

¶125 Parties

The parties to a shareholders' agreement should be described in such a manner as to completely identify them. While the correct and full legal identity of a party may not be required in order to create a valid, binding and legally enforceable agreement, there are practical reasons to sufficiently identify the parties, including facilitation of notices pursuant to the agreement and the conduct of searches of public records in relation to the parties (such as bankruptcy and personal property registries).

More important than the description of the parties, however, is the choice of parties, as this will determine who has the ability to commence proceedings, and against whom proceedings may be commenced, to enforce the agreement. Since this is a contract, the rule of privity applies and only the parties to the shareholders' agreement can enforce the agreement or be subject to its terms.

In addition, the correct choice of parties is necessary in order to ensure that a shareholders' agreement has its intended effect by obviating the indirect circumvention of its provisions. For example, shareholders' agreements will typically provide restrictions on the ability of a shareholder to transfer his or her shares. The controlling shareholder of a corporate shareholder (Holdco) that is a party to a shareholders' agreement which contains liquidity restrictions can circumvent those restrictions by merely selling the shares of Holdco. Therefore, it would be important to make the controlling shareholder of Holdco a party to the shareholders' agreement and to procure appropriate covenants from such party with respect to the disposition of shares of Holdco in order to ensure that an indirect transfer of the interest held by Holdco does not take place through a sale of the shares of Holdco by its shareholder(s). Thus, shareholders' agreements frequently include as parties persons who are not shareholders.

Parties to a shareholders' agreement might include all (if the agreement is to be a unanimous shareholders' agreement) or some of the shareholders of the corporation, as well as the individual or controlling shareholders of corporate shareholders. If there is a possibility that spouses of individual shareholders may come to have an entitlement to own shares of the corporation as a result of divorce proceedings or death and the shareholders' agreement provides a contractual arrangement which contemplates a waiver of such rights, then it may be advisable to add the spouses as parties to the agreement and ensure that they receive independent legal advice in connection therewith. In this regard, please refer to the discussion below regarding matrimonial property concerns. The corporation itself should be added as a party to all unanimous shareholders' agreements if the provisions of any shareholders' agreement are intended to be enforceable against it. If the shareholders' agreement contains buy-out provisions which contemplate payment for the purchased shares over a period of time pursuant to a promissory note and there is security granted for such payment obligations by way of a share pledge, the parties might consider adding as a party the trustee (escrow agent) holding such pledged shares pending full payment of the promissory note. As the examples discussed above illustrate, it is important for shareholders to ensure that they have achieved privity of contract with the appropriate parties in the event that they need to enforce their rights under the agreement.

¶130   Recitals

Recitals to an agreement do not have any legal effect, but they set an interpretive context for the binding provisions of the agreement which follow. Recitals may thus become decisive if a dispute arises under the agreement and an adjudicator, such as a judge or arbitrator, is called upon by the parties to interpret seemingly ambiguous provisions in the agreement. Sometimes the main body of a shareholders' agreement will contain an acknowledgment by the parties with respect to the facts set out in the recitals in order to preclude any future debate as to their truth or accuracy.

¶135   Consideration Clause

One of the elements to the formation of a binding and enforceable contract is consideration (i.e., often thought of as "value") and a shareholders' agreement which contains a clause which makes it clear that there was consideration is therefore less likely to be challenged on the basis that it is not enforceable for lack of consideration.

¶140   Business of the Corporation

The business or undertaking of the corporation may be briefly described, especially if the shareholders wish to mandate the continuation of the same business activity of the corporation without material change.

¶145   Interpretive Provisions

It is common to find basic interpretive provisions in most contracts. Though often regarded as mere "boilerplate," these provisions can become very important and should not be underestimated. For example, shareholders' agreements sometimes contain provisions which are inconsistent with the contents of corporate by-laws. In the absence of an interpretive clause which identifies the paramountcy of one document over the other, shareholders may find themselves in a quandary.

¶150   Organization and Management of the Company

Most corporate legislation in Canada, including the *Business Corporations Act* (Ontario)[1] (the OBCA) and the *Canada Business Corporations Act*[2] (the CBCA), provides that the directors of a corporation determine the manner in which the affairs of the corporation will be conducted. As stewards of corporations, directors owe fiduciary duties and certain statutory liabilities are imposed upon them. This statutory framework may be altered by an agreement amongst all of the shareholders of a corporation, referred to as a unanimous shareholders' agreement under the OBCA and the CBCA. Such legislation contemplates that a unanimous shareholders' agreement may, in whole or in part, restrict the powers of the directors of a corporation to manage its business and affairs. It is important to note that both the OBCA (subsection 108(5)) and the CBCA (subsection 146(5)) stipulate that shareholders who restrict the powers of the directors of a corporation to manage the business and affairs of the corporation assume all of the rights, powers, duties and liabilities of such directors and the directors are relieved of such rights, powers, duties and liabilities to the same extent. By contrast, an "ordinary" shareholders' agreement is merely an agreement amongst shareholders as to how, among other things, each of them will exercise their voting rights and cannot circumscribe the discretion of the directors to manage the affairs of a corporation. The law is not entirely clear on the extent to which unanimous shareholders agreements operate to excuse directors from their statutory liabilities. It is also not always clear which of the liabilities that are ordinarily incumbent upon directors are assumed by shareholders by virtue of entering into a unanimous shareholders agreement. Careful drafting may alleviate ambiguity in this regard. These concerns may be of little practical significance in many cases because shareholders are often directors as well, especially in the case of closely-held corporations. However, shareholders who intend to enter into a unanimous shareholders agreement should be aware of the risk of potential liability which goes hand in hand with the performance of the functions which are normally reserved for directors.

The array of potential organizational and management matters that may be dealt with in a unanimous shareholders' agreement is extremely broad and the precise contents of a particular unanimous shareholders' agreement will ultimately be determined by the business deal of the constituent shareholders. The OBCA and the CBCA specifically contemplate that unanimous shareholders' agreements may:

1. Provide "supermajority" approval requirements by directors or shareholders (CBCA subsection 6(3)).
2. Restrict or remove the duty and power of the directors to:
    a. issue shares (CBCA subsection 25(1));

---

[1] S.O. 1982, c. 4.
[2] S.C. 1974-75-76, c. 33.

b. declare dividends (OBCA subsection 38(1));

c. manage the business and affairs of the corporation (CBCA subsection 102(1));

d. pass by-laws (CBCA subsection 6(3));

e. appoint and remove officers (CBCA section 121);

f. borrow money (CBCA subsections 189(1) and (2)); and

g. fix the remuneration of the directors, officers and employees (CBCA section 125).

3. Require additional financial reporting to the shareholders (CBCA paragraph 155(1)(c)).

4. Provide circumstances in which the corporation should be dissolved (CBCA subparagraph 214(1)(b)(i)).

5. Provide shareholders with pre-emptive rights (OBCA section 26).

6. Provide procedures at shareholders' meetings (OBCA section 97).

A well-conceived shareholders' agreement which details the parties' expectations will minimize the potential for conflict which might ensue amongst the shareholders with respect to the organization and management of a corporation. As noted above, the matters that may be addressed in a shareholders' agreement are numerous. While they do not tend to be exhaustive, most professional advisors can provide shareholders with fulsome checklists which can serve as a framework for the discussions and negotiations amongst shareholders in connection with the entering into of a shareholders' agreement. Some of the matters which should be thoughtfully considered by shareholders with respect to the organization and management of a corporation are set out below.

Board Composition

In the absence of an agreement to the contrary, the number (subject to the articles of incorporation and the statutory residency requirements) and identity of the directors of a corporation are elected by a simple majority of the votes attaching to all of the issued and outstanding voting shares. Parties to a unanimous shareholders' agreement can alter that statutory regime by agreeing on the number of directors, the identity of the directors, the rights of the shareholders to nominate directors, the procedure for replacing directors who have resigned or who are no longer able to serve in such capacity due to death, disability or bankruptcy and the establishment of committees of the board of directors and the powers to be delegated thereto.

Officers

Unless the shareholders have agreed otherwise, the board of directors of a corporation have the power to appoint corporate officers. A unanimous shareholders' agreement can stipulate the names of the current officers, their respective positions and terms of office.

Meetings of Directors and Shareholders

Detailed procedures with respect to the conduct of meetings of directors and shareholders are set forth in corporate legislation, such as the OBCA and the CBCA. The articles of incorporation and by-laws of a corporation typically contain additional meeting procedures. Generally, caution must be exercised in drafting shareholders' agreements to ensure that their contents can be reconciled with any conflicting procedures set forth in the relevant corporate legislation, articles of incorporation and by-laws of the corporation. Subject to certain statutory limitations, some of the matters that shareholders may wish to address in their shareholders' agreement include:

1. The quorum requirements for meetings.
2. Whether the Chairperson of the meeting will have a deciding or casting vote and whether each director or shareholder will have one vote on each matter.
3. The percentage of votes required for approvals of decisions.
4. Who may requisition meetings and under what circumstances.
5. The procedures for providing notice of meetings.
6. Other regulations with respect to the conduct of meetings.

Protection of Shareholders

The power to chart a corporation's course of business and to make certain decisions with respect to the issuance of securities and the declaration of dividends and other distributions generally resides in the board of directors of a corporation. Certain other decision-making powers are specifically reserved to the shareholders, based on statutorily prescribed levels of approval. For example, certain fundamental changes to a corporation require the approval of 66 $^{2}/_{3}$ per cent of the votes attaching to all of the issued and outstanding voting shares of a corporation and still other changes permit shareholders to vote separately as a class, regardless of whether their shares have voting rights.

Minority shareholders may wish to protect their interests in a corporation, deviating from the statutory framework by imposing a requirement for unanimous (or some other supermajority) consent of the directors or shareholders of a corporation to some or all of the following matters noted below:

1. The declaration of dividends (including stock dividends).
2. Material change in the business of the corporation.
3. The issuance or sale by the corporation of its own shares and the grant of stock options or other securities convertible into shares.
4. The redemption or other purchase by the corporation of its own shares.
5. Changes in the authorized capital of the corporation.
6. The sale, lease, exchange or other disposition of all or substantially all of the assets of the corporation.

¶150

7. The repayment of shareholder loans.
8. Advances to shareholders or the securing of debts of other companies or persons by the corporation.
9. The encumbering of any assets of the corporation.
10. The winding-up, reorganization or dissolution of the company.
11. The hiring or termination of any key employees of the corporation.
12. The fixing, paying or changing of any salary, bonus or fee to any such key employee, officer, director or shareholder.
13. The authorization and filing of articles of amendment.
14. Any change in the corporation's accountants or auditors.
15. Any change in the corporation's fiscal year-end.
16. The purchase and sale of any real or immovable property by the corporation.
17. The payment of bonuses by the corporation.
18. The entering into of any contracts outside the corporation's ordinary course of business.
19. The transfer of any shares or other securities of the corporation.
20. The purchase by the corporation of securities of other companies.
21. The entering into by the corporation of any partnership or joint venture.
22. The entering into of contracts between the corporation and any person, firm or company not dealing at arm's length with the shareholders or any payments to such persons.
23. Subject to the articles of incorporation, any increase or decrease in the number of directors.
24. Any change in jurisdiction of incorporation (continuance).
25. The amendment, repeal and enactment of corporate by-laws.

Employment

It is not uncommon to include the terms of employment of one or more shareholders (or in the case of a corporate shareholder, its principal) in a shareholders' agreement, especially if one or more of the shareholders' contribution to the corporation is expected to be wholly or partly in the nature of "sweat equity," with the result that they are actively involved in the day-to-day operations of the business of the corporation, and the contributions of the other shareholders are in the nature of monetary consideration such that their involvement with the corporation will be that of passive investors. The terms and conditions of employment of one or more of the shareholders can also be dealt with in separate employment agreements. It is important to consider whether the cessation of such employment for any reason (e.g. death, disability, retirement, or dismissal with or without cause) will have consequences to a shareholder's share ownership in the form of mandatory or optional share

¶150

General Contents of Shareholders' Agreements 9

purchases by the other shareholders, a share redemption by the corporation or the ability of the departing employee/shareholder to force either event to occur. All of the salient terms of employment should be detailed in the shareholders' agreement, including a description of the duties and title of the employee-shareholder, the duration of the engagement if not indefinite, provisions relating to termination of such employment and the entitlement, if any, to notice or pay in lieu of notice in the event that such employment is terminated without just cause.

Restrictive Covenants

All or some of the shareholders may have access to proprietary information of the corporation such as trade secrets, customer lists, pricing formulae, know-how and other information which is essential to the corporation's competitive market position, especially if such shareholders are also directors, officers or employees of the corporation. Therefore, shareholders should consider whether the inclusion of certain restrictive covenants in the shareholders' agreement is appropriate. Such restrictive covenants might include covenants to maintain confidentiality with respect to proprietary information, not to solicit employees or customers of the corporation and not to compete with the business of the corporation, in each case for such reasonable period of time following the date on which a shareholder ceases to be a shareholder of the corporation as is necessary for the corporation to protect its goodwill. Caution should be had in drafting such covenants to ensure that they are reasonable and appropriate in the circumstances. Excessive covenants may be ruled unenforceable by the courts.

Execution of Documents and Instruments

Signing authorities are frequently addressed in a corporation's by-laws, but can also be addressed in a unanimous shareholders' agreement if the parties wish. Provisions with respect to the execution of instruments in writing would specify which shareholders, directors or officers (or any combination of them) are permitted to sign cheques in excess of a specified dollar amount, material contracts, promissory notes, mortgages and other evidences of indebtedness on behalf of the corporation. Note, however, that any breach of such signing provisions may give rise to contractual remedies as between the parties to the shareholders' agreement, but may not have the effect of relieving the corporation of its obligations under such instruments if any contracting third parties did not have notice of the requisite authority and the person signing on behalf of the corporation had apparent authority to act on behalf of and bind the corporation.

Books, Records and Financial Statements

Corporate statutes such as the OBCA and the CBCA require corporations to keep proper books and corporate records at the registered office of the corporation or such other place as is determined by the directors of the corporation. Shareholders generally have the statutory right to inspect such books and records at any time during normal business hours. In the absence of

¶150

an agreement (or consent) to the contrary, all non-offering or "private" corporations are required to conduct an annual financial audit and to present such audited financial statements to the shareholders annually at a meeting of shareholders held within six months of the corporation's financial year end. Furthermore, shareholders have the statutory right to appoint the auditors of the corporation's financial statements and to fix their remuneration. A unanimous shareholders' agreement may therefore designate where the books and records of the corporation are to be kept, identify who the auditors or accountants of the corporation shall be, indicate whether the corporation shall be exempt from the annual audit requirement and specify the nature and frequency of financial reporting to the shareholders.

¶155   Financing

In addition to identifying the bank or banks to be used by the corporation from time to time and the manner for making such determination, shareholders' agreements often contain provisions which reflect the parties' expectations with respect to operational financial matters in varying degrees of detail. More importantly, a shareholders' agreement should set out the mechanics for determining how, when and where additional funds required by the corporation will be obtained. If, for example, debt is not available to the corporation on commercially acceptable terms, then a shareholders' agreement might provide that additional funds may or will be provided by way of a loan or share subscription from the shareholders, either on a proportionate basis or in accordance with some other pre-determined formula.

A shareholders' agreement may provide that additional capital contributions are to be made by subscriptions for shares of the corporation or, alternatively, that such contributions shall be reflected as shareholder loans. Loans have an advantage over share subscriptions in that the lender ranks ahead of shareholders and if security has been granted by the corporation in respect of such shareholder loans, then the lenders will rank ahead of unsecured creditors of the corporation. If shareholder loans are to be utilized, the shareholders' agreement should specify whether or not such loans will bear interest and, if applicable, the rate of interest. A shareholders' agreement may also set out in advance other salient terms of any shareholder advances, including the nature and ranking of the security interest to be granted to the shareholder by the corporation in respect of such loan, the timing and source of funds for repayment of each shareholder loan, the rights of the shareholders to demand repayment, the rights of the corporation to pre-pay such loans, and whether dividends can be declared by the directors (subject to statutory solvency requirements) prior to the repayment of outstanding shareholder loans.

A shareholders' agreement should also set out the consequences in the event that any of the shareholders fail to contribute their proportionate share of the capital required to finance the ongoing operations of the corporation. Numerous options are available in this regard, but they all tend to have a punitive or dilutive impact on any shareholder who does not participate in the subsequent financing event. For example, the other shareholders may be given the option of advancing funds by way of a loan to the corporation on such shareholder's behalf. Such an advance would be interest-bearing, normally at a relatively higher rate of interest than prime, as a disincentive to the other shareholders not to make a proportionate contribution. Another possibility is that the shareholders' agreement can provide for a mandatory sale of the shares of the defaulting shareholder if the default continues after a prescribed period of time.

A shareholders' agreement should also contemplate the treatment of shareholder guarantees in respect of indebtedness of the corporation. It is not uncommon for financial institutions to require shareholders of a corporation to provide personal guarantees in respect of loans made to a corporation, especially if the corporation is in the early stages of business development or if the asset-based security which is otherwise available is perceived by such lender not to be sufficient for its purposes. A shareholders' agreement might therefore provide that each shareholder shall provide guarantees in proportion to its respective share ownership and, if guarantees are required to be given by shareholders on a joint and several basis (as opposed to a several basis), then a shareholder who is required to honour a guarantee for more than his, her or its proportionate interest in the corporation should be indemnified by the other shareholders.

¶160 Use of Surplus

The corollary to determining how future capital requirements will be met is the determination of the corporation's policy with respect to the distribution of surplus and the order of priority in respect thereof. Parties to a shareholders' agreement may therefore wish to determine in advance the relative priorities of distributions of surpluses with respect to the repayment of bank indebtedness and, subject to the articles of incorporation and statutory requirements, the redemption of preferred shares, repayment of shareholder loans and the declaration of dividends.

¶165 Share Capital

Authorized Capital

The authorized share capital of the corporation will be set forth in the articles of incorporation. However, the key elements of a shareholders' agreement are the provisions which restrict the liquidity of the issued capital of the corporation and otherwise prescribe how shareholders may deal with their shares and address the circumstances under which the corporation may issue more shares. Shareholders' agreements may also contain agreements amongst shareholders with respect to the treatment of certain attributes of share ownership, such as voting rights.

Share Certificates

Shareholders' agreements which contain liquidity restrictions should provide that certificates evidencing shares of the corporation will be stamped with a legend indicating that such shares are subject to a shareholders' agreement. Note that certain corporate legislation, such as the CBCA, deems a purchaser or transferee of shares which are subject to a unanimous shareholders' agreement to be a party to such agreement. However, the CBCA also provides that a purchaser or transferee of shares which are subject to a unanimous shareholders' agreement who has not had notice of the existence of such agreement may rescind the transaction pursuant to which they acquired such shares within 30 days of the date on which they become aware of the existence of the agreement; the OBCA does not contain similar provisions.

Both the CBCA and the OBCA provide that, if share certificates are issued, ownership of the shares represented by such certificates cannot be transferred without delivery of the share certificate, duly endorsed for transfer to the transferee. All too frequently share certificates which are delivered to shareholders are lost, stolen or destroyed and, in some cases, it is difficult to locate shareholders who own shares (such as former employees of the corporation). In order to facilitate a disposition of shares, a shareholders' agreement can provide that share certificates, endorsed in blank for transfer, are to be kept with the minute books of the corporation at the corporation's registered office or such other location as the directors of the corporation designate, or with a designated escrow agent or trustee.

General Liquidity Restriction

In terms of liquidity restrictions, shareholders' agreements usually provide that the parties may not sell, encumber or otherwise dispose of their shares or any interest therein without the prior consent of all or some of the other shareholders or the directors of the corporation, or otherwise in accordance with the terms of the agreement. As noted above under the heading "Parties," in circumstances where shareholders are corporations, the shareholders' agreement should contain restrictions on the change of control or issuance of shares of such corporate shareholders to non-family members in order to preclude the possibility of indirect dispositions of shares.

Permitted Transferees

Shareholders' agreements frequently contain special provisions to facilitate tax planning which permit share transfers to "permitted transferees," such as family holding companies, trusts or family members, provided that the new shareholder agrees to be bound by the agreement and provided that the existing shareholder continues to be principally liable for all obligations under the agreement. A transfer of shares to a holding company may be completed in a manner which does not trigger a taxable event, assuming that required tax elections are made under section 85 of the *Income Tax Act* (Canada)[3] (the Act) and, where applicable, the equivalent provision in the *Taxation Act* (Quebec)[4] and the shares issued by the holding company are structured so as not to confer a benefit on related shareholders[5].

---

[3] R.S.C. 1985 c. 1 (5th Supp.) as amended.

[4] R.S.Q. I-3 as amended.

[5] Interpretation Bulletin IT-291R3, Transfer of property to a corporation under subsection 89(1), dated January 12, 2004.

Applicable Matrimonial Property Laws[6]

Shareholders' agreements may attempt to anticipate the potential effects of applicable matrimonial property laws in order to ensure that spouses of shareholders do not become unintended shareholders of the corporation or parties to the agreement.

The definition of "spouse" and who may be entitled to a division of assets or income support on the breakdown of a marital or cohabiting relationship of some permanence has changed significantly since the mid-1990s and continues to do so. It is essential, therefore, that the drafter of a shareholders' agreement be aware of the ongoing evolution in this area of law and be prepared to adapt the provisions of any precedents on a periodic basis. In addition, the entitlement to a division of assets on breakdown of a marital or cohabiting relationship of some permanence may be addressed in a marriage contract, cohabitation agreement, domestic contract or other similar arrangement that is binding on both parties. Therefore, the drafter of the shareholders' agreement should be aware of the provisions of any such agreement or arrangements that may affect the rights of a spouse or cohabitant.

For example, if executives of the corporation own shares, then their spouses could agree in writing that such shares are not to be included in any calculation of the division of assets under the relevant provincial/territorial legislation. Alternatively, the non-shareholder spouse may be asked to agree in writing that any order obtained under the governing matrimonial property legislation or the federal *Divorce Act* will not be satisfied with the shares of the corporation. In such circumstances, the subject spouses should be parties to the agreement, should each obtain independent legal advice, and care should be taken to ensure that there is compliance with the formal requirements of the governing matrimonial property legislation. Another option available to shareholders is to provide a call right (discussed below) to either or both of the corporation and the other shareholders in respect of any shares which become the subject of matrimonial property proceedings.

If, on the other hand, spouses are shareholders, then: (a) the other spouse may wish to have the first right and option to purchase the shares on death or on breakdown of the relationship, in which case the shareholders' agreement should provide a formula for determining the purchase price, and, on breakdown of the relationship, for the settlement of outstanding loans to and from the spouse, for resignation of the spouse as an officer and director of the corporation and for the release of the spouse from any guarantees in favour of

---

[6] The authors of this text practice law in Ontario. Thus, any comments about specific matrimonial property legislation in this Chapter and others will refer to the *Family Law Act*, R.S.O. 1990, c. F.3, as amended (the "FLA"). Readers in other jurisdictions should review the provisions of the relevant matrimonial property regime when drafting, reviewing, revising, or commenting upon, a shareholders' agreement. In addition, consideration may have to be given to any orders issued under the *Divorce Act*, RCS, 1985, c. 3 (2nd Supp.).

For convenience, we are using the terms "spouse," "spouses," and "spousal" to refer to all marital or cohabiting relationships of some permanence, whether the relationship is between members of the same or the opposite sex. This terminology does not necessarily accord with that used in matrimonial property legislation across Canada, so readers should be aware of this discrepancy.

¶165

the corporation, and (b) if a spouse who is active in the business dies, withdraws, or retires, then the other spouse should be required to sell the shares to the other shareholders.

Changes in Issued Capital

Shareholders' agreements should attempt to address the effects of changes in the ownership structure of a corporation which may result from the issuance of additional shares or other securities in the future. A new or an amended shareholders' agreement may become necessary or appropriate to address such changes in ownership structure, especially in circumstances in which shares are issued to third parties; this has to be addressed on a case-by-case basis. For example, changes in proportionate shareholdings or the introduction of new shareholders may necessitate a change in the manner in which major decisions affecting the corporation are made. If the parties wish, they can include contractual rights in a shareholders' agreement through which they can preserve their proportionate ownership interests. A pre-emptive right, for example, is a contractual mechanism which provides existing shareholders with the right (but not the obligation) to participate on a *pro rata* basis in future share issuances by the corporation. This will permit interested shareholders to preserve their proportionate ownership position, provided, however, that if a shareholder declines to exercise his or her pre-emptive right then the corporation is free to proceed with the share offering and such shareholder's ownership position will be diluted. Similarly, with respect to the repurchase of shares for cancellation by a corporation, a shareholders' agreement can provide that, except as otherwise provided, all share redemptions, purchases for cancellation and other reductions of issued capital will be made proportionally, or will require the approval of all of the shareholders or of holders of a designated percentage of the issued and outstanding shares of the corporation.

¶170 Exit Provisions

Shareholders' agreements which restrict liquidity will also normally prescribe in detail the circumstances under which a shareholder may dispose of all or part of his or her shares. Customary exit provisions include: rights of first refusal, matching bid provisions, buy-sell clauses (also sometimes referred to as "shotgun" or "Russian roulette" clauses) and variations thereof, puts, calls, mandatory sale events, tag-along rights (also sometimes referred to as "piggyback" rights) and drag-along rights. Each of these exit mechanisms is described briefly in the pages which follow. A well-conceived and properly drafted shareholders' agreement will unambiguously detail the procedures relating to how and when these rights come into play and how they interact with each other in order to ensure that they are workable. Related matters of valuation and payment in the event that exit rights are exercised are discussed later under the headings "Valuation" and "General Sale Provisions," respectively.

Rights of First Refusal

A right of first refusal (also known as a right of first offer) is a prohibition against a sale of previously issued shares to a third party without first offering

General Contents of Shareholders' Agreements

to sell the shares to the other shareholders on the same terms and conditions. As with the other rights discussed below, a right of first refusal can be tailored to fit any particular circumstance. For example, if a child of a shareholder is active in the business, the shareholder parent may wish to reserve the right to sell or give his shares to his child without first offering the shares to the other shareholders. Even though rights of first refusal can be tailored to fit many different circumstances, shareholders have to consider whether it is appropriate to include such rights in a shareholders' agreement. Rights of first refusal may not be appropriate, for example, in circumstances where some shareholders are passive in relation to business operations while other shareholders are actively running the business of the corporation. In such circumstances, the passive shareholders may not want to grant rights to the active shareholders to exit from the business without them, and so an outright prohibition on transfer or a provision of "piggy-back rights" (discussed below) may be more appropriate.

There are two basic varieties of rights of first refusal, colloquially referred to as "hard" and "soft" rights of first refusal. A "hard" right of first refusal is the sort of right which provides that a shareholder who has received a *bona fide* offer from an arm's length purchaser (and, of course, such shareholder wishes to accept such offer) must first deliver notice to the other shareholders detailing the terms of the third party offer. The other shareholders receiving such notice would have the right to purchase all, but not less than all, of the shares offered on the same terms and conditions of the proposed sale on a proportionate basis, or as they might otherwise agree. By comparison, a "soft" right of first refusal will provide that a shareholder who wishes to seek out a purchaser for his or her shares must first deliver a notice to the other shareholders offering to sell all, but not less than all, of such shares to them on a proportionate basis on specific terms.

Practically speaking, it is not unreasonable to suggest that "hard" rights of first refusal are less likely to be exercised than "soft" rights of first refusal because of the reluctance an arm's length purchaser will likely have to submit an offer to purchase, subject to a "hard" right.

In either case, if the other shareholders do not exercise the right to purchase the shares offered to them, the offering shareholder is typically permitted to sell his or her shares to the arm's length purchaser (in the case of the "hard" right) or to seek out a third party purchaser to purchase his or her shares on the same terms set out in the right of first refusal notice (in the case of a "soft" right) for a prescribed period of time and, if a transaction of purchase and sale is not completed within such prescribed period of time, the right of first refusal is thereafter revived and the process must begin again.

Any purchaser of shares should be required to become a party to the agreement. Under the statutory provisions of the OBCA and the CBCA, such purchaser would be automatically deemed to be a party to a unanimous shareholders' agreement if such purchaser had actual notice of its existence (i.e., through a legend on a share certificate).

¶170

Mandatory Buy-Sell Clauses and Variations Thereof

Mandatory buy-sell arrangements, which are often referred to as "shotgun" or, less often, "Russian roulette" clauses, tend to attract a lot of controversy because they present a potentially coercive method of divorcing shareholders from each other. Further, mandatory buy-sell clauses can be difficult to negotiate and implement because of underlying tensions which can result from the divergent interests of various types of shareholders. The purpose of a mandatory buy-sell clause is to provide a liquidity option, absent which the only remedies available to the shareholders to extricate themselves from each other might be an oppression remedy application or a court ordered liquidation, both of which can involve costly litigation and uncertain outcomes.

Mandatory buy-sell clauses are typically used in circumstances in which there are only two shareholders, but they can be adapted for use in multi-party circumstances. However, these clauses tend to work best in situations in which there are only two shareholders because the addition of more participants to the buy-sell scheme increases the range of possible outcomes in the event that such right is triggered or otherwise exercised; many shareholders would not feel comfortable with the degree of uncertainty presented by a multi-party mandatory buy-sell clause in that there is less predictability with respect to the outcome of the mandatory buy-out of shares in any given case.

In short, pursuant to a buy-sell clause, a shareholder wishing to trigger the mandatory buy-sell provision would send a notice to the other shareholder(s) indicating his or her desire to purchase all of the shares of the other shareholder(s). The shareholders' agreement might provide that the mandatory buy-sell right may be exercised at any time or that it may only be exercised upon the occurrence of a triggering event, such as a deadlock with respect to a major decision affecting the corporation. The notice would set out the purchase price for such shares and possibly the terms and conditions of the transaction of purchase and sale (typically the shareholders' agreement sets out most of the terms and conditions in advance).

The shareholder receiving the mandatory buy-sell notice has only two choices: (1) agree to sell his or her shares to the offering shareholder on the terms set out in the notice; or (2) purchase the shares of the offering shareholder on those very same terms. In either case, the exercise of a mandatory buy-sell clause will result in one shareholder selling shares and the other shareholder purchasing shares. The determination of the buyer and seller, as the case may be, and the perceived fairness of the transaction of purchase and sale may be influenced by numerous factors, such as the relative financial resources available to the parties and the relative importance of the respective shareholders to the ongoing operation of the business.

Therefore, if shareholders have disproportionate shareholdings or disproportionate wealth, care must be exercised in structuring these provisions in order to ensure that one shareholder is not unduly prejudiced. For example, if one shareholder is a multi-millionaire and the other shareholder has no substantial net worth, then it might be unfair to require the latter to match the terms and conditions of any offer made by the former since sufficient financing on commercially acceptable terms may not be available to the shareholder who has less financial resources. In such a situation, it may be advisable for the shareholders' agreement to provide for a prolonged term for payment on the triggering of a shotgun clause. Even still, buy-sell clauses may operate unfairly against parties of limited means.

There can be many variations of the standard mandatory buy-sell clause described above which can be used to implement a shareholder divorce. One such variation within the same theme is a forced auction, in which all of the shareholders are required to sell their shares to the highest bidder at a private auction attended only by shareholders. One of the major drawbacks to this variation is the concern that the bidding process can inflate the price to be paid for the shares of the corporation. This method may be preferable where a shareholder wishes to retain share ownership and is therefore concerned about initiating the shotgun clause. Another variation might involve a "butterfly" scheme pursuant to which the assets of a corporation are splitup amongst shareholders, which can be particularly useful in the context of a corporation which holds real estate or has distinct operating divisions with little or no overlap.

Puts, Calls and Mandatory Sale Events

Generally, puts and calls are unilateral options or rights to purchase and sell shares. A put right is an option exercisable by a shareholder to require another party (usually the corporation or another shareholder or group of shareholders) to purchase his or her shares; a put right is thus an option to sell. A call right is an option exercisable by someone other than the shareholder (usually the corporation or another shareholder) to require the shareholder to sell his or her shares to such person; a call right is thus an option to purchase. A shareholders' agreement may provide that puts or calls can be exercised at any time or only upon the occurrence of specified triggering events.

Puts and calls can be used as a mechanism to deal with the changing circumstances of shareholders, especially where such change in circumstance is fundamental to the relationship between shareholders and affects the basis for their original agreement. Certain changes in the circumstances of the shareholders may be presented in the shareholders' agreement as "triggering" events. Depending on the nature of the specific event and whether a shareholder is at fault for causing such event, a shareholders' agreement may provide that the event gives rise to a put or call right, as the case may be, or a mandatory sale event. Some common examples of changes in circumstances which shareholders may prescribe as triggering events for puts, calls or mandatory sales include:

- death;
- insolvency;
- breach of the shareholders' agreement;
- temporary or permanent disability;
- cessation of employment as a result of retirement, termination without just cause or termination with just cause;

¶170

- special circumstances, such as loss of professional certification; and
- matrimonial property claims.

Puts, calls, and/or mandatory sale events may be structured to give rise to sales between shareholders or the corporation.

Valuation in the Context of Puts, Calls and Mandatory Sale Events

A crucial and often difficult aspect associated with negotiating put and call rights and mandatory sale events pertains to the price or the method of determining the price to be paid for the shares to be sold. The complexities associated with valuation do not arise in the context of other types of sales, such as sale events resulting from the exercise of a buy-sell clause (in which case the initiating shareholder sets the value) or a sale initiated as a result of an offer from a third party, such as a drag-along, right of first refusal or matching bid (in which case the third party sets the value). The discussion that follows relates to the valuation of common or other "fully-participating" shares. A modified approach would be required if the corporation's share capital includes preferred shares.

A shareholders' agreement can deal with the manner in which shares to be sold pursuant to puts, calls and/or mandatory sale events are valued in a number of different ways. For example, shareholders' agreements often provide that the parties will annually negotiate the value of the issued shares of the corporation, which value shall be listed on a schedule to the agreement and agreed by all of the parties. The revaluation can coincide with the issuance of the annual financial statements of the corporation. In theory, this alternative is attractive because the shareholders who are involved in and who are knowledgeable about the business ascribe a value to the shares of the corporation. Furthermore, shareholders who negotiate value from time to time can avoid the expense associated with valuation by a third party business valuator. The practical drawbacks of this approach are that shareholders often neglect to revaluate the business from time to time, with the result that the negotiated valuation can become dated, and the fact that events can occur between valuations which may have a material effect on the value ascribed to the shares of the corporation. Another concern is that minority shareholders may not have the same negotiating power or knowledge of the business and may be pressured into accepting the value set by the controlling shareholders.

A shareholders' agreement could also provide for an alternative method of valuing the issued and outstanding shares of the corporation in the event that the annual valuation schedule is not updated within a specified period of time following the corporation's financial year-end or if material changes occur between valuations such that the previously determined share price is no longer reflective of real value. In that case, the value of the issued and outstanding shares may be determined by a qualified independent business valuator or accountant, based upon book value, adjusted book value, fair market value, or any combination of the foregoing. Alternatively, such value could be determined based on a pre-determined formula, such as a multiple of earnings.

¶170

A book value determination, typically performed by an accountant based on generally accepted accounting principles, may be appropriate for a corporation that holds non-appreciating portfolio investments and where the book value of the corporation's goodwill appropriately reflects its "real" value. Simply put, it would represent the retained earnings and shareholders' equity. It would likely not reflect the "real" goodwill associated with the business, the appreciation of assets (such as real estate or liquid securities), and would not consider the value of refundable dividend tax on hand or loss carry-forwards.

An adjusted book value calculation may be more appropriate in the context of a business carried on by a corporation which has a significant goodwill component and/or appreciating assets. An adjusted book value calculation reflects a combination of the book value and fair market value approaches. Under this approach, the value of the shares will be based upon (i) a book value determination of the corporation's assets other than goodwill and specified appreciating assets (typically done by an accountant) and (ii) a fair market appraisal of goodwill and other appreciating assets (typically done by a business valuator).

Fair market value is generally defined as the highest price obtainable in an open and unrestricted market from an informed arm's length purchaser and, in this context, will typically be determined by a business valuator. In determining fair market value, a valuator can apply a premium for a controlling block of shares or a discount for a minority interest. A valuator can also have regard to other events affecting the corporation, such as the death or disability of a shareholder or the receipt of life or disability insurance proceeds in such circumstances. The valuation provisions of a shareholders' agreement should provide precise direction to a valuator to ensure that the intentions of the parties relating to the manner in which fair market value is to be determined are accurately reflected.

When a corporation owns cash value or term life insurance on the lives of one or more shareholders or key employees, the valuation process may become more complicated. In general, a term life insurance policy is deemed to have a nil value by Canada Customs and Revenue Agency (the "CRA")[7]. In contrast, the value of a cash value policy can vary a great deal, depending on the type of cash value insurance that is owned, the terms of the insurance contract, how long the contract has been in force, whether a portion of the policy's values has been borrowed by the policy owner or is being used to fund premium payments, or whether the policy has been collaterally assigned to a third party as part of a loan arrangement[8].

From the perspective of the CRA, the value of a life insurance policy can be affected by the age, life expectancy and health of the person whose life is insured. In Interpretation Bulletin IT-416R3, the CRA has stated that the value of a life insurance policy, when valuing shares on the death of a shareholder, may be up to the face value of the insurance policy if the insured individual was

---

[7] Although not enacted at the time of writing, legislation is in the works to change the Agency's name to Canada Revenue Agency. The Agency is currently referring to itself in this fashion.

[8] Chapter 3 — Life Insured Corporate Buy-Sell Arrangements contains a discussion of term and cash value life insurance, including how a policy's cash surrender value is determined.

¶170

in poor health prior to the date of death[9]. This may affect a valuation undertaken because of the death of a shareholder.

The advantage of a formula-based approach to valuation is that it will save the fees of a professional appraisal. The formula should deal with specific adjustments, including whether management bonuses are to be added back if the business is to be valued based on a multiple of earnings or whether consideration should be given to the impact on the business of the loss of the services of the departing shareholder and the treatment of redundant assets.

Some of the valuation problems which may occur on the death of a shareholder are outlined under the heading "Overview of Tax on Death" below.

Tag-Along or Piggyback Rights

Tag-along provisions generally require a majority shareholder who wishes to sell his or her shares to a third party to procure an offer from such third party to purchase the shares of all of the other shareholders on the same terms if such minority shareholders so desire, failing which the majority shareholder may not sell his or her shares at all. Tag-along provisions can also be structured to provide that minority shareholders can sell their shares to a third party offeror on a *pro rata* basis along with the majority shareholders. The minority shareholders of the corporation are thus able to "piggyback" on the offer received by the majority shareholders. Tag-along rights are generally crucial to minority shareholders in circumstances in which the majority shareholder plays a fundamental role in relation to the business and operations of the corporation and without whom the value of the business of the corporation would be seriously undermined.

Drag-Along or Carry-Along Rights and Matching Bid Provisions

Drag-along rights are the corollary of tag-along rights in that they generally empower a majority shareholder who has received a third party offer to purchase all of the issued and outstanding shares of a corporation to require all of the other minority shareholders to sell their respective shares to such third party on the terms set out in such third party offer.

Matching bid provisions generally provide that where a majority shareholder receives a third party offer to purchase all of the issued and outstanding shares of the corporation, the minority shareholder(s) will have the option to either purchase the shares of the majority shareholder on the same terms as are set forth in the third party offer or, alternatively, sell his or her shares to the third party on such terms and conditions.

Drag-along rights and matching bid provisions are crucial rights usually afforded to majority shareholders, as they are a fundamental means of providing majority shareholders with liquidity. Drag-along rights give majority shareholders the ability to negotiate with third parties, subject to other rights contained in the shareholders' agreement, with respect to a sale of all of the

---

[9] The taxation issues involving corporate-owned life insurance will be dealt with in depth in Chapter 3 — Life Insured Corporate Buy-Sell Arrangements.

¶170

issued and outstanding shares in the capital of the corporation. Similarly, matching bid provisions provide majority shareholders with the assurance of liquidity in the sense that they will have the right to either sell all of the issued and outstanding shares in the capital of the corporation to a third party, or they will be able to require the other shareholders to purchase their shares on the same terms. In each case, these rights provide majority shareholders with a liquidity alternative.

¶175
General Sale Provisions — *Inter Vivos* and *Post-Mortem* Buy-Outs

Below is a brief discussion regarding the mechanics for completing transactions of purchase and sale which might be triggered by any of the sale events discussed above. In the event that any of the rights discussed above are exercised, the terms and conditions of sale should be detailed in a shareholders' agreement, including where and when the transaction is to be completed, what deliveries are to be made at the time of closing, how and when the purchase price is to be paid and satisfied, and all such related matters.

Shareholders should consider whether the pre-determined general sale provisions shall apply in all circumstances, or only in relation to certain sale events. For example, shareholders may specify that the pre-determined general sale provisions only apply with respect to transactions of purchase and sale amongst the shareholders resulting from the exercise of puts, calls, mandatory sale events, and buy-sell clauses and not in relation to transactions of purchase and sale which result from the exercise of rights of first refusal, tag-along rights, drag-along rights and matching bids which would all be predicated on a third party offer. The pre-determined general sale provisions contained in a shareholders' agreement are likely to be consistent with the terms and conditions of purchase and sale which are contained in such third party offer and it may not be possible to negotiate consistent terms that are commercially acceptable to such third party.

Time and Place of Closing

A shareholders' agreement should provide a mechanism for choosing a time and place for completing the sale of shares.

Term

The timing specified for the payment of the purchase price may vary depending upon a number of factors, including: the quantum of the purchase price, the financial resources available to the parties and the circumstances triggering the sale of the shares. For example, a shorter period may be appropriate in circumstances in which the purchasing shareholder has immediate access to significant financial resources or where the triggering event did not involve "fault" on the part of the selling shareholder (such as disability or termination of employment without just cause). Payment over a longer period of time may be appropriate in the case of a sale event triggered by employment which is terminated for just cause, insolvency, or breach of the shareholders' agreement. The parties should consider funding options, such as various insurance products. For example, some life insurance companies sell disability buy-out insurance which provides for the payment of a lump sum under the policy upon the permanent disability of an insured. In any event, the shareholders' agreement must specify how and when the purchase price is to be paid and satisfied.

Promissory Notes and Security

It is not uncommon for shareholders' agreements to provide that the purchase price shall be paid and satisfied in whole or in part on the date of closing by way of a promissory note. In such circumstances, the shareholders' agreement should prescribe all of the salient terms of such an instrument, such as the term of the note, the applicable interest rate, the frequency of payment, whether the note is to be secured, remedies in the event of default of payment or another default, restrictions on the business of the corporation while amounts remain payable under such promissory note, prepayment privileges, extensions of time for payment (i.e., a second buy-out is triggered prior to the payment of the purchase price, such as a buy-out triggered by the death, disability or retirement of a second shareholder prior to payment in full for the shares of the first shareholder which places too onerous a financial burden on the remaining shareholders) and so forth.

If it is known in advance that all or a portion of the purchase price is to be paid over time, the parties to a shareholders' agreement should be clear on whether such deferred obligations will be secured. Common forms of security which may be set out in advance in a shareholders' agreement include share pledges, personal guarantees, mortgages or debentures of the corporation or other charges on assets, or any combination of the foregoing.

Quick Flip Protection and Acceleration

The shareholders' agreement can provide protection for a shareholder who is forced to sell his or her shares pursuant to a buy-sell clause or a call option in the event that the remaining shareholders enter into another transaction of purchase and sale with a third party within a specified period of time on substantially more favourable terms through appropriate purchase price adjustment and payment acceleration provisions.

Shareholder Loans

All loans by the corporation to the selling shareholder and vice versa should be settled on closing. For example, the purchasing shareholders may assume a loan owing by the selling shareholder to the corporation in partial satisfaction of the purchase price. Note that forgiven loans may result in an income inclusion for the debtor.

¶175

Closing Deliveries

The general sale provisions contained in a shareholders' agreement should set out clearly the deliveries which are required to be made by each party at the time of closing the transaction of purchase and sale. Among other things, the vendor will be required to deliver good title to the shares to the purchaser and, if share certificates have been issued, then the OBCA and CBCA provide that the vendor must deliver such share certificates duly endorsed for transfer to the purchaser. In order to avoid a selling shareholder frustrating the transaction of purchase and sale through non-delivery of a share certificate (whether intentionally or not), shareholders should consider providing that share certificates will be endorsed in blank for transfer and deposited with an escrow agent at their time of issue. Many shareholders' agreements purport to grant irrevocable powers of attorney in favour of an officer of the corporation to make closing deliveries and sign instruments on their behalf at a closing.

Additional closing deliveries which may be required at the time of closing might include: (1) specific indemnities for tax matters, such as interest, penalties and possible legal and accounting fees which may arise as a result of a reassessment of the corporation by the CRA or any other tax authority for a fiscal period during which the vendor was a shareholder; (2) resignations of officers, employees and/or directors of the corporation; (3) the vendor and the purchaser(s) may release each other from any liability for past actions excluding obligations arising from the transaction of purchase and sale; (4) if appropriate restrictive covenants are not already contained in the shareholders' agreement, then it may be prudent to have the withdrawing shareholder enter into reasonable restrictive covenants with respect to confidentiality, non-competition and non-solicitation in order to protect the goodwill of the business as a condition to the completion of the transaction of purchase and sale; and (5) certificates issued pursuant to section 116[10] in order to deal with the purchaser's statutory withholding tax obligations in the event that the selling shareholder is a non-resident of Canada[11].

¶178

Income Tax Implications of Buy-Sell Provisions

The buy-sell provisions of shareholders' agreements can have varying income tax consequences for the selling and purchasing shareholders. Key considerations are the relationship of the parties with one another, the buy-sell structure that is used, the timing of the purchase or sale of shares, and the chosen funding vehicle that is to be used. (The tax implications of the most common buy-sell structures will be addressed in full in Chapter 2 — Tax Considerations — *Inter Vivos* Buy-outs).

---

[10] Information Circular IC 72-17R4, Procedures concerning the disposition of taxable Canadian property by non-residents of Canada — Section 116, dated April 24, 1992.

[11] Unless otherwise indicated, all statutory references are to the *Income Tax Act* (Canada) (the "Act").

Thus, it is essential that shareholders and their advisors appreciate various "relationship" provisions contained in the Act as they affect the tax consequences of buy-sell provisions in a shareholders' agreement. The three categories are related persons in section 251, affiliated persons in section 251.1, and associated corporations in section 256[12]. Each category determines differently the nature of the relationship for tax purposes between individuals and corporations. These categories apply to both *inter vivos* and *post-mortem* transfers of shares between shareholders or their estates[13].

As noted previously, many private corporations in Canada are owned by family members. In recognition of this, paragraph 251(2)(*a*) provides that individuals who are related to one another by blood, adoption, marriage or common-law partnership are related and subsection 251(1) provides that related persons are automatically considered not to deal with one another at arm's length for income tax purposes[14].

Paragraph 251(2)(*b*) provides that the term "related persons" also includes a corporation and the person who controls it, as well as corporations controlled by a common group of shareholders or persons related to such corporations.

The category of "affiliated persons" is delineated in section 251.1, which was added by the 1995-1997 technical bill as part of the so-called "pregnant stop-loss" anti-avoidance rules. This section must be considered whenever a buy-sell arrangement utilizes the redemption of shares as a mechanism whereby ownership and control of the corporation are transferred between shareholders. In addition, planners and drafters should be aware of the effect that section 256, which contains the associated corporation rules, may have on proposed shareholders' agreements that contain buy-sell provisions[15].

---

[12] Interpretation Bulletin IT-64R4, Corporations: Association and control, dated August 14, 2001.

[13] Appendix 2 deals with these concepts in greater detail. What follows is a breif summary.

[14] Interpretation Bulletin IT-419R, Meaning of arm's length, dated August 24, 1995. It should be noted that the definition of related persons will likely be amended in the wake of the June 10, 2003 decision of the Ontario Court of Appeal in *Halpern v. Canada (Attorney General)*, (2003-06-10) ONCA C39172; C39174, which found that the federal definition of "marriage" was unconstitutional. On June 17, 2003, the Federal Government announced that it did not intend to appeal the May 1, 2003 decision of the British Columbia Court of Appeal in *Barbeau v. British Columbia (Attorney General)*, 2003bcca251, Docket(s): CA029017; CA029048; CA029017, which had reached the same conclusion. The Federal Government also announced that it will be preparing draft legislation to rectify this matter. Readers should, therefore, consider the current wording of section 251 as amended from time to time to ensure that planning for related persons issues is up to date.

[15] The association rule contained in section 256 is relevant for several purposes. The rules were primarily introduced to force Canadian controlled private corporations to share the pool of income subject to the low rate of business tax applicable to "active business" income available both at the federal and provincial level. In order to avoid the multiplication of several pools within family or commonly controlled groups, the association rules require a single pool to be shared among "associated" corporations. The association rules are also used for other purposes including requiring sharing the $2,000,000 expenditure limit for investment tax credits: subsection 127(10.2)–(10.4), the refundable tax credit provisions in subsection 127.1(2), extended final tax payment deadlines where associated corporations' taxable income do not exceed $200,000: subclause 157(1)(*b*)(i)(D)(II), Large Corporation Capital Tax deduction in subsection 181.5(7), and associated corporations which share dividend allowance for Part VI.I tax in subsections 191.1(2)–(4).

¶178

Under the related persons and associated corporation rules set out in sections 251 and 256, a person will be regarded as the owner of shares which he or she has a contractual right to acquire or to cause the corporation to redeem or cancel otherwise than on death, permanent disability or bankruptcy. In addition, where a person has the right to cause a corporation to redeem or cancel shares otherwise than on death, permanent disability or bankruptcy, those shares are deemed to have been acquired by the corporation, with the result that a relationship or association is established between the parties. Neither a right of first refusal nor a shotgun buy-sell arrangement appear to offend this rule, at least in the context of the association rules[16], but the impact on any other companies owned by the shareholders should be considered where the shareholders' agreement provides for a mandatory sale otherwise than by death, bankruptcy or permanent disability (e.g. on retirement or breach of agreement).

Shareholders' agreements can also affect the status of whether a company is a Canadian controlled private corporation, since paragraph 251(5)(*b*) applies for this purpose. Although not clear from a strictly legal perspective, the CRA is of the view that, generally speaking, a shotgun buy-sell or first refusal arrangement between non-resident and Canadian shareholders should not deem the non-resident persons to control the corporation through the *de jure* control test in the context of Canadian-controlled private corporations on the basis that the right of first refusal or buy-sell provision is simply a right to receive a right[17].

Obviously, loss of CCPC status can have significant tax implications including loss of availability of the low business rate available to CCPCs, loss of the $500,000 capital gains exemption available to qualified shares of small business corporations (which requires CCPC status as a condition precedent) and other incidental benefits such as losing status as a small business corporation rendering capital losses on shares or debt of Canadian corporations ineligible for treatment as allowable business investment losses (one-half of which are available as a deduction against other income).

Once the complex web of rules in the Act governing the relationship between shareholders has been navigated, the next step is to examine the proposed buy-sell arrangement to determine what the tax consequences will be for the vendor and the purchaser. When an individual shareholder still has part or all of the $500,000 lifetime capital gains exemption available, the selling shareholder will likely prefer a buy-sell structure that deals with the sale of shares owned by that individual. In contrast, if the exemption is no longer available, the purchasing shareholder may prefer to consider a buy-sell arrangement that calls for the redemption or purchase for cancellation of shares. In other cases, a hybrid buy-sell arrangement that permits a combination of share purchase and share redemption may be the most appropriate option as it

---

[16] See Interpretation Bulletin, IT 64R2, Corporations: Association and Control and specific release. See the CRA's View in document 9214367, in which the CRA confirmed that paragraph 251(5)(*b*) does not apply to a "right of first refusal" and does not usually apply to a shotgun arrangement. Note however that the parties must already be shareholders.

[17] See IT-419R at paragraph 13.

permits the shareholders and their advisors to determine the final structure based on the tax circumstances of the vendor and purchaser at the time of the transaction.

The last over-arching tax issue that shareholders and their advisors must be aware of when discussing the buy-sell provisions of a shareholders' agreement is the general anti-avoidance rule, or GAAR. The potential application of GAAR to a buy-sell arrangement may result in a finding that the arrangement is an avoidance transaction and, therefore, an abuse or misuse under section 245[18].

According to subsection 245(3), an avoidance transaction is any transaction that directly or indirectly results in a reduction, avoidance or deferral of tax on other amounts payable under the Act or an increase in a refund of tax unless the transaction may reasonably be considered to have been undertaken or arranged primarily for *bona fide* purposes other than to obtain the tax benefit.

The Federal Court of Appeal in *OSFC Holdings Ltd. v. The Queen*[19] determined that, when applying GAAR to a tax plan or structure, the first task of the CRA or a judge hearing the court case is to determine whether there is a tax benefit. The second step is to consider whether the tax benefit results from a transaction that is an avoidance transaction or from a series of transactions that includes an avoidance transaction.

Since most shareholders' agreements have non-tax as well as tax purposes, GAAR should not be a critical concern; however, where the proposed transaction has both *bona fide* non-tax purposes and tax avoidance components, shareholders and their advisors must determine the primary purpose of the transaction. If the primary purpose of a transaction can properly be considered to be a non-tax purpose, then GAAR is not to be applied.

Even if a transaction is an avoidance transaction, subsection 245(4) provides that GAAR does not apply to a transaction where it may reasonably be considered that the transaction would not result directly or indirectly in a misuse of the provisions or an abuse when the Act is read as a whole. In a recent decision of the Federal Court of Appeal, *Canadian Pacific Ltd. v. The Queen*, 2002 DTC 6742, the court outlined the steps to be taken in analyzing whether or not section 245 applies to a given set of facts:

> The first step is to determine whether or not the taxpayer has received a tax benefit as a result of the transaction or series of transactions. If a tax benefit has been received, it is next necessary to consider whether there has been an avoidance transaction within the meaning of subsection 245(3). Once it is determined that there is such a tax benefit, any transaction that is part of the series may be found to be an avoidance transaction. If the primary purpose of the transaction or of any transactions in a series is to obtain the tax benefit, then it is an avoidance transaction. This test is an objective one and therefore the focus must be on the relevant facts and circumstances and not on state-

---

[18] Information Circular IC 88-2, General anti-avoidance rule — Section 245 of the *Income Tax Act*, dated October 21, 1988.

[19] 2001 FCA 260, 2001 D.T.C. 5471, [2001] 4 C.T.C. 82, 17 B.L.R. (3d) 212, 275 N.R. 238, 29 C.B.R. (4th) 105, [2001] F.C.J. No. 1381, [2002] 2 F.C. 288.

¶178

ments as to the intention by the taxpayer. The primary purpose is a question of fact and is to be determined at the time the transaction in question was undertaken. It is not a hindsight assessment to be made on the basis of facts and circumstances that occurred after the transactions were undertaken. Justice Rothstein [speaking for the majority in *OSFC Holdings Ltd. v. The Queen*, 2001 DTC 5471 (F.C.A.)] said at paragraph 58:

> As a final observation, I would stress that the primary purpose of a transaction will be determined on the facts of each case. In particular, a comparison of the amount of the estimated tax benefit to the estimated business earnings may not be determinative, especially where the estimates are close. Further, the nature of the business aspect of the transaction must be carefully considered. The business purpose being primary cannot be ruled out simply because the tax benefit is significant.
>
> If a transaction or series of transactions creates a tax benefit and the primary purpose of any one of those transactions is to obtain a tax benefit, then there was an avoidance transaction. Once it has been established that an avoidance transaction occurred, subsection 245(4) must be considered. This involves determining whether it may reasonably be considered that any of the avoidance transactions or the series of transactions would result in a misuse of a specific provision or provisions of the Act. If so, the tax benefit resulting from the series will be denied. If there is no misuse, then it is still necessary to determine whether it may reasonably be considered that any of the avoidance transactions or the series of transactions would result in an abuse, having regard to the provisions of the Act other than section 245, read as a whole. If such an abuse is found, the tax benefit resulting from the series will be denied.

In *OSFC Holdings*, Justice Rothstein cautioned that, notwithstanding his finding in that case that the avoidance transactions had resulted in an abuse of the provisions other than GAAR read as a whole,

> It is important to note that there is no general rule against structuring transactions in a tax effective manner or a requirement that transactions be structured in a manner that maximizes tax. (Para. 117.)

Justice Rothstein further held that, where there has been strict compliance with the Act, a tax benefit can only be denied, on the grounds that the avoidance transaction constitutes a misuse or abuse, if the relevant policy contained in the Act is clear and unambiguous.

Consequently, there are two main defences to an application of GAAR. The first defence is to establish that the transaction was undertaken primarily for *bona fide* purposes other than to obtain a tax benefit. If the first defence cannot be established, the second defence is to establish that, even if the transaction is an "avoidance transaction," it does not result in a misuse of any specific provision or an abuse of the provisions read as a whole; that is, the results flowing from the transaction are within the object and spirit, in the sense that the results obtained are appropriate and are contemplated by the Act and its specific provisions.

However, if GAAR is found to apply to a fact situation or case, the following tax consequences may apply:

¶178

- Any deduction (whether in computing income, taxable income earned in Canada or tax payable) may be wholly or partially disallowed[20];
- A deduction may be allocated to a different taxpayer[21];
- The nature of a payment or an amount may be re-characterized[22]; and
- The tax effect that would otherwise result may be ignored[23].

If the application of GAAR results in double tax, Revenue Canada may make adjustments to eliminate the double tax. Otherwise, there is an appeal procedure which taxpayers may take advantage of in subsection 245(6).

¶180 Funding *Inter Vivos* and *Post-Mortem* Buy-outs — Alternatives

The following section of this Chapter reviews some of the alternatives that shareholders may consider when planning to fund a buy-sell arrangement. The timing of the sale may be affected by the chosen funding vehicle. Finally, Chapter 3 deals with the various buy-sell arrangements that shareholders may use when life insurance is used as the funding vehicle.

Cash on Hand

In very limited instances, the purchasing shareholder may have sufficient cash on hand personally to finance the share purchase. As this is a rare occurrence, other funding options are usually used by shareholders.

Bank Financing Obtained by the Purchasing Shareholder Personally

The purchasing shareholder may negotiate a bank loan for the purchase price. The related interest expense may be deductible under paragraph 20(1)(*c*); however, the purchasing shareholder should always discuss this issue with his or her tax advisor prior to taking out the loan. It should be noted that the successful use of this option may be affected by the purchaser's personal credit worthiness at the time of the share purchase. It will be contingent on financial and economic issues that may be beyond the control of the purchasing shareholder. Thus, reliance on this funding method may result in a purchaser not being able to obtain the requisite funds when the buy-out provisions of the shareholders' agreement are triggered.

Bank Financing Obtained by a Corporate Purchaser

A corporation may agree to borrow funds in order to finance the redemption of shares or, where the buy-sell arrangement involves holding companies, the purchaser corporation may acquire the shares of the selling shareholder. However, this option may be rendered ineffective if, at the time the buy-sell

---

[20] See paragraph 245(5)(*a*).
[21] See paragraph 245(5)(*b*).
[22] See paragraph 245(5)(*c*).
[23] See paragraph 245(5)(*d*).

arrangement is triggered, the purchaser company is insolvent or lacks the requisite credit standing to qualify for a commercial loan. It should be noted that, under corporate legislation, a redemption or purchase of shares for cancellation may not be legally possible if a company is insolvent[24]. In addition, shareholders who are considering this option should ensure that the conditions for interest deductibility are met[25].

Instalment Payments over a Period of Time

The vendor may be used as a source of financing where the vendor agrees to be paid over a number of years. The vendor would be able to defer tax on capital gains over a period of up to five years by claiming a reserve in the prescribed manner (see paragraph 40(1)(a) and Interpretation Bulletins IT-426 and IT-236R4)[26]. The vendor would expect to receive interest on the outstanding balance of the purchase price and adequate security to ensure that the purchase price and interest would be paid.

An alternative to instalment payments over time may be to undertake a reorganization of the share capital of the corporation, pursuant to section 86, in order to convert the common shares held by the vendor into fixed value preference shares which would be retractable over time pursuant to a schedule. Cumulative dividends may be paid on the outstanding shares. A taxable dividend would arise to the extent that the redemption price exceeded the paid-up capital of the shares. A capital gain may also arise to the extent that the proceeds (net of the dividend) exceed the adjusted cost base of the shares. If the shares are held by a holding company and the deemed dividend exceeds the holding company's proportional share of the operating company's post-1971 retained tax earnings, the excess may be treated as a capital gain rather than a dividend[27].

Earn-outs

The vendor may agree to be paid out of the future profits of the company. The vendor may sell his shares and receive a minimal amount on closing (perhaps equal to the book value of the shares). The balance of the purchase price may be computed as a percentage of gross or net profit over a period of years.

---

[24] For example, see the *Business Corporations Act* (Ontario), S.O. 1982, c. 4, s. 38(3) and *Canada Business Corporations Act*, S.C. 1974-75-76, c. 33, s. 34.

[25] To the extent that borrowed money used to redeem shares does not exceed the paid-up capital of the redeemed shares plus the accumulated profits of the corporation, as determined in accordance with generally accepted accounting principles, the interest expense on the borrowed money will be deductible. See Interpretation Bulletin IT-533, Interest deductibility and related issues, dated October 21, 2003, at paragraph 23, but note legislative changes proposed for 2005 and subsequent years contained in the Department of Finance News Release dated October 31, 2003 limiting deductibility of any expenses where it is not reasonable to expect that the taxpayer will realize a cumulative profit from the business or property.

[26] A ten-year reserve is available on the sale of shares of a small business corporation by a parent to children or grandchildren: subsection 40(1.1).

[27] See section 55.

¶180

Interpretation Bulletin IT-426 sets out the position of the CRA with respect to the taxation of an earn-out. Although paragraph 12(1)(g) could apply to include in income all payments under an earn-out in the vendor's income[28], the CRA will accept the cost recovery method (i.e., recover cost on a tax-free basis out of first payments) of reporting a gain or loss where the following conditions are met:

(a) the parties must deal at arm's length[29];

(b) the gain or loss must be of a capital nature;

(c) the earn-out feature must relate to the goodwill element of the purchase price which cannot reasonably be expected to be agreed upon at the date of the sale;

(d) the duration of the sale agreement cannot exceed five years so that no part of the capital gain can be deferred beyond five years; and

(e) in the year of sale, the vendor should submit with his tax return a copy of the sale agreement as well as a letter requesting the cost recovery method.

The amounts that become determinable under the earn-out formula are treated as capital gains. The cost recovery method would enable the vendor to report the determinable capital gain over a period of five years. The capital gains reserve will be available for the portion of the capital gain not due until after the end of the year. The reserve will be limited to 4/5 of the determined capital gain in the year of sale, 3/5 of the determined gain in the second year, and so on.

Reverse Earn-out

In situations where the cost recovery method is not available or is not desirable, it may still be possible to structure the transaction as an earn-out, setting a sale price of the shares and a maximum amount equivalent to the fair market value of the shares at the time of the sale, but which can be subsequently decreased if certain conditions related to sales, production or use are not met in the future. Such a structure, known as a reverse earn-out, will be treated by the CRA as being on account of capital "if there is a reasonable expectation at the time of disposition of the property that the conditions will be met, ... if subsequently, the conditions are not met then an appropriate adjustment will be made in the year in which the amount of the reduction and the sale price is known with certainty and will not vary in the future. Whether there is a reasonable expectation that conditions will be met is a question that is determined on the facts of the particular situation."[30]

---

[28] Interpretation Bulletin IT-462, Payments based on production or use, dated October 27, 1980.

[29] A planning consideration for drafters and other advisors is that all or most of the shareholders of many private corporations in Canada are family members, who are related to one another by birth, adoption or marriage/common-law partnership. Thus, this condition may be a crucial limitation in the ability of shareholders to use this buy-sell structure successfully. Readers are referred to the earlier discussion on related persons in this Chapter.

[30] See paragraph 9 of Interpretation Bulletin IT-462.

Minimizing the Value of the Company Prior to the Buy-out of a Shareholder by Annually Distributing the After-tax Profits

This arrangement is particularly attractive where the shares of the operating company are held by holding companies, each of which owns more than 10% of the voting and equity shares of the operating company or which are part of a related group which controls such a company. Such dividends would not normally be taxable to the holding companies. If the corporation requires the funds, they may be loaned back to the corporation and possibly be secured by corporate assets. This approach has the added benefit of protecting corporate profits from unsecured creditors. It may make the company more attractive as a purchaser would not be required to purchase redundant assets.

Utilizing the Retained Earnings of the Corporation to Fund the Purchase

This may be accomplished by causing the operating company to purchase for cancellation the shares held by the vendor. On a purchase for cancellation of shares, the interest expense relating to the redemption proceeds in excess of the paid-up capital should not be deductible, based on the CRA's stated position with respect to this issue[31].

Using Holding Companies

Holding companies can be used to facilitate the sale or purchase of the shares of individual shareholders, in addition to being an effective corporate planning structure. For example, the shares of an operating company may be owned by two or more holding companies, each of which is owned by an individual. One buy-sell structure involves the sale of the holding company shares owned by Shareholder A to the holding company owned by Shareholder B. This structure may result in adverse tax consequences under the provision of section 84.1[32] if Shareholder A and Shareholder B are individuals who do not deal with one another at arm's length. Another holding company structure involves having the holding company owned by Shareholder B purchase the operating company from the holding company owned by Shareholder A. The advantage of using holding companies is that the purchase price paid to the selling shareholder can effectively be funded by the operating company's existing and future earnings, allowing the purchasing shareholder to avoid having to pay the purchase price from another source. The various buy-sell arrangements using holding companies will be reviewed in Chapter 2 — *Inter Vivos* Buy-outs and Chapter 4 — Buy-outs on Death.

Sinking Fund Financing

The corporation or the shareholders may annually set aside funds as a reserve to finance the purchase of shares on the retirement (or death) of a

---

[31] See footnote 20 above.

[32] Also referred to as the "surplus stripping rules." This section will be more thoroughly discussed in Chapter 2 — Tax Considerations — *Inter Vivos* Buy-outs. See Interpretation Bulletin IT-489R, Non-arm's length sale of shares to a corporation, dated February 28, 1994.

shareholder. The investment of the funds annually set aside would create a "sinking fund" that would ultimately be used to fund the share purchase. The sinking fund option requires regular valuation of the shares of the corporation in order to ensure that the amounts being set aside are sufficient, with growth over time, to fully fund the buy-out. A significant danger of a sinking fund arrangement is that a shareholder may retire unexpectedly (or die prematurely) — at a time when inadequate funds have been set aside in the sinking fund.

In addition, the fund set aside by an individual would be considered "personal" assets and could be exposed to claims by creditors, including a claim by a spouse or former spouse under the pertinent matrimonial property legislation. Monies held in a sinking fund inside a corporation are subject to the claims of the corporation's creditors and may also be considered to be a "passive asset" of the corporation, which could cause problems for shareholders wishing to claim the $500,000 lifetime capital gains exemption for shares of a private corporation.

Disability Insurance Funding

Shareholders may opt to acquire lump-sum disability buy-out insurance to finance the purchase of shares on the permanent disability of a shareholder. The purchase of buy-out disability insurance for this purpose hinges on each shareholder being able to qualify for the disability coverage. It should also be noted that, depending on the age and health of the covered shareholders, the cost of the insurance coverage may be prohibitive. Consideration should be given to whether the insurance proceeds should be included in any valuation of the corporation for the purposes of determining the purchase price. It is essential, when using disability insurance coverage to fund the buy-out, that the definition of disability in the agreement dovetails with the definitions contained in the insurance policy.

Shareholder agreements can also provide for self-funded disability payments. For example, an agreement may provide for a disability payout by the operating company on an annual basis to a shareholder who meets the defined condition of disability in accordance with the agreement. If the payment is to be made over a reasonable period of time in a reasonable amount, the payment should be a deductible expense to the corporation. The recipient of the disability payment would include the amount as ordinary income. Although not necessarily tax effective to the recipient, it does ensure a contractually enforceable source of cash flow to the disabled shareholder. Alternatively, such disability obligation could be funded with corporate owned disability insurance.

Using Cash Values within a Life Insurance Policy

When a corporation owns cash-value life insurance on the lives of its shareholders, it is possible to access those values by way of a policy owner loan during the lifetime of the insured shareholder. Depending on the cash values that have accrued inside the life insurance policy, there may be enough to either fully or partially fund the share purchase when a shareholder retires or otherwise disposes of his or her shares on an *inter vivos* basis. This option will be discussed in greater detail in Chapter 3 — Life Insured Corporate Buy-Sell Arrangements.

Using Life Insurance Death Benefits

When a buy-sell arrangement is triggered by the death of a shareholder, a corporation may receive life insurance proceeds for the corporate-owned insurance policy on the life of the deceased shareholder. The value of the death benefit in excess of the adjusted cost basis that the corporation, as the policy owner, had in the life insurance policy can be added to the corporation's capital dividend account.

In simple terms, the capital dividend account is a notional tax account that is available to Canadian private corporations that meet the complex capital dividend account rules and is used to track the receipt by the corporation of certain types of non-taxable funds, such as the tax-free portion of a capital gain realized when the corporation disposes of certain assets that have increased in value. Part or all of the capital dividend account balance can be paid out to the shareholders of a corporation as a tax-free dividend provided the necessary election and accompanying documentation is filed with the CRA.

A capital dividend funded by the receipt of life insurance death benefits can be a means of ensuring that the purchasing shareholder has access to the requisite funding. The mechanics of the capital dividend account and its use when a corporation receives life insurance proceeds as a designated beneficiary will be discussed in Chapter 3 — Life Insured Corporate Buy-Sell Arrangements.

TWO

TAX CONSIDERATIONS — *INTER VIVOS* BUY-OUTS

¶200
Sale of Shares by Individual Shareholders

¶205 Overview

Shareholder's agreements are not mandatory but are usually recommended whenever there is more than one shareholder of a corporation. The shareholders' agreement may provide for the sale of shares by the departing shareholder to the remaining shareholders. The tax implications to the vendor would generally be the same whether the share sale is initiated by disability, retirement, voluntary withdrawal or by virtue of a shot-gun clause or right of first refusal. The tax implications to the vendor may differ, however, depending on the identity of the purchaser. For example, if the shares are redeemed or purchased for cancellation by the corporation, the tax results will differ as compared to a sale to another shareholder. Also, whether or not the purchaser deals at arm's length with the vendor will be relevant in determining the tax consequences. These differences should be considered when negotiating and drafting the shareholders' agreement. Finally, the terms of the shareholders' agreement can impact on how the corporation is classified for tax purposes, which can affect both the tax treatment of the corporation as well as the selling shareholder. The Appendix to this Chapter discusses the classification of corporations for tax purposes, the rules as to whether the corporations are associated, as well as the tests for determining whether taxpayers are related, affiliated or otherwise deal at arm's length.

¶210 Qualified Small Business Corporation

Individuals (other than trusts) who dispose of qualified small business corporation shares after June 17, 1987 are eligible to claim the $500,000 capital gains exemption.[1] (Although not discussed herein, the capital gains exemption is also available in respect of "qualified farm property.") The following is an analysis of the capital gains exemption available for shares of a small business corporation. It reviews the main technical provisions, the pitfalls and some planning opportunities.

It should be noted that the $500,000 amount refers to the whole capital gain rather than just the taxable portion. The capital gains income inclusion rate is currently 50 per cent but has also been both 66 $2/3$ per cent and 75 per cent in previous years. The capital gains exemption has been adjusted to reflect the changes in the included amount. It is reduced by any prior claim for the capital gains exemption. As the capital gains exemption may have been claimed when the capital gain income inclusion rate was 75 per cent or 66 $2/3$ per cent, adjustments are required in determining the amount of capital gains exemption that is still available to the individual. The availability of the capital gains exemption will not necessarily result in complete elimination of tax on the gain since the alternative minimum tax may result in a tax liability. This is discussed further below.

Net taxable capital gains eligible for the exemption will be reduced by an individual's "cumulative net investment loss"[2] after 1987. An individual's cumulative net investment loss at the end of a year is the amount by which the individual's investment expenses for the year and prior years (after 1987) exceed his investment income. Investment expenses of an individual generally includes interest expenses,[3] investment counsel fees, partnership losses (inactive), 50 per cent of resource expenses and property and rental losses. Investment income generally includes property income (dividends and interest), partnership income (inactive), recaptured capital cost allowance, resource property sale proceeds and rental property income.

There are three basic criteria which must be satisfied in order to qualify for the capital gains exemption:

1. At the time of disposition, shares of a small business corporation must be owned by the individual, the individual's spouse or partnership related to the individual. A small business corporation is a Canadian-controlled private corporation,[4] all or substantially all of the assets (considered by the the Canada Customs and Revenue Agency

---

[1] Subsection 110.6(2.1) of the *Income Tax Act* (Canada). The definition of "qualified small business corporation share" is found in subsection 110.6(1). Unless otherwise indicated, all statutory references are to the *Income Tax Act* (Canada) (the "Act").

[2] Defined in subsection 110.6(1).

[3] Interest deemed to be paid pursuant to section 80.5 is included in interest expenses for this purpose. Section 80.5 is applicable where an employee or shareholder is deemed under section 80.4 to have received a benefit by virtue of an interest-free or low interest loan. See Interpretation Bulletin IT-421R2, Benefits to individuals, corporations and shareholders from loans or debt, dated September 9, 1992.

[4] As discussed in the Appendix, the concept of a Canadian-controlled private corporation relies on a *de facto* control test. See subsection 125(7) and Interpretation Bulletin IT-458R2, Canadian-controlled private corporation, dated May 31, 2000.

¶210

(the "CRA")[5] to be at least 90 per cent of the fair market value of the assets)[6] at that time which were used in an active business carried on primarily (more than 50 per cent) in Canada by the corporation or a related corporation or are shares or indebtedness issued by connected corporations[7] which also qualify as small business corporations.

2. Throughout the period of 24 months immediately preceding the disposition, the shares must not be owned by any one other than the individual or a related person or partnership. Special rules are provided for determining when the person or partnership is related to the individual for this purpose. Shares issued from treasury must be held for 24 months unless the shares are issued as consideration for other shares or on a transfer of all or substantially all of the assets used in an active business or on a transfer of certain active partnership interests.[8] This relieving provision would permit a sole proprietor or partnership to incorporate a business and to sell shares which have not been owned for 24 months while still possibly qualifying for the capital gains exemption.[9] If an individual acquires shares from another unrelated shareholder and dies or disposes of the shares within 24 months, the exemption will not be available.

3. Throughout the period of 24 months immediately preceding the share disposition, more than 50 per cent of the fair market value of the Canadian controlled private corporation's assets must be attributable to:

   (a) assets used in an active business carried on primarily in Canada by the corporation or a related corporation,

   (b) certain shares or debt of connected corporations (which must be Canadian-controlled private corporations and use more than 50 per cent of their assets in an active business), or

   (c) a combination of active business assets or shares or debt of connected corporations.

Therefore, where a corporation does not hold shares or debt in connected corporations, it must use more than 50 per cent of the fair market value of its assets directly in an active business carried on primarily in Canada throughout the required holding period.

---

[5] Although not enacted at the time of writing, legislation is in the works to change the Agency's name to Canada Revenue Agency. The Agency is currently referring to itself in this fashion.

[6] While this is the CRA's administrative position, there have been cases where the courts have decided that the test cannot be so rigidly applied. For example, see *Wood v. MNR*, 87 DTC 312.

[7] See subsection 186(4). If a company controls the other company by reference to the extended definition of control in subsection 186(2) or owns issued shares with more than 10% of the votes and value of the other shares, the companies will generally be connected.

[8] Paragraph 110.6(14)(f).

[9] Where a person has disposed of all or substantially all of the assets used in an active business to a corporation in exchange for shares, the shares are deemed to be capital property pursuant to section 54.2.

If the corporation holds shares or debt of connected corporations, there are three additional tests which must be met.

Firstly, the shares or debt of the connected corporation must not have been held by anyone other than the corporation or persons or partnerships related to it throughout that part of the 24-month period ending when the shares or debt were acquired.

Secondly, throughout the 24-month period, the connected corporation must have been a Canadian-controlled private corporation (CCPC) which used more than 50 per cent of the fair market value of its assets in an active business in Canada. If the shares of a connected corporation were disposed of to an arm's length person or partnership prior to the time the determination is made, the disposition will not impact the eligibility.

Thirdly, there is a special provision which applies if a connected corporation did not have all or substantially all of the fair market value of the corporation's assets attributable to assets used in an active business in Canada. Where, for any period of time, all or substantially all of the fair market value of a corporation's assets is not attributable to assets that are shares or debt of connected corporations that meet the 50 per cent active business test or assets used directly in an active business carried on primarily in Canada, the connected corporation in which the corporation holds shares or debt must, for that period of time, use all or substantially all of the fair market value of their assets in an active business in Canada. As a result, if this provision applies, the shares or debt of connected corporations held by the corporation will qualify as active business assets only where the connected corporations are, at that time, small business corporations (i.e., at least 90 per cent of the fair market value of the assets of such corporations must be used in an active business carried on primarily in Canada), rather than only being required to use more than 50 per cent of the fair market value of their assets in such an active business.

For example, assume a holding company owns shares of a connected company which represents 70 per cent of the value of all of the holding company's assets. The other 30 per cent is made up of portfolio investments. The holding company will only be able to meet this test if the connected company (being the operating company) is a small business corporation (i.e., it has met the "90 per cent test") during the period.

The 50 per cent fair market value test ensures that the exemption will not be available on sales of shares of corporations where 50 per cent or more of the value of corporate assets are not active business assets throughout the required period prior to the disposition of the qualified small business corporation's shares. In addition, where shares or debt of a subsidiary company are held by a parent company, the subsidiary company must meet a holding period requirement and use more than half of the fair market value of its assets in an active business throughout the period in order for the parent to include those shares or debts in meeting its fair market value requirement or where the parent itself does not meet the all or substantially all (90 per cent) test, the subsidiary company must itself meet the 90 per cent test during such period. The exception to the definition is intended to ensure that the 50 per cent fair market value requirement cannot be circumvented through the stacking of several holding companies.

If a share has been substituted for another share during the 24-month period preceding the time the determination is made, the other share must also meet the other requirements in order to qualify.

The rights under a purchase and sale agreement will not be included for the purpose of determining whether the shares will qualify as a qualified small business corporation shares. Thus if an agreement is entered into where the shares are to be sold to a non-resident or a public company, the corporation will not lose its status for capital gains exemption purposes. (Note that the existence of such agreement can impact the classification of the corporation for other tax purposes.)

Special rules are provided for trusts. On a disposition of shares of a small business corporation, the capital gains exemption will be available to a beneficiary where the trust designates a taxable capital gain in favour of that beneficiary.[10] Of course, the trust must be properly structured in order to avoid various tax attribution rules. Nevertheless, for companies which are expected to grow significantly in value, the shareholders may wish to consider adding family trusts as shareholders or at least provide flexibility through the shareholders' agreement to allow for this possibility in the future.

An individual will be considered to dispose of identical shares in the order acquired.[11] This will be relevant if not all of the shares meet the holding period requirement. For example, where a shareholder purchases shares from a withdrawing shareholder and then immediately sells all of the shares of the company, only the shares originally owned by the individual for the requisite time period would qualify.

There are other pitfalls which must be considered in restructuring any corporation so as to take advantage of the exemption. Assume that an individual has never previously claimed the capital gains exemption and disposes of shares of a qualified small business corporation and realizes a capital gain of $500,000. Further assume that the individual has no other source of income or loss. At first blush, one may assume that there would be no tax payable. However, this may be true for regular tax only. For regular tax purposes, the individual would report a taxable capital gain of $250,000 which would be completely offset by the capital gains exemption. However, 4/5 of the taxable capital gain (i.e., 4/5 × $250,000) would be included for purposes of computing alternative minimum tax, leaving a net amount of $200,000. The individual would be entitled to claim the $40,000 minimum tax exemption and $160,000 would be subject to minimum tax. The federal tax rate for alternative minimum is 16 per cent. Alternative minimum tax paid in excess of ordinary tax is eligible to be carried forward seven years and deducted against regular tax payable in excess of the alternative minimum tax liability in future years.

---

[10] The amount is based on the trust's "eligible taxable capital gains" (as defined in subsection 108(1)) that is designated in favour of a beneficiary. See subsection 104(21.2).

[11] Paragraph 110.6(14)(a).

As discussed, if an individual has a cumulative net investment loss (CNIL), the capital gains exemption may not be available in the year. For example, the individual may have carrying costs with respect to passive investments, losses from limited partnerships, resource deductions from flow-through shares and rental losses. The CNIL account may create a timing problem in that the full capital gains exemption may not be available in the year. However, the CNIL account does not eliminate but only defers access to the capital gains exemption to the extent of the CNIL balance. In addition, the CNIL account may be reduced or eliminated by earning additional investment income.[12]

There are also restrictions where an individual has previously claimed an allowable business investment loss (ABIL).[13]

There are also various specific anti-avoidance rules which may deny the capital gains exemption otherwise available. For example, if a corporate reorganization is accomplished by means of a butterfly and a share sale is contemplated, then the capital gains exemption could be denied pursuant to subsection 110.6(7). The purpose of subsection 110.6(7) is to prohibit a capital gain from being eligible for the capital gains exemption where the gain was realized as part of a series of transactions to which the butterfly exception in paragraph 55(3)(b) would apply or where a "wingless butterfly" is effected at transfers of property below fair market value.

Pursuant to this subsection, the exemption may also be denied where an individual has a capital gain on a disposition as part of a series of transactions in which property is acquired by a corporation or partnership for consideration that is significantly less than the fair market value of the property.

Pursuant to subsection 110.6(8), the capital gains exemption may be denied where it is reasonable to conclude that a significant part of the capital gain is attributable to the fact that dividends were not paid on a share (other than a "prescribed" share) or the dividends were less than a certain calculated amount. Common shares and certain shares properly issued in the course of a typical "estate freeze" or "employee freeze" will generally qualify as "prescribed shares" and are, therefore, outside the scope of this anti-avoidance rule. Nevertheless, the manner in which a corporate reorganization is implemented or the terms of a shareholders' agreement could inadvertently cause shares to taint the prescribed share status of shares.[14]

As discussed above, the corporation has to meet various "active business" tests in order for its shares to qualify as qualified small business corporation shares. If the company has met the "more than 50 per cent active business test" in the prior 24 months but does not currently meet the "all or substantially all" test in order to qualify as a small business corporation, it may be possible to reorganize holdings so that the shares do qualify as shares of a qualified small

---

[12] For example, if a taxpayer had a $200,000 CNIL account but recognized a $1,400,000 capital gain, one-half of which is a taxable capital gain, the entire $500,000 capital gain exemption would be available.

[13] See Interpretation Bulletin IT-484R2, Business investment losses, dated November 28, 1996.

[14] See Section 6205 of the Regulations, which sets out the rules relating to whether a share is a prescribed share for this purpose.

business corporation. Tax practitioners refer to this type of planning as "purifying" the corporation.

Assume that a holding company has owned the shares of a small business corporation for more than two years. The fair market value of the assets of the holding company is $115,000, comprising $15,000 of investments and $100,000 representing the shares of the small business corporation. The fair market value of the assets of the small business corporation is $200,000 and the liabilities are $100,000. Assuming that more than 50 per cent of the assets of the holding company are invested in shares of a connected small business corporation at all times and assuming the subsidiary has met the "all or substantially all test" during this period, it is possible to reorganize the holding company prior to a sale in order that the capital gains exemption would be available on the sale of the shares of the holding company.

One alternative would be to have the holding company pay a dividend in kind to its shareholders. This would result in a fair market value disposition to the holding company and may trigger a taxable dividend to the shareholder. Alternatively, the small business corporation may be wound up on a tax deferred basis into the holding company pursuant to subsection 88(1) of the *Income Tax Act*. As it is the assets rather than the liabilities which are determinative for the small business corporation test, Holdco would qualify as a small business corporation. It would, after the wind up, have $200,000 of assets used in an active business and only $15,000 of passive investments. A third alternative would be for the holding company to "rollover" its investments to the small business corporation in consideration for common shares.

It may be advantageous for shareholders to "crystallize" the capital gains exemption. That is, the shareholders can reorganize their shareholdings to trigger a capital gain even though there are no current plans to sell shares to a third party. One reason for crystallizing the capital gains exemption is to obtain the benefit of increasing the cost base of the shares immediately since it is possible that the Minister of Finance may eliminate the capital gains exemption in the future. Another reason for crystallizing is to increase the cost base of the shares at a time when the shares qualify for the capital gains exemption since it may not be easy to purify the corporation at a later date. For example, where the shareholders will be involved in a "butterfly" transaction which could result in a denial of the capital gains exemption by virtue of subsection 110.6(7). Another example is if the shareholders are involved in a dispute in which a buy-sell provision in the shareholders agreement will likely be invoked. In such cases, it could be very difficult to implement the necessary reorganization strategies prior to a sale of shares. The potential that shareholders may be unwilling to cooperate in the future should be kept in mind as well when considering other clauses that may be included in the shareholders' agreement and that may result in future tax advantages or flexibility.

In terms of planning for the future, it may be advantageous to structure a new small business corporation or to reorganize an existing small business corporation so that a holding company would own a class of participating preferred shares entitled to dividends equal to the retained earnings in each year. Common shares of the small business corporation could be issued for

¶210

nominal consideration to the individuals who own the shares of the holding company. The distribution of the retained earnings in each year would not attract any tax as the dividends would be tax-free intercorporate dividends, provided the companies are connected so that Part IV tax is not applicable.[15] Such a structure would ensure that the small business corporation does not accumulate excess assets which would serve to disqualify it as a small business corporation. Assuming that the business would be sold based on a multiple of earnings, the individuals who directly own the common shares of the company would be entitled to claim a capital gains exemption at the time of sale. Of course, the capital gains exemption availability is subject to numerous technical limitations including the specific anti-avoidance rule in subsection 110.6(8) discussed above.

¶215 Tax Implications for Vendor

This section of the Chapter will discuss the tax consequences to a shareholder who sells shares to someone other than the issuing corporation. The tax consequence of a redemption or purchase for cancellation by the corporation is discussed later in the Chapter.

On a sale of shares that are considered capital property, the vendor will realize a capital gain (or capital loss) if the proceeds of the disposition exceed (or are exceeded by) the adjusted cost base of the shares and any selling expenses. If the shares were acquired by the vendor prior to 1972 or after 1972 in a non-arm's length acquisition, reference would be made to the income tax application rules to determine the adjusted cost base of the shares. One-half of the capital gain is taxable. The tax rate will depend on the individual's marginal tax rate. If the vendor is an individual resident in Canada, the capital gain exemption may be available to reduce or eliminate tax on the capital gains (up to a $500,000 lifetime maximum per individual) arising on the sale provided that the criteria described above are met.

If the shares are sold to a person with whom the vendor does not deal at arm's length, the vendor will be deemed to receive proceeds equal to the fair market value of the shares earned even if the actual consideration received is less than that amount.[16]

In some cases, a taxpayer can transfer shares on a rollover basis, which generally means that the shares are transferred at their adjusted cost base or some other elected amount. For example, a transfer to a spouse, spousal trust, "alter ego trust," or "joint partner" trust can be carried out on a rollover basis if the conditions in the Act are met.[17] There are also several possible rollovers involving transactions with corporations including sections 51, 85, 85.1, 86 and 87.

---

[15] The potential application of subsection 55(2), the specific anti-avoidance rules in section 112, Part IV.1 and Part VI.1 must also be considered to ensure dividends may be paid free of tax. As discussed below, subsection 55(2) is an anti-avoidance rule which may recharacterize an inter-corporate dividend as a capital gain. Part VI.1 tax is a special tax that applies to dividends paid on certain types of shares. This tax is also discussed below.

[16] Section 69.

[17] Subsection 73(1.01).

Where the individual agrees to be paid for his shares over time, it may be possible to defer tax by claiming the capital gains reserve pursuant to paragraph 40(1)(a)(iii).[18] This reserve allows the capital gain on a sale to be spread over a maximum of five taxation years where part or all of the proceeds of disposition are payable in subsequent taxation years. However, commencing in the year of sale, at least 1/5 of the capital gain must be reported in each year regardless of the amount of proceeds received in that year. If the balance of sale is contingent upon the profits or earnings of the company, then the taxpayer may only be required to report the portion of the gain that is determinable in each year, provided that the entire gain is reported within five years. Refer to the comments on earn-out agreements in Chapter 1.

The capital gains reserve provisions may be relevant in the context of a shareholders' agreement since the parties could agree to a deferred payment of proceeds to the departing shareholder to minimize cash-flow or financing concerns. In addition, where shares of a small business corporation are sold to a child where payment is made over time, the reserve is extended to a maximum of 10 years rather than just five years.[19] This provision may be useful where it is expected that the children of the current shareholders will eventually take over the company. It should be noted that the capital gains reserve is not available to a non-resident vendor or where, in general terms, the purchaser is a corporation or partnership that the vendor controls or holds a majority interest.[20]

Caution should be exercised where an individual sells personally owned shares to a corporation with whom the individual does not deal at arm's length. For example, where a shareholders' agreement includes an assignment clause, which allows a holding company owned by a shareholder to be substituted as a purchaser of another shareholder's shares, section 84.1 could apply where the assignment clause is invoked if the purchaser and the shareholder do not deal at arm's length. In that situation, section 84.1 could deem the immediate recognition of a dividend where the purchaser corporation and the target corporation are connected immediately after the disposition.[21] If the consideration received by the transferor exceeds the greater of the paid-up capital of the transferred shares and the adjusted cost base of the transferred shares, such a deemed dividend would arise. The other possible consequence of section 84.1 applying is that any shares issued by the purchaser corporation to the individual as consideration may be subject to a reduction or "grind" in paid-up capital for tax purposes. Section 84.1 also contains various supporting rules which modify or extend the normal rules dealing with whether parties are dealing at arm's length or for determining the adjusted cost base of shares. For example, if a person purchased shares from a non-arm's length person, the purchaser's cost base would be ground down for purposes of section 84.1 to the

---

[18] See Interpretation Bulletin IT-236R4, Reserves — Dispositions of capital property, dated July 30, 1999.

[19] Subsection 40(1.1).

[20] Subparagraph 40(2)(a)(ii).

[21] See Interpretation Bulletin IT-489R, Non-arm's length sale of shares to a corporation, dated February 28, 1994.

¶215

extent that the vendor claimed the capital gains exemption on the sale. This would prevent the purchaser from transferring the acquired shares to a holding company for debt or shares with high paid-up capital.

Therefore, when drafting shareholders' agreements and the buy-sell provisions in particular, section 84.1 must be considered since a departing shareholder's tax consequences may be significantly altered if this provision is found to be applicable. In addition, in some cases, the company which is deemed to have paid the dividend may potentially be subject to Part VI.1 tax (discussed further below).

Provided the company is a small business corporation, a loss arising on the disposition of shares or debt may constitute a business investment loss.[22] A business investment loss generally arises on a sale to an arm's length person of shares or debt of a small business corporation other than a sale to an arm's length person of a debt owing between corporations not dealing at arm's length. A business investment loss may also be claimed where the shares are not sold in certain bankruptcy or insolvency situations. One-half of a business investment loss is deductible against other sources of income.[23] (The amount may be carried back three years or carried forward seven years. If not utilized within this period, it reverts back to a capital loss with[24] an indefinite carry-forward period.) This should be contrasted with ordinary capital losses where $1/2$ of such losses may only be claimed against taxable capital gains and not other types of income. A business investment loss will reduce the capital gains exemption which could be claimed by the individual in the year.

If the vendor has an outstanding loan which was used to purchase the shares that have been sold, the interest on the loan should continue to be deductible pursuant to subsection 20.1(1). Prior to the enactment of this provision, the result would have been different.[25]

¶220

Sale of Shares by Holding Company

In many cases, individual shareholders will own their shares of an operating company through individual holding companies. Upon the disposition of the shares of the operating company (held as capital property) to another shareholder or other third party, the holding company would realize a capital gain (or capital loss) to the extent that the proceeds of disposition exceed (or are exceeded by) the adjusted cost base of the shares and any selling expenses. A holding company would be entitled to benefit from the five-year capital gains reserve subject to the restrictions noted above; that is, tax on the capital gain may be spread over a period not exceeding five years where the purchase price is payable over five years. The capital gains exemption would not be

---

[22] Paragraph 39(1)(c). See Interpretation Bulletin IT-484R2.

[23] One-half of a taxpayer's business investment loss is the taxpayer's allowable business investment loss under paragraph 38(c).

[24] The 2004 Federal Budget has proposed a 10-year carry-forward of non-capital losses.

[25] See *Emerson v. The Queen*, 86 DTC 6184 (F.C.A.).

available to a holding corporation. For this reason, individuals would normally prefer to sell the shares of the holding company rather than having the holding company sell the shares of the operating company.

A purchaser may be unwilling, however, to acquire shares of a holding company. It may be necessary to transfer the redundant assets, if any, of the holding corporation to a sister corporation on a tax-deferred basis prior to the sale of shares of the holding company. A variation would be to amalgamate the holding company and the operating company prior to the share sale. Either way, a purchaser will want an indemnity and possibly a purchase price holdback to deal with any contingent liabilities, including tax liabilities, of the holding company. The existence of holding companies often makes the negotiation of the shareholders' agreement more complicated since the buy-out options are multiplied while the individual shareholders typically will still want to maximize use of the capital gains exemption.

The tax-free portion of the capital gain (currently $1/2$) realized by a corporation would be added to its capital dividend account and could be distributed as a tax-free capital dividend to its Canadian resident shareholders upon the appropriate election being made pursuant to subsection 83(2).[26]

The corporation is subject to tax on the taxable portion of the capital gain. The tax rate will depend on the status of the corporation as well as the applicable provincial tax rate. For CCPCs and investment income, there is an additional tax of 6 $2/3$ per cent which may be refunded once sufficient taxable dividends are paid by the corporation.[27] The purpose of this additional tax is to prevent Canadian residents from realizing a tax savings or deferral by realizing capital gains through a holding company rather than personally.

An amount equal to 26 $2/3$ per cent of the taxable capital gain would generally be added to the refundable dividend tax on hand (RDTOH) of the corporation assuming the corporation qualifies as a CCPC throughout the year. The corporation would be entitled to a dividend refund equal to one dollar of RDTOH for every three dollars of taxable dividends paid.[28] Taxable dividends received by individuals who are shareholders would be eligible for the gross-up and credit mechanism. Through the capital dividend account, RDTOH and dividend gross-up and credit mechanisms, the theoretical result is that the effective overall tax rate is approximately the same whether the capital gain is realized by a Canadian resident individual personally or through a CCPC. This concept is known as "integration." Since individual and corporate tax rates differ from province to province, there are differences in the actual effective tax rate that would apply and the individual tax rate is rarely, if ever, identical to the effective tax rate on capital gains realized by a CCPC. As well, as described above, corporations are not entitled to the $500,000 capital gains exemption.

---

[26] See Interpretation Bulletin IT-66R6, Capital dividends, dated May 31, 1991.

[27] Section 123.3.

[28] Section 129. See Interpretation Bulletin IT243R4, Dividend refund to private corporations, dated February 12, 1996.

¶225 Tax Implications for Purchaser of Shares

The purchaser should be entitled to deduct the interest expense on funds borrowed to purchase common shares from the vendor (although see comments below). If the purchaser wishes to pay the purchase price out of the earnings of the operating company, a new corporation could be formed to acquire the shares from the vendor. If the vendor does not deal at arm's length with the purchaser, section 84.1 may deem the vendor to receive a dividend rather than a capital gain.

The new corporation could borrow funds from the bank in order to finance the purchase. After the purchase is completed, the new corporation could be amalgamated with the operating corporation on a tax-free basis in order that the amalgamated company incur the interest expense and discharge the bank loan out of its operating profits. The CRA has indicated that the general anti-avoidance rule would not be applied to the formation and amalgamation described above (see Information Circular IC 88-2). One consequence of this plan is that the cost base of the shares acquired from the purchaser would disappear on the amalgamation, although a "bump" in cost base of non-depreciable capital property owned by the target company may be available pursuant to paragraph 88(1)(d). Another consequence of amalgamating the purchaser and target corporation is that the provincial capital tax and federal Large Corporations Tax liabilities may be increased after the amalgamation.

It should be noted that any comments made herein with respect to interest deductibility are subject to proposed changes to such rules announced by the Department of Finance on October 31, 2003. At the time of writing, it is not clear whether these rules will be enacted as currently drafted. Indeed, the interest deductibility rules under the Act have been in a state of flux since the early 1990s. The recent proposals are largely a legislative response to certain Supreme Court of Canada decisions[29] where taxpayers have been successful. The proposed legislation requires that in order to claim a loss, the taxpayer must assess annually the expected profitability of the business. In addition, income or loss from a business does not include capital gains or losses. Since the rules will likely continue to change, it is prudent for a taxpayer to review the applicable rules in any year where interest expense will be incurred.[30]

On a straight purchase of shares by an existing shareholder, the adjusted cost base of the shares to the purchaser would be based on an average of all identical shares owned by the purchaser.[31] Unless the purchaser forms a new corporation in the manner outlined above, the purchaser will be using after-tax dollars to pay for the shares of the vendor (assuming no insurance funding). The purchaser acquires the shares with the same paid-up capital of the shares regardless of the purchase price with the result that the funds could not be

---

[29] See *Ludco et al. v. The Queen*, 2001 DTC 5505, *Stewart v. The Queen*, 2002 DTC 6969.

[30] The current position of the the CRA is set out in Interpretation Bulletin IT-533, Interest deductibility and related issues, dated October 31, 2003.

[31] Section 47. See Interpretation Bulletin IT-387R2, Meaning of "identical properties," dated July 14, 1989.

distributed from the corporation to the individual without incurring a tax liability. However, subsequent to the purchase, the purchaser could transfer the shares to a new holding company for either debt equal to the value of such shares or for shares of the new holding company with paid-up capital equal to the adjusted cost base. Section 84.1 will not apply in such situations unless the purchaser purchased the shares from a non-arm's length person and that person claimed the capital gains exemption or a capital gains reserve or where the shares were owned prior to 1972. The funds could then be paid as a dividend from the operating company to the holding company permitting the holding company to either repay the debt owed to the purchaser or make a tax-free return of paid-up capital thereby allowing the purchaser to receive funds from the operating company to pay for the purchase of the shares.[32] GAAR should not apply since the purchaser is simply obtaining a return of his or her cost base, which can generally be done on a tax-deferred basis with any other investment or business asset rolled into a company.

If the purchaser is a holding corporation, it will not be able to increase its share of the safe income (discussed below) of the operating corporation.

If a holding company incurs a capital loss on the disposition of shares, the capital loss will be reduced by taxable dividends and capital dividends previously paid on the shares.[33] Dividends include dividends deemed to have been paid on a redemption or purchase for cancellation of shares pursuant to subsection 84(3).

The capital loss to the holding company may also be denied where the holding company or an affiliated person acquires the shares (or an identical property) during the period that begins 30 days before and ends 30 days after the disposition. In such cases, the loss will be suspended in the hands of the holding company[34] and generally only realized when the property is no longer owned by an affiliated person.

¶230
Purchase for Cancellation or Redemption by Corporation

¶235 Shares Owned by an Individual

The tax consequences on a purchase for cancellation or redemption by the corporation are more complicated than a sale to another person. The reason for this is that, in addition to the vendor's adjusted cost base, the paid-up capital of the shares also becomes relevant. The adjusted cost base of shares need not be, and often is not, identical to the paid-up capital of the shares.

---

[32] The reduction of paid-up capital will reduce the adjusted cost base of the shares on a dollar for dollar basis.

[33] Subsection 112(3). See Interpretation Bulletin IT-328R3, Losses on shares from which dividends have been received, dated February 21, 1994.

[34] See subsection 40(3.4).

On a purchase for cancellation or redemption of shares of a privately held corporation, a dividend will be deemed to have been paid to the extent that the amount paid exceeds the paid-up capital of the shares.[35] The deemed dividend will be treated as a taxable dividend, unless the corporation elects (where possible) to treat the dividend as a capital dividend. If dividends are received by an individual, they will be eligible for the gross-up and credit mechanism. As a result of this mechanism, the tax rate on dividends for individuals is lower than the tax rate for ordinary income.[36] For purposes of calculating any capital gain or loss as a result of the redemption or purchase for cancellation, the proceeds of disposition would be reduced by the amount of the deemed dividend.[37] Generally, if the paid-up capital of the shares exceeds the adjusted cost base of the shares, a capital gain will be triggered.

If the paid-up capital of the shares is less than the adjusted cost base of the shares to the vendor, a capital loss will be realized. The capital loss will be denied if the individual is affiliated with the corporation immediately after the disposition.[38]

If the shares are purchased for cancellation and the vendor is issued a promissory note to be paid over a number of years as part or all of the consideration, it would not be possible for the vendor to claim a reserve or otherwise defer the tax on any taxable dividend thereon.[39] An alternative which would permit a deferral of tax is discussed below.

¶240   Shares Owned by Holding Company

A private company which receives, or is deemed to receive, a dividend, may be subject to Part IV tax. Assuming that the holding company owns more than 10 per cent of the voting shares and shares having a fair market value of more than 10 per cent of all of the issued shares of the operating company or controls, or is related to other persons which control, the operating company, no Part IV tax would arise on any deemed dividends resulting from the purchase for cancellation or redemption of shares except to the extent that a dividend refund is triggered to the operating company as a result of such deemed dividends. In such cases, therefore, the holding company would receive tax-free intercorporate dividends. The capital gains stripping provisions of section 55 can, however, be a major obstacle.

Subsection 55(2) applies where one of the results of the purchase for cancellation is to effect a significant reduction in the portion of the capital gain that would have arisen on the sale of the shares at fair market value if it were not for the dividend. The purpose of this anti-avoidance rule is to prevent taxpayers from structuring transactions that would allow them to receive tax-free dividends instead of taxable capital gains. Where this anti-avoidance

---

[35] Subsection 84(3).

[36] For 2004, the tax rate for an Ontario resident taxpayer at the highest marginal tax rate is 46.4% for ordinary income, 31.3% for dividend income, and 23.2% for capital gains.

[37] See the definition of "proceeds of disposition" in section 54.

[38] Subsection 40(3.6).

[39] See *Cabezuelo v. M.N.R.*, 83 DTC 679.

rule applies and no exceptions apply, the dividend is recharacterized as a capital gain. (There is an exception for any portion of the dividend that is subject to Part IV tax that is not refunded as a consequence of the payment of a dividend to another corporation where the payment is part of the series of transactions relevant for purposes of subsection 55(2).) The result is that the holding company will realize a taxable capital gain rather than tax-free inter-corporate dividends. The tax consequences of a capital gain realized by a holding company are discussed above. Subsection 55(2) does permit the holding company to receive its share of the safe income without triggering a capital gain.[40]

Subsection 55(2) does not apply in certain related party reorganizations. If the criteria in paragraph 55(3)(a) are met, dividends (and deemed dividends) will not be recharacterized as capital gains. This exception to subsection 55(2) may allow family businesses to restructure the corporate group on a tax deferred basis. For example, if a parent wanted to split assets owned by one company into two companies with the intention of having different children taking part in the companies, it is possible to structure this result relying on the related party exception in paragraph 55(3)(a). Caution should, however, be exercised when relying on this exception as the rules are very technical. In addition, brothers and sisters are not considered to be related for this purpose. Another exception to the application of subsection 55(2) is the "butterfly" provision in paragraph 55(3)(b). Once again, the rules are very technical and, as a result, it is often not possible to easily separate corporate business interests or assets on a tax-deferred basis.

Were it not for subsection 55(2), it would be possible for a vendor shareholder to defer tax on the sale of shares by having the shares owned by a holding company purchased for cancellation and by retaining the proceeds in the holding company. As a result of subsection 55(2), a corporate shareholder is permitted to receive an ordinary or deemed (e.g., on a redemption) dividend equal to the shareholder's proportionate share of the safe income without triggering a capital gain. In the case of any sale of shares owned by a holding company, the safe income dividend should almost always be paid before the sale (as it would not be available to the purchaser). In the case of a share redemption, any dividend not paid out of safe income may be designated in the tax return as a separate taxable dividend pursuant to paragraph 55(5)(f).[41] Absent this designation where a deemed dividend arising on a redemption of the shares exceeds the holding company's proportionate share of the safe income of the operating company by even one dollar, the entire deemed dividend would be deemed to be proceeds of disposition of the share with the

---

[40] For further discussion as to the computation of safe income, see John R. Robertson, *Capital Gains Strip: a Revenue Canada Perspective on the Provisions of Section 55*, 1981 Conference Report, and Michael A. Hiltz, Section 55: an Update, 1984 Corporate Management Tax Conference, p. 40. See also Ted Harris, "An Update of Revenue Canada's Approach to the Butterfly Reorganization," in *Report of Proceedings of the Forty-Third Tax Conference*, 1991 Conference Report (Toronto: Canadian Tax Foundation, 1992), 14:1-15, and also, Michael A. Hiltz, "Income Earned or Realized: Some Reflections," in *Report of Proceedings of the Forty-Third Tax Conference*, 1991 Conference Report (Toronto: Canadian Tax Foundation, 1992), 15:1-24.

[41] This is required since only part of the deemed dividend arising on the share redemption will be considered to be paid out of safe income in such cases.

result that a capital gain would arise.[42] Since the CRA takes the position that the value of each share is partly attributable to safe income and partly attributable to non-safe income amounts, it is not possible to stream safe income payments by first redeeming shares with a value equal to the safe income on hand.

Another option to take advantage of the safe income without making the paragraph 55(5)(*f*) designation includes increasing the paid-up capital of the shares equal to the safe income amount. An increase in paid-up capital results in a deemed dividend but it also increases the adjusted cost base of the shares by an equal amount.[43] This approach is often preferable in that it avoids the potentially greater scrutiny involved where a designation in the tax return pursuant to paragraph 55(5)(*f*) is made. Therefore, the tax-free deemed dividends will reduce the amount of capital gain on the subsequent sale of shares since the holding company will have a higher cost base in its shares. As long as the deemed dividends do not exceed the permissible amount (i.e., safe income), subsection 55(2) will not recharacterize the dividends as capital gains. In practice, the dividends or deemed dividends are triggered in stages since it is often difficult to calculate safe income with absolute precision.

It should be noted that the payment of intercorporate tax-free dividends out of safe income only results in a tax deferral. In order for a Canadian resident shareholder to obtain personal use of the safe income proceeds, the holding company would normally be required to pay taxable dividends. Based on current tax rates, the overall tax rate payable on a dividend may be higher than the tax rate on a capital gain. Therefore, while safe income planning can result in a deferral of tax, there may be an absolute tax cost to pursuing this strategy. Of course, the value of the tax deferral increases the longer the proceeds are expected to remain at the holding company level.

¶245 Tax Implications for Remaining Shareholder

In the case of a share redemption, as the remaining shareholder will not acquire the shares directly, there will be no increase in the adjusted cost base of the shares. If the remaining shareholder is a holding corporation, there would be no increase and generally no decrease in the holding company's proportionate share of the operating company's safe income.

The operating company may be entitled to deduct all or part of the interest expense relating to the purchase for cancellation of the shares. Based on jurisprudence as well as the CRA's published position, a company can deduct interest on funds borrowed to pay dividends out of accumulated profits or to return capital (used by the company in its business) by way of redemption or purchase for cancellation. This is based on the "filling the whole" theory on the basis that the debt is incurred to replace capital withdrawn from the business. To the extent the purchase price exceeds the contributed capital and accumulated profits, however, interest on money borrowed to make the purchase would likely not be deductible. In situations where interest deduction

---

[42] Paragraph 55(2)(*b*).

[43] See subsection 84(1) and paragraph 53(1)(*b*).

may be problematic, a shell company, which borrowed funds to purchase the shares directly, could be amalgamated with the operating company, thereby making interest expense fully deductible.[44]

As indicated above, a deemed dividend would arise on the redemption or purchase for cancellation to the extent that the redemption price exceeds the paid-up capital. A deemed taxable dividend arising on the purchase for cancellation may result in the operating company receiving a dividend refund, to the extent that it had refundable dividend tax on hand. This may trigger Part IV tax to a corporate shareholder whose shares are to be redeemed. Depending on the other dividends paid by the corporation in the year, the resulting Part IV tax liability to the corporate shareholders may have unexpected results. For example, since the shareholders may receive unequal dividends, they may bear a disproportionate share of the Part IV tax liability. These issues will be important to the remaining shareholder since such shareholder will continue to own the corporation entitled to the dividend refund and may share in the Part IV tax liability if it is a corporate shareholder and it also receives a dividend or deemed dividend in the same year. In addition, the paid-up capital returned to the shareholder may have a distorting effect to the extent that the shareholders own the same class or series of shares and have contributed different amounts for the subscription of such shares. In order to avoid such paid-up capital distortion or dilution issues, it would be necessary to reorganize the capital to realign the paid-up capital in an appropriate manner. Of course, it is possible to avoid this problem from inception by issuing different classes or series of shares to the shareholders.

The remaining shareholder will also want to ensure that Part VI.1 tax does not apply to the corporation purchasing the shares for cancellation. Part VI.1 tax is a tax that applies to a company which pays (or is deemed to pay) a dividend rather than a tax that applies to the recipient of the dividend. Part VI.1 can apply where dividends are paid or deemed to be paid on "taxable preferred shares" or "short-term preferred shares."[45] This tax was introduced as an anti-avoidance measure to curb the use of certain after-tax financing arrangements. Unfortunately, tax can apply in unexpected situations. These rules must be kept in mind when drafting shareholders' agreements, particularly when there are buy-sell provisions that can result in dividend or deemed dividend consequences. In some cases, there will be shares which were issued on an "estate freeze" type transaction which will fall within the definition of "taxable preferred shares" or "short-term preferred shares." Even in cases where a company has only issued common shares, it is possible that such shares will also be considered "taxable preferred shares" or "short-term preferred shares" by virtue of terms in the shareholder agreements. For example, particular attention should be paid to any "guarantee agreements" or put options in respect of a share or fixed liquidation or disposition entitlement with respect to the share. While there are exceptions to the application of Part VI.1 tax, such

---

[44] See paragraph 21 of Interpretation Bulletin IT-533, *Interest Deductibility and Related Issues*, dated October 31, 2003.

[45] These terms are defined in subsection 248(1).

as the exception that applies where a person has a "substantial interest"[46] in the corporation, these exceptions may be difficult to rely on in certain cases. The result is that the possibility of Part VI.1 tax has to be considered in situations where it may not be expected to apply, including owner-manager private businesses.

¶250 Staggered Redemption

Rather than redeeming the shares owned by a departing shareholder or his holding company in a single transaction, the share capital of the operating company could be reorganized so as to permit the redemption of the shares over time. This would overcome the timing problem whereby a taxable dividend or a capital gain may arise in the year of purchase for cancellation of the shares with no reserve (i.e., no tax deferral) being available even if there are

---

[46] Part VI.1 tax will apply to taxable dividends paid on taxable preferred shares that are not excluded shares to the extent the dividend exceeds the dividend allowance. The basic tax under Part VI.1 is 25% of the taxable dividend, or if an election is made, a rate of 40%. Where the election to pay the Part VI.1 40% tax is made by the payer corporation, a public corporation or its subsidiaries who receive the dividend from the payer will not be liable for the special 10% tax under Part IV.1. Where a dividend is paid on a short term preferred share the tax rate, formerly $66^{2}/_{3}$, will be 50%.

A deduction is available under paragraph 110(1)(k) equal to three times the Part VI.1 tax paid which will generally offset the effect of the Part VI.1 tax provided the payer company has sufficient taxable income in the year.

As previously noted, Part VI.1 tax is only payable to the extent the taxable dividend exceeds the dividend allowance. The dividend allowance is $500,00 for a taxation year, but with a claw-back rule. The rule requires that the dividend allowance for the current year is reduced by one for every dollar of dividends paid in the immediately preceding calendar in excess of $1,000,000. The dividend allowance is allocated among associated corporations by filing an agreement in prescribed form.

As noted, dividends paid by a corporation that are "excluded dividends" will not be subject to Part VI.1 tax. The dividend will be an excluded dividend based either on a "substantial interest" exemption or a 25% share test.

Where a corporation receiving the dividend has a "substantial interest" in the paying corporation, no Part VI.1 tax will be payable. This will arise where the shareholder and the paying corporation are related other than a right or other option set out it paragraph 251(1)(b).

Alternatively, where the corporation receiving the divedend owned shares to which are attached at least 25%of the votes of all shares and owns shares which are worth at least 25% of the fair market value of all shares and owns at least 25% of the fair market value of each class of shares or at least 25% of the fair market value of all shares that are not taxable preferred shares, a substantial interest will arise. This latter test usually means the taxpayer must own 25% of the common shares and if the shares do not have a value of 25% of all the shares, then ownership of at least 25 per cent of the shares of each class.

An excluded dividends will also include dividend paid by a private holding corporation. A private holding corporation is defined as a corporation the only undertaking of which is the investing of its funds. If the private holding corporation has a substantial interest in another corporation, that corporation must as well be a private holding corporation. Therefore, a private holding corporation will not include a holding company that has a substantial interest in an operating company.

Part VI.1 tax can arise with respect to a deemed dividend on any corporate redemptions of taxable preferred shares. However, susection 191(4) deems a dividend that arises on a corporate redemption to be an excluded dividend if the terms of the shares specify an amount at which the shares are to be redeemed at the time of the issue provided the amount does not exceed the fair market value of the shares at the time. The CRA has indicated that a formula amount is not a specified amount. Price adjustment clauses may create problems particularly where the price adjustment claus permits a downward adjustment since the intitial payment will have exceeded the fair market value of the share as finally adjusted downward.

deferred proceeds. As in the case of an ordinary purchase for cancellation, the operating company would use after-tax dollars to redeem the shares and the remaining shareholders would not be afforded a step-up in the cost base of the shares.

The common shares owned by a holding company in the operating company could be reorganized and exchanged for fixed value preference shares pursuant to either section 86 or section 51. Shares to be redeemed which are held personally could be transferred initially to a holding company for this purpose. The preference shares received on the reorganization would be entitled to the same percentage of safe income as the common shares prior to the reorganization. Therefore, in most cases, the fair market value of the preference shares may exceed this safe income with the result that a capital gain could arise on the redemption of each preference share owned by the holding company. It is therefore recommended that, prior to a share reclassification or exchange, the paid-up capital of the common shares be increased to reflect the safe income. The increase in paid-up capital should be effected after the common shares have been transferred to a holding company (and prior to a share reorganization) as a deemed dividend would arise where the increase in paid-up capital is not matched by an increase in net assets.[47] The deemed dividend would be free of Part IV tax where the holding company and operating company are connected for tax purposes and would not give rise to a section 55 problem where the increase in paid-up capital represents the safe income.[48]

After the paid-up capital has been increased to reflect the safe income, the common shares would be exchanged for preference shares having the same paid-up capital but having a redemption price equal to the fair market value of the common shares. The full amount of any dividend arising on the subsequent purchase for cancellation would be treated as additional proceeds of disposition of the shares (i.e., as a capital gain) on the redemption as the safe income would be reflected in the paid-up capital of the preference shares. In other words, safe income is crystallized at the time of the reorganization and is not increased by future earnings.

A possible variation of the foregoing plan is to implement a two-stage reorganization in order to isolate the full adjusted cost base in one class of preferred shares. For example, after the paid-up capital of the common shares is increased, the first reorganization can occur pursuant to section 85 where the common shares held by the company are exchanged for preference shares which are redeemable for an amount equal to the adjusted cost base of the exchanged shares and new common shares. Pursuant to section 85, the cost base of the exchanged common shares will be allocated to the preference

---

[47] Subsection 84(1).

[48] Part VI.1 tax would not apply if the shares are not taxable preferred shares or short-term preferred shares. This tax would also not apply if the shareholder had a "substantial interest" in the corporation as determined pursuant to subsection 191(2).

¶250

shares.[49] After the reorganization, the new common shares may be exchanged for a second class of preference shares.

By redeeming the preference shares received on the section 85 transaction first, the tax consequences will be deferred since these shares will have full cost base. Arguably, GAAR should not apply since the taxpayer is relying on a specific provision in the Act which requires the cost base to be allocated to the preferred shares.

Particular attention is required as to the attributes to be attached to the preference shares where they are owned by a holding company. The preference shares may be voting in order to ensure that Part IV not be eligible on any dividends arising and to possibly retain control of the business until the preference shares have been redeemed. In order to avoid Part IV tax where the shares are to be redeemed over time, the final redemption must comprise ownership of more than 10 per cent of the issued shares having full voting rights with more than 10 per cent of the value of the operating company. If voting control is retained by the holding company, the operating company would be associated with the holding company and any other companies owned by the same shareholders.

The preference shares may provide for a cumulative dividend (in order to provide the vendor with the equivalent of interest on the unpaid portion of the purchase price) which may be at a rate which is less than the borrowing, as the vendor would be entitled to a deferral of tax where dividends are paid to a holding company. The cumulative dividend may be monthly, quarterly or annually. More frequent dividends may be preferred for cash flow purposes and in order to reduce the risk to the vendor. The preference shares may also be entitled to a participation feature over the cumulative dividend in recognition of the risk assumed by the vendor. There should be a redemption schedule for the preference shares, perhaps providing for an acceleration of the redemption without penalty, should the corporation have the required funds. The retraction may also be accelerated should the assets of the company be sold or should a cumulative dividend not be paid in a year. The difficulty is in securing the redemption proceeds and the cumulative dividend. It may be possible to accomplish this result by providing the preference shareholder with a put to the remaining shareholders in the event that the shares are not redeemed on schedule. The put may be secured.

¶255
Change of Control

It should be noted that the sale of shares or purchase for cancellation of shares could result in an acquisition of control of the corporation. An acquisition of control does not occur where shares are acquired by a related party (other than a person who is related by virtue of a right under paragraph 251(5)(*b*)), by an executor or trustee under a will or by a beneficiary, related to

---

[49] Paragraph 85(1)(*g*). See Interpretation Bulletin IT-291R3, Transfer of property to a corporation under subsection 85(1), dated January 12, 2004.

Tax Considerations — *Inter Vivos* Buy-outs

the deceased, under a will. If a corporation controlled by non-residents becomes a Canadian controlled private corporation as a result of a change of control, the capital dividend account of the corporation accumulated before that time disappears.[50] An acquisition of control can have other significant tax implications. Perhaps the most significant relates to the use of losses carried forward from previous years. Capital loss carry forwards and losses from property income would cease to be deductible and non-capital losses would be deductible only against profits from the same or similar business, provided the business which generated the loss continues to be carried on with a reasonable expectation of profit. The carry-forward of scientific research and experimental development expenditures[51] and the resource accounts[52] are affected. An acquisition of control will also result in a deemed year-end[53] requiring the filing of short-year tax returns where the acquisition does not occur at the normal year-end. The amount by which the adjusted cost base of non-depreciable capital property exceeds the fair market value immediately prior to the change of control would be deemed to be a capital loss for the year deemed to end on the change of control.[54] The amount by which the undepreciated capital cost of depreciable property exceeds the fair market value immediately prior to the change of control is deducted from income for that period and deemed to be allowed as a capital cost allowance. It could result in the write-down of non-depreciable capital property.[55] Similarly, eligible capital property losses[56] and doubtful debts[57] are recognized in the deemed year-end and immediately prior to the acquisition of control. There is a reduction in investment tax credits following an acquisition of control.[58] There are other anti-avoidance rules which apply to transfers of assets in anticipation of an acquisition of control.[59] An acquisition of control may result in the association of the corporation with other corporations controlled by the purchaser.

---

[50] Subsection 89(1.1). The capital dividend account will not disappear if CCPC status arises solely by virtue of the change of residency of the non-resident shareholders.

[51] Subsection 37(6.1). See Interpretation Bulletin IT-151R5, Scientific research and development expenditures, dated October 17, 2000.

[52] Section 66.7.

[53] Subsection 249(4).

[54] Subsection 111(4). See Interpretation Bulletin IT-302R3, Losses of a corporation, the effect on their deductibility in changes in control, amalgamation and winding up, dated February 28, 1994.

[55] Paragraphs 53(2)(b.2) and 111(4)(c), (d) and (e).

[56] Subsection 111(5.2).

[57] Subsection 111(5.3).

[58] Subsections (9.1) and (9.2).

[59] Subsections 13(24), 66(11.4), 69(11) and 111(5.5).

¶255

¶260
Non-Compete Payment, Retiring Allowance or Consulting Fee

When drafting and negotiating the shareholders' agreement, consideration should also be given to other types of payments that might be paid to the departing shareholder and the tax consequences of such payments to the payer and recipient.

When a shareholder sells his or her interest in a company, the company and remaining shareholders may wish to obtain a non-compete covenant from the departing shareholder. While recent jurisprudence has confirmed that non-compete payments received by a selling shareholder may not be subject to income tax, the Department of Finance announced proposed amendments on October 7, 2003 to eliminate such tax benefits. After the date of announcement (subject to certain grandfathering provisions), taxpayers who receive non-compete payments will be taxed on such payments as they will be treated either as ordinary income or as dispositions from the sale of capital property or eligible capital property. The proposed amendments announced on October 7, 2003 do not deal with the tax consequences to the payer of non-compete payments. However, further proposed amendments were released on February 27, 2004 which deal with the treatment to payers of non-compete payments. Under the new proposals, the treatment to the payer of the non-compete mirrors the tax treatment of the non-compete to the recipient. For example, if the amount paid by the payer is employment income to the recipient, the payment will be considered wages to the payer.

A retiring allowance is defined as an amount received as a consequence of death or on or after retirement of a taxpayer from an office or employment in recognition of the employee's long service, or in respect of a loss of an office or employment of a taxpayer, whether or not received as damages for wrongful dismissal. It may be possible for an employee to transfer certain retiring allowance amounts to an RRSP free of tax. This will only apply if the employee was employed with the employer prior to 1996. There is also an annual limit of $2,000 for every year of employment prior to 1996, plus up to an additional $1,500 for each year of employment before 1989 (subject to certain other limitations where there is a company pension plan).[60]

In many private companies, both the shareholder and his or her spouse receive a salary. A retiring allowance should be considered wherever possible as the payment would generally be deductible to the corporation making the payments and tax would be deferred to the recipient (i.e., until funds are withdrawn from the RRSP). For example, on the purchase for cancellation or sale of shares of a corporation, a retiring allowance could be paid by the corporation in the year of sale. Where the shareholder is to remain for a period of time pursuant to a contract of employment, the retiring allowance could be incorporated into the contract and could be paid on the termination thereof.

---

[60] Paragraph 60(j.1).

As an alternative to a retiring allowance, a departing shareholder may be paid a consulting fee. Such a fee would not be eligible for a direct transfer to an RRSP, although it would constitute earned income. If the departing shareholder, in fact, ceases to be an employee, the corporation would not be required to withhold tax.

Care must be exercised to ensure that a retiring allowance or a consulting fee not be perceived by the CRA as a reduction in the purchase price for the shares, in which case there is a risk that the deduction to the corporation would be challenged by the CRA as being unreasonable or as not constituting a retiring allowance.

In cases where a shareholder becomes disabled, the shareholders' agreement may provide for disability payments to be made to such shareholders. Such payments are generally subject to tax. Note that, unlike life insurance proceeds, proceeds from disability insurance do not form part of the capital dividend account.

¶265
Non-Resident Vendor

It should be noted that there are additional tax considerations where the vendor is a non-resident. If the buy-sell agreement is in respect of shares of a private company, such shares would be taxable Canadian property, with the result that a certificate would be required under section 116 in respect of any disposition thereof.[61] The section 116 certificate is required whether or not the vendor is liable to pay Canadian income tax on the disposition. In the absence of a certificate, the purchaser is required to withhold and remit generally 25 per cent of the purchase price (or the fair market value in some cases) to the CRA. Failure to comply will result in penalties to the purchaser. This requirement would apply to both the sale of shares as well as a redemption or purchase for cancellation of shares. The individual may be entitled to treaty protection in respect of any capital gain. If so, the capital gain will generally not be subject to Canadian income tax. Where an individual is claiming treaty protection, the section 116 requirements still apply. The CRA may, however, issue a certificate without payment of tax provided the vendor provides the required information including an undertaking to file a federal return and report the disposition.

Most treaties contain exceptions for companies whose primary asset value is Canadian real estate. Therefore, the shares of such companies generally remain subject to Canadian income tax even if the vendor shareholder resides in a treaty country.

If a non-resident disposes of shares of a Canadian corporation to another Canadian corporation with whom the non-resident does not deal at arm's length, a deemed dividend may arise equal to the difference between the non-share consideration received and the paid-up capital. This result arises

---

[61] See Information Circular IC 72-17R4, Procedures concerning the disposition of taxable Canadian property by non-residents of Canada — Section 116, dated April 24, 1992.

where section 212.1 applies.[62] Section 212.1 is similar, but not identical, to section 84.1. Both these sections are designed to prevent shareholders from engaging in what is referred to as "surplus stripping." Where applicable, both provisions can result in the shareholder receiving deemed dividends rather than tax-preferred (in some cases) capital gains.

A non-resident vendor would not be entitled to a capital gain reserve where the price is paid over time, nor would a non-resident be entitled to benefit from the capital gains exemption. A non-resident individual will be subject to minimum tax in respect of Canadian source income. Capital gains would be included in the calculation of minimum tax.

Dividends and deemed dividends paid to non-residents would be subject to withholding tax under Part XIII. This would include capital dividends. The rate of withholding tax would be determined with reference to the country of residence of the vendor and the relevant tax treaty, if any. In the absence of any treaty, the rate of withholding tax is 25 per cent. The rate of withholding is reduced to as low as five per cent under various treaties. For example, the Canada-U.S. Tax Convention reduces the dividend withholding tax rate to five per cent where the beneficial owner of such dividends is a company which owns at least 10 per cent of the voting shares of the company paying the dividends. It may be beneficial to "stream" capital dividends to Canadian resident shareholders since non-residents are not entitled to receive them tax-free.[63]

---

[62] See Interpretation Bulletin IT-489R.

[63] This planning may be possible although there are anti-avoidance rules in section 83 which must be reviewed.

THREE

BUY-SELL AGREEMENTS AND LIFE INSURANCE

¶300
Overview

This Chapter begins with an assessment of why a buy-sell agreement that is triggered on the death of a shareholder is a key business continuation planning tool. Buy-sell agreements, which may be triggered on the retirement, disability or death of a shareholder, may be part of a comprehensive shareholders' agreement or may be "carved out" as a separate agreement between the shareholders. In the latter case, it is important that the main shareholders' agreement does not include provisions that may conflict with the terms of the stand-alone buy-sell agreement. A well-drafted buy-sell agreement can ensure the smooth transfer of shares between shareholders, whether as part of the transition of a business from one generation to the next in a family-owned corporation or between arm's length shareholders.

The effectiveness of any buy-sell agreement can be hampered or severely restricted if the funds for the purchase are not available at the time of the triggering event. Accordingly, shareholders and their advisors should be aware of the primary funding options. There are various funding options that shareholders may choose to consider when they are discussing the buy-sell portion of their shareholders' agreement or of a stand-alone buy-sell agreement.

Life insurance can be used to help finance the acquisition of the shares of one shareholder by another because it can be an extremely cost-effective funding option. The discussion in this Chapter on the role that life insurance can play as a funding option is followed by a brief overview of the most common types of life insurance available to shareholders. This is followed by a review of the key taxation issues that may affect life insurance owned by shareholders directly or through a corporation.

Finally, this Chapter addresses some of the planning concerns that confront the sole shareholder and problems that may be encountered where there are non-resident shareholders.

¶305
Buy-Sell Agreements and Business Continuation Planning

Whenever a corporation has more than one shareholder, it is recommended that the shareholders enter into a buy-sell agreement addressing the sale or transfer of shares when a shareholder dies.

Some issues that arise when a shareholder dies are:

- Can the business survive without one of the key contributing owners or employees?
- How will creditors react to the news of an owner's death, disability or critical illness?
- Can the surviving co-owners afford to purchase the shares or interest? If so, can a fair market price be agreed upon?
- If the business is to go to the family, can the inactive family members be kept from meddling in the affairs of the business?

A well-planned buy-sell agreement can satisfactorily address each of these issues and provide a solution. The buy-sell agreement can provide for a smooth transition of the business, thus satisfying the concerns of employees and of creditors and maintaining the value of the company for the purchaser. Without a buy-sell agreement, it is possible that employees would leave the company or that creditors would call loans if there was uncertainty as to the transition.

By providing for a sale on death to the surviving shareholder(s) or to the company, the likelihood of a confrontation between the estate and the surviving shareholder(s) will be minimized. A mandatory buy-sell agreement will preclude a sale by the estate to a third party. In addition, a buy-sell agreement serves to ensure stability of management and control of the corporation, especially in cases where neither the estate's legal representative nor the deceased's heir are qualified to be involved in the business or to participate in management decisions. In large part, this is an essential part of business continuation planning as the interests of the estate and of the surviving shareholder(s) are not likely to be the same.

The estate is protected as the buy-sell agreement provides for the payment of a fair price for the shares. By negotiating the terms of the buy-sell agreement when all parties are in good health, it is more likely that a fair price would be set for the shares as the parties do not know who will be the first to die. A mandatory buy-sell agreement creates a market for the shares of the deceased shareholder, which is important as it is possible that an alternate purchaser would not be found for the shares, especially if the estate receives a minority interest or the deceased was a sole shareholder.

In many cases, the shares may be the major financial asset of the estate. The estate may be in need of cash not only to discharge the expenses on death but also to provide a source of income for the family to replace the salary which was earned by the deceased. In many small businesses, the bulk of the profits are distributed by way of salary rather than dividends, so there may be an immediate need for income for the deceased's family.

If no provision is made for the sale of the deceased's shares, the estate may find itself in the unenviable position of owing capital gains tax (arising from the deemed disposition of the shares on death under subsection 70(5)[1]), while not receiving any proceeds for the sale of the shares.[2] That situation may be worsened if there is little or no expectation of receiving dividends from the corporation in the future. It is unlikely that the estate or any of the deceased's heirs would receive a salary from the corporation in the absence of someone actually doing work for the corporation.

By entering into a buy-sell agreement, arrangements may be made for the determination of the price, the funding and the structure of the buy-out. The buy-out may be structured to minimize the cash flow drain to the company and to the surviving shareholder(s), and to minimize or defer the tax liability of the estate.

¶310
Funding *Inter Vivos* and *Post-Mortem* Buy-outs — Alternatives

An unfunded buy-sell agreement may cause almost more harm than good as it results in shareholders being obliged to sell or purchase shares in the absence of a guaranteed source of funding. A review of the most common funding options can provide some direction for shareholders and their advisors when deciding on the structure that best suits their needs and circumstances.

At times, the preferred funding option may determine which buy-sell structure is chosen, while in other instances, the funding structure is only one consideration examined by the shareholders in their decision-making process. Once the preferred funding option is selected, steps should be taken to ensure that the funding will be in place when it is required. Then, the buy-sell agreement should be drafted to incorporate the advantages of the preferred funding option.

¶315   Funding from Outside the Corporation

Cash on Hand

As noted in Chapter 1, in rare instances, the purchasing shareholder may have sufficient cash on hand personally to finance the share purchase. This funding option has the virtue of being simple and does not require any pro-active steps to be taken by either the selling or purchasing shareholders.

---

[1] Unless otherwise indicated, all statutory references are to the *Income Tax Act* (Canada) (the "Act").

[2] See Interpretation Bulletin IT-416R3, Valuation of shares of a corporation receiving life insurance proceeds on the death of a taxpayer, dated July 10, 1987.

The cost to the purchasing shareholder is 100 per cent of the cost of the shares being acquired.

It should be noted that the shareholders of private corporations frequently sign personal guarantees for the corporation's liabilities. When a shareholder dies, the surviving or remaining shareholders may be called upon to use personal resources to meet those obligations, which may further limit the purchaser's ability to use cash on hand to fund the buy-out.

However, the most significant drawback of this funding option is that the purchaser may not actually have enough cash on hand at the time the buy-sell is triggered. Thus, this is perhaps the least viable method of funding a buy-sell agreement.

Sale of Assets

Like using cash on hand to finance a buy-out, the sale of assets has significant drawbacks. Firstly, the purchaser must have valuable assets that could be liquidated on a timely basis to finance the buy-out. This means that the sale depends on the nature and value of property owned by the purchaser at the time of the buy-out. In the case of a corporation considering this funding option, an asset sale may not be possible, especially if the primary assets are required for the daily operation of the business. Secondly, the purchaser would also have to pay the cost of disposing of the assets, including any capital gains tax that may arise on the disposition of capital property.

This funding option cannot be used successfully if the purchaser does not own enough valuable assets at the time the buy-out is triggered, if the assets cannot be disposed of in a timely manner, or if the costs of disposition result in a short-fall of proceeds to finance the share purchase.

Sinking Fund Financing

Once the shares of a corporation have been valued, the corporation or the shareholders may choose to create a fund from which the purchase price will be paid when the buy-sell triggering event occurs. Annual deposits are made to the "sinking fund" with the intention that the annual deposits plus the income and growth due to the investment of the sinking fund will be enough to finance the purchase of shares.

The sinking fund option means that there must be a periodic valuation of the shares of the corporation. This must be done to ensure that the amounts being set aside are sufficient, with growth over time, to fully fund the buy-out.

There are several disadvantages to using a sinking fund. Firstly, there is always the risk that a shareholder may die prematurely or retire unexpectedly — usually at a time when inadequate funds have been set aside in the sinking fund. Even with regular share valuations, it is not unlikely that the deemed disposition arising on the death of a shareholder will be for more than the value of the sinking fund — leaving the purchaser to find a way to make up the short-fall.

Secondly, the value of a sinking fund held within a corporation means that the sinking fund is considered on a share valuation — unless the shareholders' agreement expressly states that a corporate sinking fund is excluded. In the absence of such an exclusion, the corporation's sinking fund will never be enough to fully fund a share purchase. For example, assume that Opco's fair market value ("fair market value") is $1,000,000 and there are two equal shareholders. Over time, Opco's sinking fund accumulates the requisite $500,000 which is earmarked for the purchase of the shares of a deceased shareholder. However, since the sinking fund is an asset of the corporation, the shares of Opco will now be worth $1,500,000. The fair market value for 50 per cent of Opco's shares will, therefore, be $750,000, which means the purchasing shareholder will have a shortfall of $250,000 of purchase funds.

Further, creditors of an individual shareholder or of the corporation may be able to bring a successful claim against a sinking fund held by an individual or a corporation. In the case of individuals, the sinking fund would be deemed to be a personal asset and could be the subject of a successful claim by a spouse or former spouse under the pertinent matrimonial property legislation. Similarly, a sinking fund held inside a corporation is an asset of the corporation and, therefore, subject to the claims of the corporation's creditors.

Finally, a corporation's sinking fund will be considered to be a passive asset since it is not used by the corporation in the course of business. As noted in Chapter 2, when the passive assets of a corporation exceed 10 per cent of the corporation's value, there is a significant risk that the shares will no longer qualify for the $500,000 lifetime capital gains exemption available to the holders of shares of a private corporation.

When examined in the context of a holding company structure (with Holdco owning all of the shares of Opco), the use of a sinking fund approach may provide mixed outcomes. On the death of a shareholder, the holding company could purchase the deceased's shares using after-tax corporate dollars that have accumulated within the company (which are generally taxed at a lower rate than the top marginal tax rate for individuals). However, the shares of the holding company would still be an asset of the individual shareholder, which may expose the sinking fund to the personal creditors of the individual shareholder. In addition, the sinking fund will likely be considered a "passive" asset which could make the shares of the holding company ineligible for the $500,000 capital gains exemption.

Thus, the use of a sinking fund as a funding option is not generally recommended as long as alternatives such as insurance are available to the shareholders.

Loan Financing from a Financial Institution

Many parties to unfunded buy-sell arrangements intend to rely on loan financing from a bank, trust company or other financial institution, whether the loan is taken out by an individual shareholder or a corporation.

This funding option may not be viable if the corporation or the purchaser's personal credit worthiness or solvency at the time of the share purchase is questionable. The insolvency of the purchasing shareholder will make a commercial loan unlikely. As stated in Chapter 1, under corporate legislation, a redemption or purchase of shares for cancellation may not be legally possible if a company is insolvent.[3]

The purchasing shareholder, whether an individual or a corporation, may be able to deduct the interest expense on a commercial loan under the provisions of paragraph 20(1)(c). If the borrowed funds are used to finance a share redemption, the interest expense will generally be deductible so long as the amount of the loan (used to redeem shares) does not exceed the paid-up capital of the redeemed shares plus the accumulated profits of the corporation, as determined in accordance with generally accepted accounting principles.[4]

The carrying costs of the loan financing are, in effect, an additional cost to the purchaser, which increases the effective purchase price to the amount of the loan plus the cost of all interest payments. Servicing the debt will divert corporate earnings from being reinvested in the business, which may have an adverse effect on the long-term vitality of the corporation. This funding option may also mean that the purchaser will be unable to acquire loan financing for business expansion or other purposes of the corporation until the buy-out loan has been fully or partially paid.

Loan financing for a buy-sell agreement is contingent on financial and economic issues that may be beyond the control of the purchasing shareholder/corporation. Thus, reliance on this funding method may result in a purchaser not being able to obtain the requisite funds when the buy-out provisions of the shareholders' agreement are triggered.

Instalment Payments over a Period of Time

The vendor may be used as a source of financing if the vendor is willing to accept payment over a number of years. There are two principal versions of this structure: payment via a promissory note and the staged purchases of shares on an annual basis. Two further variants are the earn-out arrangement and either a section 86 or a section 51 reorganization.

The promissory note arrangement means that the purchaser buys the shares for the agreed-upon price using a deposit in partial payment of the purchase price, along with a promissory note that sets out the terms upon which the balance of the purchase price will be paid. The vendor will typically expect to receive interest payments on the unpaid balance of the purchase price during the payment period. In addition, the vendor will expect to receive adequate security to ensure that the promissory note and interest are both paid in full. The promissory note will be a debt of the purchaser (individual or corporation), which the vendor will be entitled to legally enforce through all steps permitted to a creditor in the purchaser's place of residence.

---

[3] For example, see the *Business Corporations Act* (Ontario), S.O. 1982, c. 4, s. 38(3) and *Canada Business Corporations Act*, S.C. 1974-75-76, c. 33, s. 34.

[4] See Interpretation Bulletin IT-533, Interest deductibility and related issues, dated October 31, 2003, at paragraph 23. Note legislative changes proposed for 2005 and subsequent years contained in the Department of Finance News Releases dated October 31, 2003 limiting deductibility of any expenses where it is not reasonable to expect that the taxpayer will be realizing cumulative profit from the business or property.

Under a promissory note arrangement, the vendor can claim a capital gains reserve,[5] thereby deferring payment of capital gains tax over a period of up to five years. The capital gains reserve will be available for the portion of the capital gain not due until after the end of the year. The reserve will be limited to 4/5 of the determined capital gain in the year of sale, 3/5 of the determined gain in the second year, and so on.

The successful use of the capital gains reserve hinges on the fact that the proceeds due to the vendor are readily determinable at the time of the sale. The Act only permits a reserve "in respect of the proceeds of disposition of the property that are payable to the taxpayer after the end of the year."[6] Therefore, the buy-sell agreement must include details of when each installment of the purchase price will be payable to the vendor, together with particulars of interest payment dates.

The vendor ceases to be a shareholder once the purchase transaction has closed. Thus, the purchaser only has to be concerned with making the requisite interest and principal payments under the promissory note and does not have to consider issues such as control of the corporation or minority shareholder concerns.

A staged purchase of shares occurs when the parties to the buy-sell agreement determine that the vendor will sell a specified number of shares to the purchaser in accordance with a schedule. The vendor will claim any capital gain or loss as each block of shares is sold. Alternatively, the corporation may agree to redeem the vendor's shares in accordance with the schedule. Under this structure, the vendor will be deemed to have received a taxable dividend to the extent that the proceeds exceed the paid-up capital of the shares sold.

Unlike the promissory note method, the vendor remains a shareholder during the staged buy-out process and can, therefore, insist upon receiving dividends or participating in the management of the corporation. If the vendor is dissatisfied with what the other shareholder does with the corporation, the vendor may bring a minority shareholder's oppression remedy application, which could disrupt the ongoing management and control of the corporation. It should be noted, however, that former shareholders of a corporation may well have status to bring an oppression remedy application where they continue to hold debt issued by the corporation and received by them as part of a sale of their shares.

A third instalment payment structure, known as an earn-out arrangement, occurs when the vendor agrees to accept payment of the purchase price out of the future profits of the corporation. The vendor will sell the shares and receive a minimal amount on closing (perhaps equal to the book value of the shares). The balance of the purchase price is usually computed as a percentage of gross or net profit over a period of years.

---

[5] See subparagraph 40(1)(a)(iii) and Interpretation Bulletin IT-236R4, Reserves — Disposition of capital property, dated July 30, 1999.

[6] See clause 40(1)(a)(iii)(C). Subsection 40(1.1) permits the capital gains reserve to be extended to 10 years in the case of a sale of shares by a parent to a child (both of whom are resident in Canada at the date of the transfer) where the shares are of either a "small business corporation" or a "family farm corporation."

Canada Customs and Revenue Agency's (the "CRA")[7] administrative position with respect to earn-out arrangements is quite clear and is set out in Interpretation Bulletin IT-426. The CRA is of the view that paragraph 12(1)(*g*)[8] will apply to include all payments under an earn-out in the vendor's income unless the vendor adopts the cost recovery method of reporting a gain or loss, which results in the recovery of the cost base of the shares on a tax-free basis out of first payments. As set out in Interpretation Bulletin 426 ("IT-426"), the vendor must satisfy the following conditions:

1. The vendor and purchaser are dealing with each other at arm's length[9].
2. The gain or loss on the sale is clearly of a capital nature.
3. It is reasonable to assume that the earn-out feature relates to underlying goodwill the value of which cannot reasonably be expected to be agreed upon by the vendor and purchaser at the date of the sale.
4. The duration of the sale agreement does not exceed five years.
5. The vendor submits, with his or her return of income for the year in which the shares were disposed of, a copy of the sale agreement. He or she also submits with that return a letter requesting the application of the cost recovery method to the sale, and an undertaking to follow the procedure of reporting the gain or loss on the sale under the cost recovery method as outlined below.

The cost recovery method gives the vendor the ability to report the determinable capital gain over a period of five years in accordance with the capital gains reserve mechanism under subparagraph 40(1)(*a*)(iii). Thus, the capital gains reserve will become available for the portion of the determinable capital gain not due until after the end of the year. As with the promissory note structure, the reserve is set at 4/5 of the determined capital gain for the year of sale, 3/5 of the determined gain in the second year, and so on. The amounts that become determinable under the earn-out formula are treated as capital gains. Where the earn-out proceeds are not determinable, no reserve is available. However, such amounts would not be included in income until actually received. The capital gains reserve available under subparagraph 40(1)(*a*)(iii) will not apply as the ultimate purchase price cannot be determined at the time of the sale; it is dependent upon the uncertain future performance of the corporation. Thus, according to the CRA:

> In this type of situation, no amount is considered "payable" as proceeds of disposition at the time of the disposition. An amount is not "payable" until

---

[7] Although not enacted at the time of writing, legislation is in the works to change the Agency's name to Canada Revenue Agency. The Agency is currently referring to itself in this fashion.

[8] This section requires that amounts received by a taxpayer that was dependent on the use of property or the production of property (other than agricultural land) are to be included as ordinary income of the taxpayer, even though the asset being sold was capital in nature. Although the application of paragraph 12(1)(*g*) to a sale of shares is not clear, in view of the CRA's stated position, prudence suggests following either the cost recovery method or the reverse earn-out approach wherever possible. See Interpretation Bulletin IT-462, Payments based on production or use, dated October 27, 1980.

[9] A discussion of the meaning of "arm's length" can be found in Chapter 2 — Tax Considerations — *Inter Vivos* Buy-outs.

¶315

there is a "legally enforceable" right to receive the amount. The "legally enforceable'" entitlement to proceeds of disposition pursuant to the earn-out agreement cannot be established until certain future events have occurred such that no amount is "payable" at the time the property is disposed of.[10]

It should be noted that paragraph 12(1)(g) may also be avoided by structuring the sale as a reverse earn-out under which a maximum purchase price is set in the sale agreement. The maximum purchase amount would be subject to reduction in the event that certain criteria contained in the buy-sell agreement are not met. This approach is set out in more detail in Interpretation Bulletin IT-462, Payments based on production and use.

The fourth instalment payment structure involves the reorganization of the share capital of the corporation pursuant to either section 86 or section 51. The common shares held by the vendor will be converted into fixed value preference shares, which would be retractable over time in accordance with an agreed-upon schedule.

The spousal rollover under subsection 70(6) may be used to defer tax when the shares of the deceased shareholder are redeemed over time.[11] The spousal rollover may be available when the shares are bequeathed to a spouse or common-law partner or to a trust for the exclusive benefit of the spouse or common-law partner. The use of the spousal rollover will defer the capital gains tax arising on the death of the shareholder until the date upon which the spouse/common-law partner dies or the shares are disposed of during the lifetime of the spouse/common-law partner.

In order to qualify for the spousal rollover, the shares must vest indefeasibly in the spouse/common-law partner or the trust for the benefit of the spouse/common-law partner within 36 months of the date of death of the deceased shareholder. Accordingly, it is important that the shareholders' agreement not create a binding obligation on the estate of the deceased shareholder to sell the shares, such that it could be found that the shares did not vest in the surviving spouse/common-law partner or the trust for the benefit of the spouse/common-law partner. The use of put/call options can be an effective method of dealing with this issue.

Cumulative dividends may be paid on the outstanding shares held following the conversion. Under subsection 84(3), a taxable dividend would arise to the extent that the redemption price exceeds the paid-up capital of the shares. In addition, the vendor may also have a taxable capital gain equal to the amount by which the proceeds of the redemption (less the dividend deemed to arise on the redemption) exceed the adjusted cost base of the shares. The capital gains exemption may offset all or part of the capital gain. If the shares of an operating company are held by a holding company and the deemed dividend exceeds the holding company's proportional share of the operating company's post-1971 retained tax earnings, the excess may be treated as a capital gain rather than a dividend.[12]

---

[10] Technical Interpretation 2000-0051115 — Capital Gains Reserve.

[11] See Interpretation Bulletin IT-305R4, Testamentary spousal trusts, dated October 30, 1996.

[12] See subsection 55(2).

The principal drawback to all of the instalment payment arrangements is that the vendor is dependent on the continuance of the business in order to realize the full proceeds, unless adequate security is provided. In the case of a buy-out on death, this may leave the estate of the deceased shareholder in the position of having to rely on the ability of the purchaser to generate profits and growth in the corporation over the term of the pay-out period following the death of the selling shareholder. Further, the estate must remain "open" and under administration for as long as any portion of the purchase price remains unpaid. This may give rise to administration difficulties for the executors and family of the deceased shareholder, especially if the Will provides for an outright distribution of the estate assets, once the debts and other obligations of the deceased have been paid.

¶320 Funding from Within the Corporation

Annual Distribution of After-tax Profits to Minimize the Value of the Company prior to the Buy-out of a Shareholder

While this is not a true funding option, the annual distribution of after-tax profits keeps the value of the shares lower than they would be if the corporation has significant retained earnings. Thus, the purchase price set out in the buy-sell agreement will be lower than it might otherwise be, yet would still reflect the fair market value of the shares.

As noted in Chapter 1, this arrangement is particularly attractive in situations when holding companies own the shares of an operating company. The holding companies must each own more than 10 per cent of the issued shares and fair market value equity of the operating company or be part of a related group which controls such a company.[13]

The after-tax profits of the operating company will be paid to the holding companies as an inter-corporate dividend, on a *pro rata* basis. The dividend is included in the holding companies' income but an offsetting deduction is generally available under subsection 112(1).[14] Thus, the holding companies do not pay tax when they receive the dividend that reflects the after-tax profits of the operating company. Tax is only payable when dividends are paid to the individual owners of the holding company shares.

If the operating company subsequently requires the funds, the holding companies can lend the funds that were paid as dividends back to the operating company. The holding companies may elect to have these shareholder loans secured by corporate assets of the operating company. This approach can

---

[13] No Part IV tax would arise in these circumstances unless the operating company receives a dividend refund as a result of the payment of dividends: see subsection 186(1) and Interpretation Bulletin IT-269R3, Part IV Tax on taxable dividends received by a private corporation or a subject corporation, dated November 29, 1991. The possible application of Part VI.1 tax should be considered whenever a corporation pays a dividend or redeems a taxable preferred share. The possible application of this tax is discussed in Chapter 2 — Tax Considerations — *Inter Vivos* Buy-outs.

[14] Section 112 contains specific provisions which deny the deduction in certain circumstances in the context of preferred shares issued as part of a financing arrangement. In addition, subsection 55(2) may apply to treat a dividend as a capital gain in certain circumstances.

have the additional benefit of protecting the profits of the operating company from unsecured creditors.

The principal appeal of dividending out the after-tax profits of the operating company is that it may make the company more affordable. When the share value is kept low by the annual distribution of after-tax profits, the purchaser will not be required to purchase redundant assets.

Funding the Share Purchase from the Retained Earnings of the Corporation

This funding option requires the operating company to purchase for cancellation the vendor's shares. When shares are purchased for cancellation, the interest expense that relates to the redemption proceeds in excess of the paid-up capital are generally provided the redemption proceeds do not exceed the paid-up capital and the accumulated profits are deductible. See the preceding discussion on Instalment Payments for the potential disadvantages of this funding option.

Holding Companies as a "Funding Source"

In addition to being an effective corporate planning structure, holding companies can be used to facilitate the sale or purchase of the shares of individual shareholders.

Typically, the shares of the operating company will be owned by one or more holding companies. The buy-sell agreement can be structured so that the holding company of one individual is required to purchase the holding company shares owned by the other individual. When this structure is used by individuals who together with certain related persons own at least 10 per cent of the shares of the company and who do not deal at arm's length with the purchasing holding company, section 84.1 will be applied. If section 84.1 applies, a taxable dividend will arise to the extent that any cash or debt received exceeds the greater of the paid-up capital of the shares of the operating company and the adjusted cost base of the shares. The adjusted cost base of the shares will be adjusted downward to exclude any portion of the former $100,000 lifetime capital gains exemption or the $500,000 capital gains exemption for shares of a private corporation previously claimed in respect of shares held by the selling shareholder and any individual who is not dealing at arm's length with the selling shareholder. The adjusted cost base of the shares will also be ground down or reduced to the extent of any 1972 valuation day value in respect of such shares where the shares were owned prior to 1972 by the selling shareholder or any person not dealing with the selling shareholder at arm's length.[15] Where no cash or debt is received, section 84.1 will reduce the

---

[15] See subsection 84.1(2). Any capital gains reserves claimed in non-arm's length transactions may also grind the adjusted cost base of the operating company.

¶320

paid-up capital of any share issued by the purchasing corporation in the fashion described above.[16]

Numerous rules apply in section 84.1 to deem shareholders to not deal at arm's length when the selling shareholder is part of the purchasing group. The rules are wide-ranging, including the attribution of share ownership rules among related family members and trust situations.[17]

An alternative holding company structure involves having the holding company owned by Shareholder B purchase the operating company shares owned by the holding company owned by Shareholder A. Generally speaking, based on tax rates in effect at the time of writing, the tax paid by the holding company on the capital gains arising on the sale of the shares of the operating company followed by a distribution of the after-tax proceeds to the individual shareholder or his or her estate will be about the same or slightly higher than the tax payable on a sale of the holding company shares by the individual shareholder. The exception is that the holding company will not be able to claim the capital gains exemption. However, the sale of the shares of the holding company may not be desirable if the holding company owns other significant assets, especially if those assets have appreciated in value.

When holding companies are used, the purchase price paid to the selling shareholder can be funded from the current and future earnings or profits of the operating company. This means that the purchaser will not have to explore the use of other funding options, such as a sinking fund, a loan from a financial institution, the sale of assets, or cash on hand, if any.

¶325 Insurance Funding

Disability Insurance Funding

The use of disability insurance to fund the buy-out of a shareholder's interest is not as common as life insurance funding. Interestingly, actuarial studies show that the probability of a shareholder's long-term or permanent disability is greater than that of premature death.

Disability buy-out insurance can be used to finance the purchase of shares on the permanent disability of a shareholder and is generally available on a lump-sum basis. Disability buy-out insurance can usually be acquired only if each shareholder can qualify for the personal disability coverage. The cost of disability insurance for buy-sell purposes is generally higher than that of an

---

[16] Even if section 84.1 is not applicable, consideration should be given to whether GAAR will apply to the transaction. For example, in *McNichol v. The Queen*, 97 DTC 111 (T.C.C), the Tax Court ruled that GAAR applied to treat the proceeds from the sale of shares as taxable dividends in the hands of the selling shareholder when the shares of a corporation were sold to an arm's length corporation in circumstances where section 84.1 did not apply. If this decision is allowed to stand, it will hopefully be limited to its facts. In *McNichol*, the sale of shares occurred after the company had sold certain real estate assets, leaving only cash remaining in the company. The selling shareholders claimed the $100,000 capital gains exemption on the share sale.

[17] Paragraphs 84.1(2)(*b*) and (*d*), subsections 84.1(2.01), and 84.1(2.2). Interpretation Bulletin IT-489R, Non-arm's length sale of shares to a corporation, dated February 28, 1994.

equivalent amount of life insurance coverage. This, of course, reflects the higher probability of disability, particularly as shareholders age.

The definitions of disability (whether long-term, partial, recurring or partial) in the buy-sell agreement must match the definitions in the insurance policy. Otherwise, there is a risk that there could be a pay-out under the policy without there being a mandatory share purchase. Even worse, the terms of the buy-sell agreement could be triggered while those of the disability buy-out policy are not.

Consideration should be given to whether the disability buy-out proceeds should be included in any valuation of the corporation for the purposes of determining the purchase price. It should be noted that, while the disability buy-out proceeds may be received by the corporation on a tax-free basis, the disability buy-out proceeds do not get added to the corporation's capital dividend account.[18] Thus, although the disability buy-out proceeds are not subject to tax, there is no mechanism in the Act to permit the corporation to pay out the disability buy-out proceeds as a tax-free capital dividend to shareholders. This serves to restrict the use of disability buy-out insurance on a wider basis.

If the disability buy-out policy does not provide for a lump sum pay-out, the corporation may have to spread the purchase price of the disabled shareholder's shares over a period of time consistent with the duration of the benefit period under the disability policy. Under this arrangement, the disabled shareholder may be faced with cash shortages as buy-out funds would be received over a number of years, but the disabled shareholder would no longer be able to work.

In addition, if the disability buy-sell agreement were to be based on an immediate redemption of all of the shares of the disabled shareholder, the shareholder would face the fiscal hardship of having the full amount of the dividend on redemption being subject to tax in the year in which the sale of the shares occurred. A staged redemption (using a section 51 or section 86 reorganization converting common shares into preferred shares, for example) of a disabled shareholder's shares by the company over a number of years would avoid this tax problem since the deemed dividend resulting from the redemption of shares would be spread over the redemption period, thus obviating the selling shareholder's need to fund all the tax dollars in one year. The influence that the disabled shareholder might exert as a shareholder could be detailed in the shareholders' agreement.

Finally, when a share redemption disability buy-out arrangement is used, the remaining shareholder does not receive an increase in the adjusted cost base of the remaining shares. The purchase and cancellation of the shares of a disabled shareholder by the company results in a reallocation of the intrinsic share value among the remaining shares. For example, assume that the two shareholders of Opco each own 50 per cent of the issued shares. If the fair market value of Opco's shares is $1,000,000 with an adjusted cost base of nil, when one-half of the shares are purchased for cancellation, the aggregate value

---

[18] See the section later in this Chapter on Taxation of Life Insurance for an explanation of the capital dividend account and how it works.

of the post-redemption shares is still $1,000,000 and the adjusted cost base remains at nil. However, the remaining shareholder now owns shares worth $1,000,000 instead of $500,000. When the remaining shareholder disposes of the shares, the "pregnant" capital gain has been increased by $500,000.

Inter vivos Funding using Cash Values within a Life Insurance Policy

A corporation that owns cash-value life insurance on the lives of its shareholders may opt to access values within the policy during the lifetime of the insured shareholder.

The corporation may elect to take a policy loan[19] against the cash value in the policy from the insurance carrier to fund an *inter vivos* buy-out. The corporation may borrow any amount up to the adjusted cost basis of the policy on a tax-free basis. Amounts borrowed from the policy over the policy's adjusted cost basis[20] are considered to be a partial disposition of an interest in a life insurance policy under subsection 148(9) and are included in the corporation's income in the year the policy loan is taken. This serves to reduce the adjusted cost basis of the life insurance policy. If, however, the amount in excess of the adjusted cost basis is repaid within the same calendar year as the policy loan was taken, there will be no income inclusion and the policy's adjusted cost basis will be reduced to nil. When a policy loan is repaid, the policy's adjusted cost basis is replenished. The insurance carrier is entitled to receive interest on the amounts borrowed from the policy.

Whenever the life insured dies while there is an outstanding policy loan against the policy, the insurance carrier is entitled to full repayment from the death benefit. From a practical perspective, the insurance carrier will issue a cheque to the designated beneficiary that is equal to the death benefit minus the value of the outstanding policy loan together with any accrued interest on the policy loan. Thus, the corporation as the designated beneficiary will only receive the net amount. However, under the provisions of the *Uniform Insurance Act* and the Quebec Civil Code, taking out a policy loan does not affect any existing beneficiary designation in force at the time of the policy loan or on the date of death of the person whose life is insured.

Alternatively, the corporation may opt to use the accrued cash values of the policy as collateral for a loan or line of credit from a financial institution.[21] This arrangement is often referred to as "leveraging the policy." Under current tax rules, the loan from the financial institution is received on a tax-free basis,

---

[19] This arrangement is more accurately described as an advance against the death benefit payable under the policy — an important consideration as the legal formalities are not the same as taking out a loan from a financial institution. Thus, the terms "policy loan" and "borrow" are used for convenience only. See David Norwood & John P. Weir, *Norwood on Life Insurance Law in Canada*, 3rd ed. (Toronto: Carswell, 2002), at p. 128 for a lucid and brief review of "policy loans."

[20] Readers should note that the tax cost of a life insurance policy is referred to as "adjusted cost basis" in the *Income Tax Act* (Canada) unlike the definition "adjusted cost base" which is used to describe the tax cost of other property.

[21] See Norwood & Weir at pp. 369 — 371 for a discussion of collateral assignment of life insurance policies.

while a policy loan from the insurance carrier may not be. In addition, the corporation may be able to deduct a portion of the interest expense under paragraph 20(1)(e.2) if the loan arrangement can be characterized as being for business or investment purposes.[22] In order to qualify, the policy must be assigned to the financial institution as collateral for the loan. The collateral assignment of the life insurance policy must also be a condition of the loan.

In the common law jurisdictions in Canada, the collateral assignment of a life insurance policy does not result in any limitation being placed on how much of the death benefit can be credited to the capital dividend account. Thus, the corporation will receive the entire amount of the death benefit as the designated beneficiary and will use a portion of the death benefit to pay off the loan. However, the amount of the death benefit in excess of the policy's adjusted cost basis may still be credited to the capital dividend account.

In Quebec, the use of life insurance as collateral for a loan results in the creation of a movable hypothec. As with collateral assignment in the common jurisdictions in Canada, the movable hypothec does not require the actual transfer of title to the policy to the lender. Instead, the lender is granted a security interest in the death benefit up to the amount of the loan.

At the date of the writing of this Chapter, the law in Quebec remains unresolved about whether an individual can enter into a movable hypothec for a personally owned life insurance policy. This is because a valid movable hypothec must be "with delivery," which means that the lender is to receive physical possession of the property that is governed by the movable hypothec. It is unclear whether an individual policy owner can provide full delivery of the life insurance policy.

In contrast, a corporation may enter into a valid movable hypothec of a life insurance policy because there is no requirement for delivery of the policy. The key planning issue for corporations is that, when a life insurance policy is assigned as collateral for a loan, the Quebec Civil Code expressly provides for the revocation of existing beneficiary designations up to the amount of the loan. This means that, while the corporation receives the death benefit on the death of the insured shareholder, the amount of the insurance proceeds that can be credited to the capital dividend account is severely restricted. As a result, while the corporation may receive the death benefit on a tax-free basis, the capital dividend account may not be available to provide for a tax-free capital dividend payment to the purchasing shareholder.

Using Life Insurance to fund a Buy-out on Death

When a shareholder dies, a corporation may receive life insurance proceeds from a corporate-owned insurance policy on the life of the deceased shareholder. The amount of the death benefit in excess of the adjusted cost basis of the life insurance policy that the corporation, as the policy owner, had in the life insurance policy can be added to the corporation's capital dividend account.

---

[22] See Interpretation Bulletin IT-309R2, *Premiums on life insurance used as collateral*, dated February 28, 1995.

The insurance proceeds can be used by the corporation to fund the purchase of shares in a variety of structures, which will be discussed in a later section of the Chapter.

¶330
Types of Life Insurance

When the time comes to consider the role of insurance products, many business owners and their advisors overlook the fact that the distinction between "family" or "personal" insurance and "business" insurance is largely one of convenience rather than fact. The welfare of the business and the family are, in may ways, inter-related and integrally linked. The continued economic well-being of the business owner and the family depends upon the income flow from the income earning owner as well as the on-going financial good health of the business in which the owner and the family are engaged. Conversely, disruptions in the family often cause problems in the business. This is particularly true if the dissension reaches the stage where family members stop communicating with one another on a meaningful basis.

The motivation for buying life insurance in a business context is, fundamentally, the same as that for buying personal insurance: protection. Shareholders want to minimize the disruption that may be caused as a result of death, disability, critical illness, or retirement of a family member, business owner, or key employee. When the primary insurance need is personal, the family is involved in the planning and decision-making. In contrast, the employees, fellow shareholders and other business associates and their families, along with creditors and, on occasion, competitors, are considered when the main need is business-related.

Term Insurance

A term life insurance policy is one that is issued by the insurance carrier for a specific term or period of years. The shortest period offered is a yearly renewable term, with other common coverage periods being five, ten, fifteen and twenty years. The premium for term insurance is based on a combination of the age and health of the life insured and will be locked in for the term of the policy. If the policy can be renewed, the contract will be extended for the renewal term and the premium will increase (to reflect the increased age of the person whose life is insured) according to a schedule contained in the policy contract. The life insurance company will pay the face value of the policy to the beneficiary of the policy on the death of the life insured, provided that the death occurs during the term. If a policy is cancelled at any time prior to death, no portion of the premium paid is refunded to the owner.

Term insurance premiums are generally less costly than permanent life insurance premiums, especially if the insured person is under age 40. This is because the premiums represent the pure cost of insuring a person of a given age without any liquid investment or savings element.

In general, the insurance carrier will require varying degrees of proof of insurability as part of the application process. This may range from the proposed life insured simply answering a number of medical questions on the application form to having to undergo a full medical examination. In addition, the insurance carrier will ask for financial evidence to support the amount of proposed coverage, especially in a business context. When a term insurance policy contains a guaranteed renewability clause, the life insured does not have to undergo a medical examination when the policy is renewed.

Many, but not all, term insurance policies give the policy owner the option to convert to a permanent form of insurance during the term of the policy. The policy owner may opt to convert to any type of permanent policy offered by the insurance carrier at the time of conversion or may be limited to a specific type of permanent coverage. A medical examination will not be necessary, unless the policy owner also wants to increase the amount of coverage at the time of conversion. The amount of the premium generally will be the same as a person of the same current age and health would pay for a new permanent life insurance policy. Since most insurance carriers only offer term coverage to a specified age (typically somewhere between ages 65–75), the right to convert to permanent insurance is a useful option. Shareholders and their advisors should ensure that a right to convert is offered whenever they or the corporation acquire term insurance.

Permanent Life Insurance

Like term insurance, this type of life insurance is insurance payable on the death of the insured person whenever that event may occur, provided that the policy is still in force. However, unlike term insurance, a permanent policy will be issued on a lifetime basis, subject to premium deposits being made. The premium payable under a permanent life policy depends upon the type of permanent coverage that is being applied for. The primary types of permanent life insurance include the following:

- **Whole life insurance** is a permanent life insurance policy that provides a guaranteed death benefit with premiums that are usually guaranteed to remain level regardless of age or health changes throughout the lifetime of the insured person. Whole life insurance typically accumulates cash values that may be borrowed against, used to continue coverage if premiums are not paid by the policy owner, or withdrawn on a permanent basis. The premiums for whole life are based on estimates of various factors, including the insurance carrier's return on investments, its operating expenses, and the cost of paying out death benefits. *Participating whole life insurance* (also known as "par insurance") policies will usually pay dividends to the policy owners, with the dividends reflecting the overall performance of the insurance company based on the factors previously mentioned. In contrast, *non-participating whole life insurance* (also known as "non-par insurance") provides lifetime coverage for a guaranteed premium. However, no dividends are paid and cash values may or may not develop, or may be limited, depending on the insurance carrier and the specific plan design of the policy.

¶330

- **Universal life** (also known as "UL insurance") is a permanent interest-sensitive policy that contains two elements: basic yearly renewable term insurance and an investment account. The premiums and benefits can be readjusted at specified times, depending on the policy owner's insurance needs and the choices that the policy owner makes with respect to the investment side of the policy.

- **Index-linked life insurance** contracts are another type of permanent life insurance in which the cash values vary based on the performance of an investment fund or other index. The premiums are usually guaranteed in these policies. The death benefit is a hybrid of a guaranteed death benefit and a non-guaranteed (or variable) component that varies, depending on the performance of the selected investment fund or index, subject to a guaranteed minimum.

- **Term-to-100 insurance** (also known as "T-100 insurance") is considered to be a type of permanent insurance; however, T-100 policies closely resemble traditional term insurance in that they do not build significant cash values or pay dividends. T-100 policies provide a death benefit to age 100, if the policy is kept in force, and have level premiums, regardless of changes in the age or health of the life insured.

Insurance on Two or More Lives under a Single Policy

Most types of life insurance can be issued on two or more lives, either on a joint basis or under a multiple lives provision. Joint life policies provide insurance payable on either the death of the first to die of the lives insured or on the second death. Typically, joint first-to-die insurance is used to provide coverage on the lives of two or more individuals and the policy terminates on the first death with the full amount of the death benefit being paid at that time. Joint second-to-die is usually only offered on two lives and is, therefore, often used when shareholders are spouses and the spousal rollover will be used to defer tax until the death of the second spouse. Joint life insurance can be used when one individual is uninsurable or suffers from impaired health. The premiums are set at a blended rate that reflects the ages and health of the lives insured and will reflect any medical underwriting on both of the insured lives done at the time of the policy application. An uninsurable shareholder can potentially "borrow a life" by using a joint second-to-die life insurance policy with a spouse or common-law partner where the shares are to be transferred to the survivor outright or in trust.

In contrast, multiple lives insurance provides for payment of a death benefit (or a refund of premiums) when each of the lives insured dies, with the payment being for a specified amount. Each life insured undergoes a medical examination and the premium for coverage on that individual is based upon the age and health of that specific life insured. Unlike joint first-to-die insurance, the policy is not dissolved on the first death. Shareholders and their advisers should consult with an insurance professional to determine if a joint life or multiple lives option makes sense for their situation.

¶330

¶335
How Life Insurance Policies are Taxed

No discussion of the use of life insurance in a corporate context would be complete without a review of the essential taxation provisions that affect the policies and their owners, whether the policy owner is a shareholder or a corporation. Interpretation Bulletin IT-87R2 deals with income received by policy owners from life insurance policies, while Interpretation Bulletin IT-430R3 addresses the issue of life insurance proceeds received by private corporations and partnerships.

Adjusted Cost Basis

The adjusted cost basis of a life insurance policy is defined in subsection 148(9) and is the result of a complex formula that takes into consideration all premiums paid into a life insurance policy, all withdrawals from, dividends declared under and policy loans from the policy, and the cost of the insurance provided under the policy. There are thirteen components referred to in subsection 148(9) that are used to calculate the adjusted cost base of a life insurance policy.

The adjusted cost basis of a life insurance policy is increased by the following events:

- the cost of all interests in the policy acquired by the policy owner;
- for policies last acquired before December 2, 1982, the full amount of the premiums paid, including the premiums paid for all policy riders;
- for policies last acquired after December 1, 1982, the premium paid for the basic policy and any term insurance riders that have been paid by the policy owner (or on the owner's behalf) minus the net cost of pure insurance;[23]
- policy gains that have previously been included in the policy owner's income, such as dividends, policy loans received by the policy owner, etc.;
- certain policy loan repayments; and
- the mortality gain, if any, arising on the death of a policy owner if an interest in the policy is rolled over to a surviving spouse; this will typically occur when the deceased taxpayer was the owner of a life insurance policy on a life other than his or her own.

Reductions in the adjusted cost basis of a life insurance policy occur under the following circumstances:

- for policies in force before March 31, 1978, the amount of any policy loan outstanding on that date;
- for policies last acquired after December 1, 1982, the total premium paid that relates to policy riders and ancillary benefits (i.e., waiver of

---

[23] See the explanation of "net cost of pure insurance" later in this section of the Chapter.

premiums if the policy owner becomes disabled, an accidental death benefit, a guaranteed insurability option, an age rating or an extra premium charge on a substandard life); and

- the total of all amounts which are defined as proceeds of disposition of an interest in the life insurance policy that have been received by the policy owner prior to the date on which the adjusted cost basis is being calculated.

The adjusted cost basis of a permanent life insurance policy will generally be higher in the early years but will, generally, be reduced to zero by life expectancy of the life insured. This is in large part because the annual net cost of pure insurance of the policy increases year over year until, in most cases, it exceeds the amount of the annual policy premium. Once the adjusted cost basis of a life insurance policy reaches zero, every dollar of value withdrawn from the policy is taxable as income. The adjusted cost basis of a life insurance policy cannot be less than zero.

Capital Dividend Account[24]

The capital dividend account is a notional tax account, unlike an actual account at a bank, trust company or other financial institution. Certain capital receipts of an eligible corporation can be credited to the capital dividend account, after which the corporation may elect to declare a capital dividend, which will be received tax-free by the shareholders. The capital dividend account is only available to certain private corporations that are resident in Canada. Key criteria in determining whether a corporation qualifies for a capital dividend account are the following:

- the corporation must be a Canadian corporation throughout the taxation year;
- the corporation must also be a private corporation throughout the taxation year; and
- the corporation must receive certain tax-free receipts, such as the tax-free portion of certain capital gains realized by the corporation (net of the non-allowable portion of any capital losses),[25] capital dividends received by the corporation, tax-free amounts received by the corporation on the sale of "eligible capital property,"[26] and the mortality gain

---

[24] See subsection 89(1). Under paragraph 89(1)(b.2), a corporation was permitted to elect to treat dividends declared before May 23, 1985 which reflected a tax-free receipt of life insurance proceeds net of the policy's adjusted cost basis as a capital dividend payable from the corporation's Life Insurance Capital Dividend Account ("LICDA"). This section has been repealed. However, LICDA and LICDA dividends are still used for limited transitional purposes under subsection 83(2.1), including determining adjusted cost base under subparagraph 53(1)(e)(ii) and limiting capital losses under subsections 112(3) — (3.2). The tracking occurs through amalgamations under paragraph 87(2)(x) and wind-ups under clause 88(1)(d)(i.1)(B).

[25] Since capital losses reduce the capital dividend account it is prudent to pay out amounts equal to the capital dividend account before realizing any capital losses.

[26] For example, the goodwill of a business. See also sections 54 and 248(1) and Interpretation Bulletin IT-123R6, Transactions involving capital property, dated June 1, 1997.

¶335

on life insurance proceeds received by the corporation as a beneficiary.[27]

The capital dividend account credit is the total of all such receipts minus capital dividends paid by the corporation from time to time. Under subsection 83(2), tax-free capital dividends may be paid out on a *pro rata* basis to the shareholders of the class of shares on which the capital dividend is declared, provided Form T2054 is filed on or before the date the dividend becomes payable together with the required accompanying documentation.

Cash Surrender Value

When a permanent life insurance policy with accrued cash values is surrendered or disposed of during the lifetime of the person whose life is insured, the cash surrender value is the amount received by the policy owner, net of the repayment of any outstanding policy loans and accrued interest on the policy loan(s) and after any surrender charges levied by the insurance carrier have been deducted.[28] The cash surrender value in excess of the policy's adjusted cost base is a taxable income receipt of the policy owner.

Disposition

According to subsection 148(9), the "disposition" of an interest in a life insurance policy includes:

- a surrender of the policy, including a partial surrender such as a policy withdrawal or the transfer of funds to a segregated fund[29] of the insurance carrier;
- policy loans made after March 31, 1978, including automatic premium loans (which occur when the insurance carrier uses values within the policy to pay premiums if premiums are not deposited into the policy by the policy owner) and capitalized interest on unpaid policy loans;
- dissolution of the policy owner's interest in the policy due to its maturity;
- a disposition by operation of law, such as when a policy is voided for fraud committed by the policy owner;
- lapse due to the non-payment of premiums where the policy is not reinstated during the calendar year of the lapse, or within 60 days thereafter; and
- annuitization of a life insurance policy acquired after December 2, 1982.

Mortality Gain

When a corporation that is eligible to maintain a capital dividend account is the beneficiary of a life insurance policy and receives the death benefit on

---

[27] See Interpretation Bulletin IT-430R3, Life insurance proceeds received by a private corporation or a partnership as a consequence of death, dated February 10, 1997.

[28] See subsection 148(6).

[29] As defined in subsection 138(1). It should be noted that some index-linked life insurance policies are effectively taxed on surrender as if they were a segregated fund policy.

the death of the life insured, the amount that can be credited to the capital dividend account is calculated. In the context of the capital dividend account, the mortality gain is the amount by which the death benefit exceeds the policy's adjusted cost basis.

Net Cost of Pure Insurance

The net cost of pure insurance (NCPI) of a life insurance policy is a tax concept that does not necessarily have a relationship with the actual calculation of mortality charges under a life insurance policy. The NCPI is determined according to the formula in Regulation 308 and reflects the prescribed mortality charge applied to the at-risk amount (i.e., total death benefit minus the accumulating fund or investment component of the policy). In effect, the at-risk amount is the policy face amount minus the cash surrender value. The NCPI of a policy cannot be less than zero.

Proceeds of the Disposition of an Interest in a Life Insurance Policy

Under subsection 148(9), the proceeds of the disposition of an interest in a life insurance policy is the amount that the policy owner is entitled to receive on: the surrender of a policy; a policy loan made after March 31, 1978; a payment by a life insurance carrier under a life annuity contract entered into after November 16, 1978 and before November 13, 1981 of any amount other than an annuity payment, a policy loan or a policy dividend;[30] or the value of a policy arising from the deemed disposition of the policy on the death of the policy owner or life insured/annuitant.[31]

Value

The value of an interest in a life insurance policy under subsection 148(9) at any time is the cash surrender value, except where the policy has no cash surrender value, in which case the value is nil.[32]

¶340
Insurance Planning Issues

¶345 The Exempt Test and Life Insurance

Under subsection 12.2(1), policy owners of life insurance policies last acquired after 1989 are required to include in their annual income the amount

---

[30] Other than an annuity payment, a policy loan or dividend payment. See the definition in paragraph (e) of subsection 148(9) of "disposition".

[31] See subsections 148(2)(b) and 148(9).

[32] It should be noted that the value under subsection 148(9) is not always the relevant amount, particularly when a life insurance policy is sold or transferred to an arm's length purchaser or acquirer. See the section "Transfer of Life Insurance Policies" for more details.

by which the policy's accumulating fund[33] exceeds the policy owner's adjusted cost base in the policy. The three exemptions to this accrual taxation requirement are:

- exempt policies;
- prescribed annuity contracts;[34] and
- proceeds from policies issued before December 2, 1982 which have been received by the policy owner in the form of an annuity contract.

Under Regulation 306 each life insurance policy will be allocated an exemption test policy, which is a notional policy used to determine if a life insurance policy qualifies as an exempt policy and is therefore exempt from accrual taxation. In paragraph 4(a) of Interpretation Bulletin IT-87R2, the following comments are found with respect to life insurance policies last acquired after 1989:

> An exempt policy is a policy which is issued mainly for insurance protection and not for investment purposes. Policyholders must generally rely on the issuer of a life insurance policy to determine if it is an exempt policy because the determination requires information which may not be available in life insurance contracts themselves.

The insurance carrier is responsible for ensuring that the exempt status of a life insurance policy can be determined every year. The actual calculation of the exempt test involves a determination of the policy's accumulating fund, which requires consideration of the provisions in paragraphs 1401(1)(*a*) or (*b*) of the Regulations in respect of certain deposit administration fund policies and group life insurance policies. In contrast, paragraph 1401(1)(*c*) of the Regulations determines the reserve for other types of life insurance policies and can generally be described as the greater of:

- the cash surrender value of the policy less outstanding policy loans in respect of the policy; and
- the excess of the present value of future benefits over the sum of outstanding policy loans and the present value of future modified net premiums.

Exempt policies must meet current exempt test requirements and must also meet prospective exempt test requirements for future anniversaries. The exempt status of a policy can change for a variety of reasons and each has different consequences.

An exempt policy that does not meet the exemption test is then granted a 60-day grace period to return the policy to its exempt policy status. The policy owner may take one or more of the following steps to bring the policy within the exempt test guidelines:

- cashing in dividend additions for a participating life insurance policy;

---

[33] In general terms, the "accumulating fund" of a life insurance policy is a measure of the accumulated savings that have built up within the policy. Regulation 307 defines "accumulating fund" for the purposes of subsection 12.2(1). See Interpretation Bulletin IT-87R2, Policyholders' income from life insurance policies, dated February 15, 1996.

[34] Prescribed annuity contracts are defined in Regulation 304.

- partial surrender of an interest in the policy;
- increasing the death benefit, subject to a mandatory maximum; or
- not paying premiums.

The accumulating fund of an exempt policy can be increased if the death benefit under the policy is increased (subject to contractual provisions) — provided that the insurance carrier will permit a percentage increase under the terms of the contract. The tax on non-exempt policies must be paid at least every three years. Policy owners of non-exempt policies acquired after 1989 must pay tax annually. When the life insured who is covered under a non-exempt policy dies, any investment income generated from the policy that has not been taxed prior to the date of death will be considered taxable income for the year of death.

In general, Canadian life insurance carriers do not issue polices that are not exempt at the time of issue or that are projected to become non-exempt over time.

¶350 Transfers of Life Insurance Policies

In general, transfers of life insurance policies are dispositions and will, depending on the cash value and the policy's adjusted cost basis, usually attract tax consequences. Exceptions occur when an interest in a life insurance policy is transferred to a spouse or common-law partner[35] on a rollover basis. *Inter vivos* transfers may take place on a tax-deferred basis under subsection 148(8.1), while transfers following the death of a spouse or common-law partner to the surviving spouse or common-law partner fall under subsection 148(8.2). The CRA has indicated that a rollover under subsection 148(8.1) will not occur on the breakdown of a marriage or common-law partnership when a life insurance policy is split into two separate policies, as this is not a transfer of an interest in a policy. Instead, the division of the original policy results in the creation of a new policy.[36]

An interest in a life insurance policy can be transferred on a rollover basis to a child of the policy owner, during the policy owner's lifetime, if the person whose life is insured is a child of the policy owner or a child of the transferee.[37] However, there is no equivalent provision to subsection 148(8.2) for a testamentary rollover of an interest in a life insurance policy to a child or grandchild. Unless arrangements are made to effect the transfer of the ownership rights in the life insurance policy through the appointment of a successor owner,[38] the

---

[35] See subsection 248(1).

[36] See Technical Interpretation 2001-0073505.

[37] See subsection 148(8). Note that this provision applies the extended definition of "child" in subsection 248(1).

[38] See the discussion in Norwood & Weir on "Transfers At Death Distinguished," found at pp. 360–361. Both the uniform *Insurance Act* of the common law provinces/territories and the Quebec Civil Code expressly permit the owner of a life insurance policy to transfer his or her ownership rights in the policy on the policy owner's death. See also Technical Interpretation 9618075 which confirmed that the transfer via the successor owner provisions of the Uniform Insurance Act would qualify for the rollover.

policy forms part of the estate of the deceased taxpayer and the potential rollover is forfeited.[39] In Technical Interpretation 9826715, the CRA also indicated that there will be no rollover when a life insurance policy is transferred to a trust of which the child is the sole beneficiary or if someone other than the child is the life insured.

Other transfers of an interest in a life insurance policy that may attract tax are:

- where a policy is transferred by way of a gift, either during the lifetime or under a Will, to any other person;
- where a policy is transferred by operation of law to any person;
- where a policy is transferred by means of a corporate distribution to a person; and
- where a policy is transferred to anyone with whom the policy owner does not deal at arm's length.[40]

Thus, there will be a taxable gain to an individual whenever the cash surrender value of a permanent life insurance policy exceeds the policy's adjusted cost basis on a transfer. However, if the policy's adjusted cost basis is more than its cash surrender value at the time of the transfer, the transferee will have a lower adjusted cost basis for the life insurance policy than the original policy owner as the transferee's adjusted cost basis will be the original owner's cash surrender value. If a life insurance policy is transferred while there is an outstanding policy loan, the policy's value is reduced by the amount of the loan.

Since term life insurance has no value within the meaning of subsection 148(9), the transfer of an interest in a term life insurance policy will usually not result in taxable income to the transferor. An exception to this general principle occurs when the fair market value of the policy may be found to be more than the cash surrender value. This may occur when a life insurance policy is transferred when the death of the life insured is foreseeable and imminent.

Another exception to the general rule that transfers of interests in life insurance policies usually result in taxable income for the transferor arises when the transfer is the result of a sale for consideration to an arm's length transferee. The transferor's proceeds of disposition and the transferee's adjusted cost basis for the life insurance policy will equal the actual proceeds.

As noted above, the deemed disposition rules regarding transfers of life insurance apply to policies that are transferred to individuals on a distribution from a corporation. This may capture transfers arising from the payment of a life insurance policy as a dividend or salary in kind. The simple sale of a life insurance policy by a corporation to a shareholder or employee may also be

---

[39] See Technical Interpretation 9433865 in which Revenue Canada stated that subsection 148(8) did not apply to the transfer of a life insurance policy to the child of the deceased taxpayer under the deceased's Will.

[40] An interest in a life insurance policy is not property that is eligible for a tax-deferred rollover when an individual transfers property to a corporation under section 85 . Thus, that transaction is caught by the provisions of subsection 148(7).

¶1350

caught, depending on whether the transfer is characterized as a shareholder or employee benefit.[41]

The CRA's views on the valuation of life insurance policies in circumstances where the Act is silent are found in Information Circular IC 89-3. Thus, when a shareholder has died, pursuant to subsection 70(5.3), the value of corporate owned life insurance for the deemed disposition under subsection 70(5) will be the cash surrender value. However, in order to determine the value of the life insurance policy for all other shareholders, factors other than the policy's cash surrender value must be considered:

- cash surrender value;
- the policy's loan value;
- face value;
- the state of health of the insured and his/her life expectancy;
- conversion privileges;
- other policy terms, such as term riders, double indemnity provisions; and
- replacement value.[42]

As a result, the CRA has stated that the age, health and imminent death of a shareholder may result in a finding that the value of the corporate owned life insurance policy exceeds the policy's cash surrender value. Mitigating factors will be: the fact that the ill shareholder may still recover and not die; an increase or decrease in the share value because of a majority or minority shareholding; the importance attached to factors other than asset value in the circumstances (such as the future earnings expectations and the prospects for dividends); and the effect that the loss of a key person would have on the business operations.

Where a life insurance policy does not develop cash values until a predetermined time/date and the policy is transferred just prior to that time/date, the CRA may find that the policy's value is greater than the official cash surrender value of zero and may impose a benefit on the transferee. Similarly, if a corporate owned life insurance policy on the life of a shareholder with limited life expectancy is transferred, the value of the policy could be more than the deemed proceeds of disposition because of the shareholder's imminent death. If the CRA finds that the purchaser did not provide adequate consideration in view of the limited life expectancy, a shareholder benefit may be assessed.

Tax planning strategies to avoid or minimize an adverse valuation determination by the CRA include:

- *Owning the life insurance through a holding company.* The life insurance is owned by each shareholder's holding company, rather than the operating company. When the interest in the operating company is disposed

---

[41] See sections 15 and 16 respectively for income inclusions of shareholders and employees.
[42] See paragraph 40 of IC 89-3.

of, the life insurance policy will not have to be transferred as part of the transaction.

- *Split dollar ownership.* Having the shareholder own the cash surrender value of the policy from the date of issue may mitigate this problem. The shareholder will hold the ownership rights to the cash surrender value, while the corporation will own the death benefit. The transfer of the corporation's interest in the death benefit can usually been done without attracting tax consequences.[43]

- *Payment of life insurance policy as a dividend.* This in-kind dividend will result in a disposition to the corporation, with tax being due on the income inclusion (cash surrender value minus adjusted cost basis), if any. Unless the shareholder is a holding company, this will be a taxable dividend for the transferee shareholder — but tax will be paid at dividend rates, rather than ordinary marginal rates. If the corporation has refundable dividend tax on hand, a dividend refund will occur. Caution, however, is advised as the CRA may deem the value of the transferred policy to exceed its cash surrender value as noted earlier.

- *Purchase of the policy at fair market value.* A shareholder may purchase the life insurance policy at its fair market value, which is generally the policy's cash surrender value. This approach is not, however, recommended when the shareholder is ill and not expected to recover, as the CRA may deem the fair market value to be in excess of the cash surrender value or even an amount approaching the policy's face amount.

¶355 Life Insurance and Share Valuation[44]

Under paragraph 70(5)(*a*), the deemed disposition of all shares owned by a shareholder occur immediately prior to death and, if the shares are not transferred to a surviving spouse or common-law partner (or a trust for the benefit of the surviving spouse/common-law partner), any increase in the value of the shares over their adjusted cost base will be subject to capital gains tax. If the full value of the death benefit of corporate-owned life insurance were included in the share valuation, it would artificially inflate the value of the shares.

In order to deal with this possibility, subsection 70(5.3) was enacted to impose a deemed disposition of property on (i) the death of a taxpayer, for deaths occurring after December 1, 1982, (ii) the departure of a taxpayer from Canada, and (iii) property owned by a trust on the death of a spouse or in respect of the 21-year cycle.[45] This provision deems the value of the life insurance policy on the life of the deceased shareholder immediately prior to death

---

[43] See Glenn Stephens, *Estate Planning with Life Insurance* (Toronto: CCH Canadian Limited, 1999) at pp. 92–96 for a discussion of split dollar insurance.

[44] See Chapter 2 — Tax Considerations — *Inter Vivos* Buy-outs for a discussion on the effect that cash value life insurance owned by a corporation may have on the $500,000 capital gains exemption.

[45] Under subsections 104(4) — (5.2), imposition of the 21-year deemed disposition rule can be deferred for trusts that are solely for the benefit of the spouse or common-law partner of the settlor of the trust or the testator whose death gives rise to the trust.

to be the policy's cash surrender value as determined in accordance with subsection 148(9).

For the purpose of determining the cash surrender value of a corporate-owned life insurance policy on the death of a shareholder, subsection 148(9) provides that the cash surrender value is to be calculated without reference to outstanding policy loans, any policy dividends payable as of the date of death and any interest payable upon policy dividends that are payable but not paid as of the date of death. The CRA has also determined that prepaid premiums and dividends left on deposit with the insurance carrier do not form part of the policy's cash surrender value. However, the value of the assets represented by outstanding policy loans, unpaid dividends and the interest thereon, along with the value of prepaid premiums and dividends on deposit, will be additional assets of the corporation and may affect the value of the shares of a corporation which is the owner and beneficiary of the policy. In other words, the policy on the life of the deceased shareholder may not have a value limited to the policy's cash surrender value.

Because the effect of the provisions in subsection 70(5.3) are limited to the valuation of the life insurance policy on the life of the deceased shareholder, other valuation issues arise when there are two or more shareholders and corporate-owned life insurance was acquired to fund the buy-sell agreement. Thus, on the death of a shareholder, the value of the life insurance policies on the lives of the surviving shareholders must also be determined. As set out in Information Circular IC 89-3,[46] factors to be considered in determining the value of such policies are the cash surrender value of the policy, the policy loan value, the face value, the life expectancy of the life insured shareholder based on mortality tables, and the known state of health of the insured life insured shareholder. If the life insured shareholder is known to be terminally ill or was critically injured and not expected to recover, the CRA takes the position that the value of the policy might be as high as the face value of the policy.

If the death of a healthy individual occurred suddenly, the CRA has conceded that the insurance would have little added value over its cash surrender value. This position is consistent with the reasoning of the Federal Court of Appeal in *Mastronardi v. The Queen*,[47] which held that the share valuation for income tax purposes had to occur "the instant before death." In the *Mastronardi* case, the death of the insured shareholder was sudden and unexpected. Accordingly, since the insurance proceeds would not be receivable at that time, the death benefit was not to be included in the share valuation. The CRA has not, to our knowledge, undertaken a medical assessment of surviving shareholders where a death has occurred and corporate-owned life insurance is in place on the lives of the surviving shareholders.

---

[46] See discussion of IC 89-3 in the section *Transfers of Life Insurance Policies.*
[47] 77 DTC 5217 (F.C.A.).

¶355

Because the valuation provisions of subsection 70(5.3) only apply to the valuation of the life insurance at the time of the deemed disposition,[48] when the shares transferred to the deceased's estate are subsequently sold under the terms of the buy-sell agreement, the value of the remaining corporate-owned life insurance policies may not be the same as at the time of the deemed disposition.

There is jurisprudence to the effect that the valuation of shares for the purposes of the buy-sell agreement determines the fair market value of the shares.[49] The valuation formula in the agreement should specifically exclude the insurance proceeds from any *post-mortem* share valuation. Since the agreement will restrict the marketability of shares, the buy-sell agreement's price should be considered to reflect the highest price obtainable for the shares.

A possible exception to this general rule is when non-arm's length shareholders enter into a buy-sell agreement which sets out the fair market value of the shares. Where shareholders do not deal with one another at arm's length, paragraph 69(1)(*b*) may be applied to conclude that the fair market value of the shares will be determined without reference to the provisions of the buy-sell agreement. Since the life insurance death benefit will have been received by the corporation by the time the estate sells the deceased's shares to the surviving shareholders, the insurance proceeds could increase the share value, in some cases, significantly.

The Supreme Court of Canada considered the effect that a buy-sell agreement could have on the valuation of shares under the old *Federal Estate Tax Act* in *Beament v. M.N.R.*[50] The deceased's estate was bound by a contractual obligation that required the wind-up of the deceased's corporation at a price set in an agreement between the deceased and his sons, who were minority shareholders. After reviewing the facts of the case and the then current legislation, Cartwright, C.J.C. stated:

> Once it is established (and it has been conceded) that the contract binding the deceased and his executors to have the company wound-up was valid, the real value of the shares cannot be more than the amount which their holder would receive in the winding-up. To suggest that they have in fact any other value would be altogether unrealistic. When the true value of the shares in the circumstances which exist is readily ascertainable, I can find nothing in the Act that requires the computation of the value they would have had under completely different circumstances followed by an inquiry as to whether any deductions should be made from that value.[51]

The Court held that the contractual obligation to wind-up the company was determinative of the share value for the purposes of levying estate tax.

---

[48] Subsection 70(5.3) was amended by the 2001 technical bill, effective for dispositions occurring after October 1, 1996. An excellent review of the 2001 technical amendments to subsection 70(5.3) can be found in Philip Friedlan, "Revised Valuation Rules for Life Insurance," VIII(1) Insurance Planning (Federated Press) 492–495 (2000).

[49] See the decision of the Supreme Court of Canada in *Beament v. M.N.R.*, 70 DTC 6130 (S.C.C.).

[50] 70 DTC 6130 (S.C.C).

[51] See [1970] S.C.R. 680 at p. 687.

Interpretation Bulletin IT-140R3, Buy-sell agreements, dated April 14, 1989 addresses the valuation of shares that are subject to a buy-sell agreement. The provisions of subsection 70(5) apply, such that the fair market value of the shares must be determined at the time immediately before death. The CRA, in paragraph 2 of IT-140R3 states that "where the deceased and the surviving party to the buy-sell agreement (survivor) did not deal at arm's length, it is a question of fact whether the fair market value for the purpose of subsection 70(5) will be determined with reference to the buy-sell agreement." At paragraph 3, the CRA states that, in the view of the Department, paragraph 69(1)(*b*) will apply to non-arm's length share transfers under a buy-sell agreement and that "it is a question of fact whether fair market value under paragraph 69(1)(*b*) will be determined with reference to the buy-sell agreement."

This problem may be resolved by altering the corporation's share structure so that each shareholder subscribes to a class of preferred shares, the sole right of which is to receive a capital dividend on the death of one or more of the other shareholders. The preferred shares would have a nominal adjusted cost base and paid-up capital. When a shareholder dies, the buy-sell agreement will provide for the redemption of the deceased's preferred shares at their paid-up capital, which triggers minimal tax, if any. The corporation will then declare a capital dividend to the remaining preferred shareholders, who will use the dividend monies to purchase the deceased's remaining shares from the estate.

The buy-sell agreement should also contain a price adjustment clause, which states that the purchase price of the deceased's shares will be adjusted, should the CRA or the Courts determine that the fair market value is something different than that set out or agreed upon in the buy-sell agreement.

We are not aware of a case where the CRA has exercised its prerogative to apply paragraph 69(1)(*b*) to a sale of shares under a buy-sell agreement where the vendor and purchaser do not deal at arm's length. Given the potential adverse effects if the share value is re-assessed under paragraph 69(1)(*b*), non-arm's length shareholders should give this issue serious consideration when determining the fair market value of shares for the purposes of a buy-sell agreement.

¶360 Life Insurance as Collateral, Capital Dividend Account Planning, and Quebec Concerns

Other insurance issues arise when a life insurance policy owned by an individual or a business is assigned as security for a loan, line of credit or other lending arrangement.[52] If the loan is for investment or business purposes (but not to finance the payment of life insurance premiums) and qualifies for interest deductibility under paragraph 20(1)(*c*), a portion of the insurance premiums can be deducted by the policy owner/borrower if the policy is

---

[52] See Norwood & Weir at pp. 369–371 for a discussion of collateral assignment of life insurance policies.

assigned to a restricted financial institution[53] as security and the assignment is required by the lender.[54]

As set out in Interpretation Bulletin IT-309R2, the deductible portion of the premium is the lesser of the premium actually paid in that year and the NCPI for the year. The deduction calculation is derived from the average loan balance, the value of any other security provided, the amount of the death benefit, the premiums paid, and the net cost of pure insurance (NCPI).[55] For example, assume that Opco has an average loan balance of $500,000, has provided other security worth $100,000, and has assigned a life insurance policy on the sole shareholder that has a death benefit of $1,000,000, together with annual premiums of $4,000 and an NCPI of $4,500.[56] The deductible portion of the premiums would be:

$$\frac{\$500{,}000 - \$100{,}000}{\$1{,}000{,}000} \times (\text{Lesser of } \$4{,}000 \text{ and } \$4{,}500) = \$1{,}600$$

Thus, when a corporation has made a collateral assignment of a life insurance policy, it may only be able to deduct a portion of the insurance premium. In addition, there will be no deduction unless the policy owner actually makes a premium payment during the taxation year of the loan. If the corporation is using the accrued cash values within a policy to fund the annual premium cost — rather than making a premium payment — the deemed premium payment is zero and no portion of the annual premium "cost" can be deducted. This approach also applies if the life insurance policy's contractual terms only require premium payments for a specified number of years and the loan arrangement and collateral assignment of the policy occur after the end of the required payment period.

The collateral assignment of a corporate-owned life insurance policy may affect the amount that can be credited to the capital dividend account when the corporation receives life insurance death benefits. Interpretation Bulletin IT-430R3 deals with the treatment of life insurance proceeds received by a Canadian private corporation or partnership. The CRA issued a revision to Interpretation Bulletin IT-430R3 on 10 February, 1997 in which, at paragraph 6, it was stated that only the lender corporation could claim a credit to its capital dividend account on the receipt of insurance proceeds when the policy was used to secure indebtedness and the proceeds were paid directly to the lender as a beneficiary or as an assignee for security. The revised IT-430R3 was to apply even though the debtor corporation had directly or indirectly paid the premiums. Not surprisingly, the revision raised a furor in the insurance community as it represented a dramatic change in the CRA's position on collateral insurance policies.

---

[53] Subsection 248(1). See also the earlier discussion on "leveraging" under the section *Inter vivos funding using cash values within a life insurance policy*.

[54] Paragraph 20(1)(e.2). See Interpretation Bulletin IT-309R2.

[55] See Regulation 308 and the previous discussion on NCPI.

[56] It should be noted that, in general, the NCPI of a policy in the early years will be less than the premiums paid for the policy. However, the NCPI increases over time (to reflect, in part, the increasing age of the life insured) and will generally be more than the premiums within approximately 10 years of the date of issue of the policy.

In response to representations by the Conference for Advanced Life Underwriting (CALU), the CRA issued Income Tax Technical News No. 10 (ITTN No. 10), dated July 11, 1997, which stated:

> It was not intended that there be a change in the Department's position with regard to situations where a life insurance policy has been assigned as collateral for securing indebtedness, as opposed to an absolute assignment of the policy, and the debtor remains a beneficiary under the policy. In such a case, as the proceeds of the insurance policy would be constructively received by the debtor/beneficiary, even though paid directly to the creditor in accordance with the assignment, the proceeds in excess of the adjusted cost basis of the policy would be included in the capital dividend account of the debtor. Paragraph 6 of IT-430R3 will be revised in this regard.

In Technical Interpretation 2002-0127475, the CRA confirmed that its 1997 position still reflects the Department's current administrative position with respect to the capital dividend account credit available to corporations receiving life insurance death benefits where the policy had been assigned as collateral for security. In addition, the CRA confirmed that it was still considering a request to reassess the Department's position that the position set out in ITTN No. 10 does not apply to hypothecary claims in Quebec.

In summary, when a corporation receives life insurance death benefits from a policy that has been assigned as collateral for security, the capital dividend account treatment will vary, depending on whether the policy is subject to the rules of the Uniform Insurance Act or the Quebec Civil Code. Policies that fall under the common law regime will receive preferential capital dividend account treatment, as the entire death benefit in excess of the policy's adjusted cost base will be eligible for a credit to the corporation's capital dividend account. In contrast, since Quebec's hypothecation and collateral assignment rules revoke the beneficiary designation to the extent of the indebtedness, a corporation receiving life insurance death benefits under the civilian regime may not be able to claim as large a capital dividend account credit.

¶365
Non-Insurance Planning Issues

¶370 The Sole Shareholder

The sole shareholder of a corporation is often placed in a predicament as there may not be prospective purchasers to acquire his or her shares on death. If the shareholder's spouse is involved in the operation and management of the corporation, a transfer of the shares under his or her Will to the spouse can provide for tax deferral on the capital gains tax arising under the deemed disposition on death under subsection 70(5). If, however, the surviving spouse is not involved in the business and there are no children, an alternative structure would be for the sole shareholder to appoint an independent board of directors to run the corporation and ensure that the surviving spouse obtains voting control. When the spouse is not involved in the business but adult children are, the sole shareholder may wish to bequeath the shares to the children instead. However, since this plan would leave the surviving spouse without an income source, it is often recommended that the shareholder consider entering into a life insurance funded buy-sell agreement with the children who are active in the business.

In cases where there are children involved in the business and children who are not, the sole shareholder must determine the most appropriate business succession plan — ideally, the shares of the business will go to the active children and the non-active children will either receive other assets or life insurance proceeds in lieu of assets.

This arrangement reflects the need for all parents involved in a family business to consider the distinction between an estate plan that makes an equal distribution to the children and one that makes an equitable distribution. A strictly equal distribution of assets will generally mean that children who are not involved in the business will become shareholders. This dilutes control of the corporation and may result in a minority shareholder oppression remedy application. It may also give rise to family disharmony as the profits of the corporation are paid out to non-active shareholders instead of being reinvested in the on-going growth of the corporation or being applied solely for the benefit of the active shareholders.

In contrast, an equitable distribution will ensure that ownership and control of the corporation are given to the active children. Typically, the corporation will be the single most valuable asset in the parent's estate. Thus, an equitable distribution may mean that the non-active children receive far less value from the estate. Alternatively, if the sole shareholder is insurable, life insurance can be used to provide for the non-active children's inheritance.

One possible problem when shares are bequeathed to family members, other than a spouse, is that there will be a deemed disposition on the shareholder's death. At the time of death, the value of the business may be at its peak and a substantial capital gain may be triggered. Assume that the family heirs are not able to operate the business successfully and it gradually declines in value. After more than a year the business is closed down. Unfortunately, in such a fact situation, there would be no method to offset the capital gain arising on death. The beneficiaries may be permitted to claim a business investment loss with respect to the shares of a small business corporation but the benefit of such a loss would be dependent on their personal tax rates and would not result in a refund to the estate.

Another problem which could occur in a closely held company is the inadvertent association of other companies on the death of a shareholder. While the shareholder is alive, steps may have been taken to keep various companies disassociated. For example, the husband may have owned all the shares of one operating company and a wife or adult child may have owned all the shares in another operating company. On the death of the husband, the acquisition of his shares by his spouse or child may result in the association of both companies. Reference should be had to the discussion of the associated company rules in Appendix 2.

¶370

If there are no family members capable of carrying on the business, the sole shareholder approaching retirement should consider selling the corporation to employees or to a third party. In limited cases, it may be possible to enter into a buy-sell agreement with a competitor who would agree to purchase the business for a predetermined price on the death of the shareholder. Insurance funding may be available. Another alternative would be to take the company public in order to create a market for the shares.

The shareholder may wish to provide for the transfer of the business to key employees. The Will of the shareholder may provide that the shares of the company are to be reclassified on death into voting fixed value preference shares (having a value equal to the value of the business on death) yielding a cumulative dividend and which are to be redeemed according to a redemption schedule. If the shares were not bequeathed to a spouse or to a spouse trust, the full capital gain may be taxable in the year of death, subject to any relief afforded by the capital gains exemption. No capital gains reserve would be available. The common shares would be issued to a trust for the employees and would be released on final redemption of the shares. This could be combined with a life insurance program.

The final option when there are no logical heirs or purchasers would be to provide for the liquidation of the corporation on the death of the sole shareholder. If the corporation maintained life insurance on the shareholder's life, a capital dividend could arise on liquidation.

¶375 What about Partnerships?

A partnership is an association of two or more individuals carrying on a business for their mutual benefit. An insurance-funded buy-sell agreement will work quite well in a partnership situation. The partners can enter into a buy-sell agreement and have the partnership own, pay the premiums on, and be the beneficiary of insurance policies on the lives of the partners. Unlike corporations, a partnership does not have a capital dividend account through which the mortality gain on insurance proceeds received by the corporation can be paid out as a tax-free capital dividend to the surviving shareholders. However, the income and capital receipts of a partnership retain their original character for tax purposes when distributed to the partners. Therefore, the insurance proceeds can be flowed out tax-free to the surviving partners, who will use the proceeds to purchase the deceased partner's interest in the partnership.

¶380 Issues for Non-Resident Shareholders

There are a number of complications where non-resident shareholders are involved in a corporation. Firstly, under subsection 212(2), capital dividends are subject to Canadian withholding taxes at a rate of 25 per cent, unless reduced by treaty. So-called direct inter-corporate dividends are often subject to a reduced 10 per cent treaty withholding rate, which has been reduced to 5 per cent in the context of the U.S.–Canada Tax Treaty. The benefit of a tax-free dividend is thus removed. Companies having non-resident shareholders should not elect to treat the deemed dividend arising on a purchase for cancellation as a capital dividend for the non-resident shareholders.

The optimum share structure may be dependent on the tax treatment for the non-resident of dividends or capital gains both under the relevant tax treaty and under domestic law in the country of residence.

A non-resident shareholder is required to comply with section 116 when on the disposition of the shares. A non-resident vendor is not entitled to a capital gain reserve if the price is paid over time, nor will a non-resident be entitled to benefit from the capital gains exemption.

A corporation may become a Canadian-controlled private corporation when a non-resident controlling shareholder either dies or otherwise disposes of the shares. Under subsection 89(1.1), any existing capital dividend account balance of the corporation will be eliminated immediately prior to the date of death or disposition. If the shares of a non-resident controlling shareholder are acquired before the corporation receives any death benefit payable on the death of the non-resident shareholder, it can be argued that the resulting change of control would not result in the inability to credit the mortality gain of the insurance to the capital dividend account.[57]

¶385
Summary

Shareholders who are concerned about the successful transition of ownership of the corporation to family members, arm's length shareholders, or a third party purchaser will often look at methods of funding the share transfer. The tax implications of the various funding options, including life insurance, will often influence the choice of the funding vehicle. In many instances, life insurance on the lives of the shareholders is the most cost-effective and least restrictive funding option for both operating companies and holding companies.

Fundamentally, the motivation for buying business insurance is the same as that for buying personal insurance: protection. Shareholders want to minimize the disruption that may be caused as a result of the death, disability (or critical illness), or retirement of a family member, business owner, or key employee. Business-related insurance decisions will be affected by considerations about employees, business associates and their families, along with creditors and, on occasion, competitors.

This Chapter provided a detailed review of key planning considerations for business continuation, various funding options and, finally, an examination of life insurance as the funding vehicle of choice. The next Chapter will cover the most common buy-sell structures on death and the tax implications for the deceased shareholder, his or her estate and the surviving/purchasing shareholder.

---

[57] Subsection 89(1). See Interpretation Bulletin IT-430R3.

FOUR

BUY-OUTS ON DEATH

¶400
Overview

In the following sections, the traditional structures for buy-outs on death of a shareholder, being criss-cross insurance, deferred sales and corporate share repurchases, will be analyzed both from the perspective of the estate of the deceased shareholder and the surviving shareholders. Each section will be divided into two parts, the first dealing with the situation where individuals personally own shares in the operating company and the second dealing with holding companies.

Each section will commence with an overview and an analysis of the tax implications to the estate and to the survivors. The advantages and disadvantages of each alternative follow. For the purposes of comparison, the same example is used throughout wherever a numerical example is provided; that is, the shares owned by the deceased have a fair market value of $100,000 (which corresponds to the price in the buy-sell agreement) and an adjusted cost base and paid-up capital of $100. For purposes of discussion, we will generally assume that the shareholders deal with each other at arm's length for purposes of the Act.

¶405
Criss-Cross Insurance

¶407 Criss-Cross Insurance — Individual Shareholders

Overview

Under this structure the shareholders' agreement would provide for criss-cross insurance, each individual shareholder undertaking to obtain and maintain a life insurance policy on the life or lives of the others. Each shareholder would be responsible for the payment of the life insurance premiums.

On the death of a shareholder, the shareholders' agreement would provide for the purchase by the surviving shareholders of the shares held by the deceased. The life insurance proceeds would be paid to the survivors to be applied towards the purchase price of the shares of the deceased. If several shareholders are involved, the arrangement may be simplified by involving a trustee who would collect and discharge the insurance premiums, receive the insurance proceeds and pay the insurance proceeds to the estate in consideration for the shares of the deceased.

Tax Implications for the Estate

The tax implications for the Estate will depend on whether the shares are eligible for a rollover on death because such shares are left to the deceased shareholder's spouse or a trust for such spouse's benefit that qualifies as a "spousal trust."[1]

If the shares are eligible for the spousal rollover on death, there would be no deemed disposition on death.[2] However, the spouse or spouse trust would acquire the shares at the adjusted cost base to the deceased.[3] The subsequent sale by the spouse or spouse trust of the shares under the terms of the shareholders' agreement would give rise to a capital gain to the extent that the purchase price exceeds the adjusted cost base of the shares.[4] If the purchase price is payable over time, the capital gains reserve may be available to defer the tax over a period not exceeding five years.[5] Assuming that there was adequate life insurance, the price would be paid in full on closing and no reserve would be available or required.[6]

If the shares of the corporation held by the deceased qualify as shares of a qualified small business corporation, the estate could elect not to have the rollover apply to shares having an accrued gain equal to the unused capital gains exemption of the deceased shareholder so as to fully utilize such exemption.[7] The balance of the shares may then be rolled over to the deceased's spouse who would claim his or her own capital gains exemption on the actual sale of shares. If the shares were owned by a spouse trust, the trust may designate that a portion of the trust's capital gain that is eligible for the

---

[1] The requirements for a spousal rollover on death are set out in subsection 70(6) and generally apply where the deceased transfers property on death to a spouse or common-law partner resident in Canada immediately before death or to a trust created under the deceased's Will, where the spouse or common-law partner is entitled to all of the income of the trust during the spouse's lifetime and no one other than the spouse is entitled to the capital of the trust during the spouse's or common-law partner's lifetime and the property has become indefeasibly vested in the spouse, common-law partner or trust within 36 months of the death of the deceased. (Unless otherwise indicated all statutory references are to the *Income Tax Act* (Canada) (the "Act").)

[2] Subsection 70(6). See Interpretation Bulletin IT-305R4, Establishment of testamentary spousal trust, dated October 30, 1996.

[3] Paragraph 70(6)(*d*).

[4] Paragraph 40(1)(*a*).

[5] Subparagraph 40(1)(*a*)(iii). Interpretation Bulletin IT-236R4, Reserves — Dispositions of Capital property, dated July 30, 1999.

[6] Paragraph 70(5)(*d*).

[7] Subsection 70(6.2).

¶407

exemption be treated as earned by the spouse directly for purposes of claiming the spouse's capital gains exemption.[8]

If no spousal rollover is available, there would be a deemed disposition of the shares immediately prior to death for their fair market value at that time.[9] The unused capital gains exemption of the deceased may be used to reduce or eliminate the taxable capital gain arising from the deemed disposition. The estate would be deemed to acquire the shares for an adjusted cost base equal to the deemed proceeds.[10] Assuming that the shares are then sold for a price equal to the increased adjusted cost base, no additional gain or loss will arise. The estate may pay the tax arising as a result of the deemed disposition over a period of ten years.[11] The tax would be subject to interest and the placement of adequate security with the Canada Customs and Revenue Agency (the "CRA").[12]

Tax Implications for the Survivor

The surviving shareholder or shareholders would not be taxable on the receipt of the insurance proceeds under an exempt policy.[13] The full amount of the insurance proceeds would be used to acquire the shares from the deceased shareholder's estate.

The adjusted cost base to the survivor of the shares acquired from the estate would equal the purchase price. If the survivor owned other shares which are identical to the shares acquired from the estate, then the tax cost of all the shares (including the acquired shares) would represent the average price paid for the shares.[14] In the event that the survivor does not want to average the cost of the shares purchased from the estate with the adjusted cost base of shares already owned personally, one alternative would be to effect a tax-free reorganization pursuant to section 86 after the death of a shareholder and prior to the sale in order that the shares held by the deceased be reclassified into a separate class of shares. As the shares would not be identical to the other shares owned by the survivor, it would not be necessary to average the adjusted cost base of all the shares owned by the survivor. Instead, the shares acquired from the deceased would have a separate adjusted cost base.

---

[8] The requirements for claiming the capital gains exemption are set out in section 110.6 and generally require that the shareholder claiming the exemption meet a holding period test for the shares and that the corporation meet an asset test for the period. In the case where the shares are held by a spousal trust, there are provisions which permit, in certain circumstances, the beneficiary of the trust to claim the exemption which are set out in subsections 104(21), (21.2) and 110.6(12).

[9] Paragraph 70(5)(a).

[10] Paragraph 70(5)(c).

[11] Subsection 159(5).

[12] Although not enacted at the time of writing, legislation is in the works to change the Agency's name to Canada Revenue Agency. The Agency is currently referring to itself in this fashion.

[13] The definition of "disposition" in subsection 148(9) excludes such a payment from constituting a disposition. Subsection 148(1) only provides for an income inclusion where there has been a disposition. Paragraph 56(1)(j) includes in income an amount required by subsections 148(1) or (1.1).

[14] Section 47. See Interpretation Bulletin IT-387R2, Meaning of "identical properties," dated July 14, 1989.

¶407

For example, assuming that the survivor owns 100 common shares having an adjusted cost base of $100 and that he or she acquires an additional 100 shares from the estate of the deceased shareholder for $100,000 (or $1,000 per share), the average cost per share (to the survivor) would be increased from $1 to $500.50. If the survivor subsequently sells 100 of his 200 shares for the same $1,000 per share purchase price, a capital gain of $499.50 would be realized. If the shares of the deceased were first reclassified into fully participating Class A shares that qualified as shares of a separate class which were then sold to the survivor, such Class A shares would have an adjusted cost base to the survivor of $100,000 and could be sold separately from the common shares. In order to qualify as a separate class of shares, the Class A shares should have a distinguishing feature from the common shares. In our example, there would be no gain on the subsequent sale. This technique may be useful if the survivor contemplates the sale of a part interest in the company.

Advantages

The criss-cross method is of greatest advantage to the survivor in that the insurance proceeds are received tax-free and are reflected in the adjusted cost base of the shares acquired from the deceased shareholder. This higher adjusted cost base can then be used to shelter any gain on a subsequent sale of the shares by the surviving shareholder or may, in certain circumstances, be extracted from the corporation through an additional reorganization involving the surviving shareholder transferring such shares to a holding corporation for shares or debt of the holding corporation.[15]

From the perspective of the estate, the life insurance proceeds would not be exposed to creditors of the corporation as the insurance policy would be held outside of the corporation. The capital gain arising either on the death of the shareholder or on the actual sale by the surviving spouse or spousal trust may be sheltered by the capital gains exemption.

As the insurance proceeds are not payable to the corporation, the insurance proceeds would not affect the status of the corporation as a small business corporation. As well, the insurance proceeds would not be included in valuing the corporation for the purposes of the *Family Law Act* (Ontario). Insurance proceeds are also excluded property under the *Family Law Act* (Ontario) with the result that they would not be exposed to a claim by a spouse of the survivor.[16]

Disadvantages

The major disadvantages are that the deceased or estate may realize a taxable capital gain under this alternative (in excess of any claim under the capital gains exemption), and there are a number of potential problems with

---

[15] The use of the adjusted cost base as a "pipeline" to extract cash from a corporation tax-free through such a reorganization depends on many considerations including the relationship of the surviving shareholders and the deceased, whether any portion of the $500,000 capital gains exemption was claimed on the death of the deceased, and the percentage of shareholdings in the corporation of the survivor.

[16] Section 4(2)(4).

¶407

respect to the insurance funding. As after-tax dollars must be used in order to discharge the insurance premiums, the shareholders may be required to take additional funds by way of a bonus or a taxable dividend in order to finance the premium payments.

One of the drawbacks is that the insurance premiums would be shared disproportionately based on the age and health of the insured rather than on the percentage of shares owned by the beneficiary. For example, a 30 per cent shareholder may find himself paying more than 30 per cent of the total premiums as a result of the age and health of the other shareholders. It may be possible to compensate a shareholder in that instance with an adjustment by way of a bonus.

It also becomes complex to administer this type of insurance arrangement where there are more than two or three shareholders. Each shareholder would own a portion of the policy on the lives of the other shareholders and several policies may be required. To some extent, the complexity may be relieved by having a trust arrangement. A trust arrangement may permit the parties to acquire joint life insurance policies rather than separate policies.

As well, each shareholder must take steps to ensure that the other is paying the premiums to maintain the life insurance.

An alternative structure that may deal with the policing of the payment of premiums is to have each shareholder hold a policy on their own life with the other shareholder as the beneficiary. In this scenario, each shareholder will be able to ensure, by payment of their own premiums, that there is life insurance in place to fund a purchase by the other surviving shareholder. On death, the insurance proceeds would be paid to the other surviving shareholder who would then use the proceeds to acquire the shares from the deceased who funded the premium payment. If the insurance is no longer required to fund a buyout (i.e., the last surviving shareholder), the designation of the beneficiary under the policy can be changed without a taxable disposition.

An Income-splitting Opportunity

A variation of the foregoing would be to involve the spouses of the shareholders (or a trust for the benefit of spouses or other family members) as parties to the buy-sell agreement. Under the terms of the buy-sell agreement the spouse (or trust for the benefit of a spouse or other family members) of the survivor could be afforded the first option to acquire the shares from the deceased. The insurance proceeds could be payable to the spouse(s) (or trust(s)) of the surviving shareholder(s)), provided that he or she is living with the surviving shareholder at that time. Otherwise, the insurance could be payable directly to the surviving shareholder(s). In the case where only spouses are used, the option may be subject to the condition precedent that the individual be married to and living with the surviving shareholder at the time of exercise. This would afford surviving shareholder(s) the ability to split income by allowing the spouse to receive dividend income on the acquired future capital gains and shares.

¶407

As the shares would be acquired directly from the estate of the deceased rather than from a spouse, the attribution rules in subsection 74.1(1) and 74.2(1) would not be applicable with respect to dividends subsequently paid on the shares or any capital gain realized on the disposition of such shares.[17] In the event that the spouse of the surviving shareholder declines or is unable to exercise the option, then the surviving shareholder personally could be obligated to purchase the shares.

¶409 Criss-Cross Insurance — Holding Companies

Overview

Assuming that each of the shareholders has incorporated a holding company to own their respective shares in the operating company, the holding companies would enter into an agreement whereby each holding company would undertake to purchase the shares of the operating company owned by the other holding company on the death of the shareholder of the other holding company.[18] The shareholders' agreement would normally contain restrictions on transfers or issuance of shares of the holding companies. Each holding company would acquire and pay for the premiums for a life insurance policy on the life or lives of the shareholder(s) of the other holding company(ies). The life insurance premiums could be financed by dividends paid by the operating company. Assuming that the companies are connected and that the operating company does not receive a refund of refundable dividend tax on hand ("RDTOH"), there should be no income tax to the holding companies on receipt of the dividend under the Act.[19] On the death of a shareholder, the holding company of the survivor would receive the insurance proceeds and use the insurance proceeds to purchase the shares of the operating company owned by the holding company of the deceased.

Tax Implications for the Estate

If a spousal rollover is available there would be no tax on the death of the shareholder of the holding company.[20] Instead, the shares of the holding company would be acquired by the spouse or the spouse trust for a cost equal to the adjusted cost base to the deceased.[21] On the actual sale of shares of the operating company by the deceased's holding company to the survivor's holding company, a capital gain would be realized. As the capital gain would be

---

[17] See Interpretation Bulletin IT-511R, Interspousal and certain other transfers and loans of property, dated February 21, 1994.

[18] We are assuming for purposes of this discussion that the holding corporation owns assets other than the shares of the operating company that cannot be distributed so that a sale of the shares of the deceased's holding company to the surviving shareholder is not an option. If a sale of the shares of the holding company can be effected, then the considerations are the same as those discussed in the previous section for criss-cross life insurance and the purchase of the shares of a company by a surviving shareholder from the estate of the deceased shareholder.

[19] There should also be no tax under Part VI.1 of the Act provided that the dividends are paid on shares that do not qualify as taxable preferred shares.

[20] Subsection 70(6).

[21] Paragraph 70(6)(d).

realized by a company, the capital gains exemption would not be available. The non-taxable portion of the capital gain would be added to the capital dividend account of the deceased's holding company and would be eligible for tax-free distribution as a capital dividend. [22] A portion of the corporate tax payable on the capital gain equal to $26^2/_3$ per cent of the taxable capital gain would be included in the RDTOH account of the corporation and would be eligible for a refund on the payment of sufficient taxable dividends.[23]

If no spousal rollover was available, the deceased would be deemed to dispose of his shares of the holding company at their fair market value immediately prior to death.[24] If the shares of the corporation qualify as shares of a qualified small business corporation, the capital gains exemption may be available to shelter part of the taxable gain. Assuming that the holding company has never held property, other than the shares of the operating company which was a small business corporation, then the $500,000 capital gains exemption would be available. The estate would be deemed to acquire the shares of the holding company for a cost equal to their fair market value immediately before the death of the taxpayer.[25] If the sole asset of the holding company were shares of the operating company, the deemed proceeds would be based on the fair market value of the shares of the operating company owned by the holding company. The holding company of the deceased would also realize a capital gain on the sale of the shares to the holding company owned by the survivor pursuant to the shareholders' agreement, assuming that the purchase price exceeded the adjusted cost base of the shares. The tax-free portion of the capital gain realized by the deceased's holding company would be added to its capital dividend account and would be eligible for distribution to the estate or beneficiary (i.e., the shareholder) as a tax-free capital dividend.[26] The remaining portion of the capital gain would be subject to tax in the holding company at a rate of approximately 50 per cent.[27] A portion of the corporate tax payable on the capital gain equal to $26^2/_3$ per cent of the taxable capital gain would be added to the RDTOH account of the holding company which would be refunded to the holding company on the payment of a taxable dividend.[28]

Dealing with Double Taxation

If no spousal rollover is available on the death of the deceased, there is a potential for double tax. The deceased may have a tax liability arising from the deemed disposition of the shares of the deceased's holding company on death.

---

[22] Subsections 89(1) and 83(2).

[23] Subsection 129(1).

[24] Paragraph 70(5)(a).

[25] Paragraph 70(5)(b).

[26] Subsection 83(2) and 89(1). See Interpretation Bulletin IT-66R6, Capital dividends, dated May 31, 1991.

[27] Based on the combined federal-provincial corporate tax rates applicable in the province of Ontario for 2004.

[28] Subsection 129(3) and 129(4) and paragraph 129(1)(a). See Interpretation Bulletin IT-243R4, Dividend refund to private corporations, dated February 12, 1996.

The holding company may also have a tax liability arising from the sale of the shares of the operating company to the survivor's holding company under the shareholders' agreement. In order to avoid or minimize such double tax, consideration can be given to the estate winding-up the holding company. This can be effected either before or after the sale of the shares of the operating company by the deceased's holding company to the survivor's holding company, but must be completed in the deceased's estate first taxation year.[29] Alternatively, the estate can reorganize the shareholdings of the deceased's holding company prior to the sale of its shares of the operating company by inserting a new company between the estate and the deceased's holding company and winding-up the deceased's holding company or amalgamating it with the new company to obtain a "bump" in the adjusted cost base of the holding company's shares of the operating company.[30]

The choice between a winding-up of the deceased's holding company by the estate or an insertion of a new company followed by a winding-up or amalgamation will depend on the facts and circumstances of each case, including the prevailing tax rates for dividends and capital gains.

Winding-up the holding company

Winding-up the holding company within the first taxation year of the estate may avoid double taxation by creating a capital loss in the estate which may be applied to eliminate the capital gain of the deceased shareholder on the deemed disposition on death.[31]

The tax consequences of a winding-up of the holding company are as follows. A deemed dividend would arise to the estate on the wind-up of the holding company equal to the difference between the cash and the fair market value of other property distributed and the paid-up capital of the shares. If the holding company had not previously distributed the capital dividend arising from the sale of the shares of the operating company, it may do so as part of the winding-up dividend.[32] In other words, the deemed dividend would comprise a separate capital dividend and taxable dividend. An election is required pursuant to subsection 83(2) to treat part of the dividend as a capital dividend. The taxable dividend would generate a refund of RDTOH to the corporation.[33] The taxable dividend would be subject to ordinary treatment (i.e., it would be eligible for gross-up and credit) in the hands of an individual shareholder. The capital dividend would be received free of regular tax and would not reduce the cost base of the shares held by the shareholder.[34]

---

[29] Since a taxation year can be chosen for the deceased's estate that may be shorter than 12 months, care must be taken to ensure that the reorganization occurs within the required time.

[30] The paid-up capital of the shares of the new company held by the estate will be equal to the adjusted cost base of the shares of the operating company, subject to any reduction under section 84.1.

[31] Subsection 164(6).

[32] Paragraph 88(2)(b). See Interpretation Bulletin IT-149R4, Winding-up dividend, dated June 28, 1991.

[33] Subsection 129(1). See Interpretation Bulletin IT-243R4, Dividend refund to private corporations, dated February 12, 1996.

[34] Subsection 83(2).

¶409

As a result of the winding-up, the estate would no longer hold shares in the holding company and would be deemed to have disposed of the shares for proceeds of disposition equal to the amount of the winding-up distribution net of the deemed dividend.[35] Generally, this will result in the proceeds of disposition being equal to the paid-up capital of the shares. A capital loss or business investment loss would be realized as the proceeds of disposition, as adjusted, would be less than the estate's high adjusted cost base of the shares arising from the deemed disposition on death. Provided the capital loss is incurred within the first taxation year of the estate, it may, subject to certain stop loss rules, be carried back to offset the taxable capital gain arising on death with respect to the shares of the holding company.[36] As a result, the only tax payable by the estate should be the tax payable on the portion of the deemed dividend received on the winding up that is treated as a taxable dividend.

The foregoing is best understood by way of a numerical example. Assume that the shares of the operating company are to be sold for proceeds of $100,000 and that the adjusted cost base and paid-up capital of the shares of both the holding company and the operating company (owned by the holding company) are $100. A spousal rollover is not available. Assume also that the capital gains exemption is not available. The deceased would be deemed to have disposed of the shares of the holding company for $100,000 immediately prior to death with the result that a capital gain of $99,900 and a taxable capital gain of $49,950 would be realized. The estate would be deemed to re-acquire the shares of the holding company for an adjusted cost base of $100,000. The deceased's holding company would dispose of the shares of the operating company for $100,000 to the survivor's holding company pursuant to the shareholder's agreement and would trigger a capital gain of $99,900 and a taxable capital gain of $49,950. An amount equal to $49,950 would be added to the capital dividend account of the deceased's holding company. The deceased's holding company would be required to include in income the taxable capital gain of $49,950 and would pay tax of approximately $24,865.[37] The sum of $13,320 would be added to the deceased's holding company's RDTOH account. On the wind-up of the corporation, there would be a deemed dividend of approximately $88,455 ($100,000 - $24,865 + $13,320 - $100) of which $49,950 would be a capital dividend (assuming that the election is made).[38]

The estate would receive a taxable dividend of approximately $38,505 and a return of capital of $100. Assuming that the estate is in the top marginal taxable bracket, the tax on the dividend would be approximately $12,067.[39] For

---

[35] Section 54 and the definition of "proceeds of disposition."

[36] Subsection 164(6). The stop loss rules in subsection 40(3.6) and 112 are discussed in a later section of this chapter.

[37] Based on the combined federal-provincial corporate tax rate applicable in the Province of Ontario in 2004.

[38] For purposes of illustration, we have assumed that a sufficient dividend can be paid by the company to fully recover RDTOH. In practice, a company may not have sufficient cash to pay a dividend to fully recover RDTOH which may result in a slightly higher effective tax rate.

[39] Based on the top combined federal-provincial personal tax rate on dividends applicable in the Province of Ontario.

¶409

purposes of determining the proceeds of disposition of the shares, the proceeds would be deemed to be $100. As the adjusted cost base to the estate was $100,000, a capital loss of $999,950 would be incurred which, subject to the stop loss rules, could be carried back to offset the capital gain on death.[40] Effectively, the estate would be taxable only on the taxable portion of the deemed dividend distributed on the wind-up. The total tax payable by the corporation and the estate would be approximately $23,612. The estate would net approximately $76,388.

Insertion of holding company

A variation would be for the estate to transfer the shares of the deceased's holding company to a new company at fair market value for either shares with paid-up capital equal to the purchase price or debt. Because the estate's adjusted cost base of its shares of the deceased's holding company should be high as a result of the deemed disposition on death, little or no gain should generally arise on such transfer.[41] The deceased's holding company may then be wound up or amalgamated with the new company as part of a pre-sale reorganization and the cost of the shares of the operating company held by the deceased's holding company could be increased pursuant to paragraph 88(1)(c) and (d) to reflect the fair market value of the shares of the operating company immediately before the death of the deceased shareholder.[42] The new company could then sell the shares of the operating company to the survivor without incurring a capital gain or capital loss.[43] Under this alternative, the only tax would be on the capital gain arising from the deemed disposition on death of the deceased or $23,177 in our example. The proceeds received by the new company can then be distributed tax-free to the estate as a return of paid-up capital (if shares were issued as consideration) or repayment of the debt (if debt was issued).[44]

---

[40] The stop loss rules are discussed in a later section of this Chapter. In this example, the stop loss rules would not be applicable.

[41] Section 84.1 should be reviewed to ensure that it does not apply. Section 84.1 is an anti-avoidance rule designed to prevent corporate surplus stripping which is applicable where a shareholder transfers shares of a company to a non-arm's length corporate purchaser and the transferred company and the acquisition company are connected following the transaction. If the provision applies, the estate would be deemed to have received all or part of the proceeds as a taxable dividend rather than a tax-free sale. In general, section 84.1 should not apply to a buy-sell structure if the shareholders deal with each other at arm's length or if the deceased shareholder did not claim the capital gains exemption with respect to the gain on the shares.

[42] The availability of the "bump" should be reviewed in all circumstances. There is an array of complex "bump denial" rules which may restrict the availability of the bump set out in subsection 88(1)(c)(iii) to (vi) and related provisions.

[43] Assuming that there has been no increase in the value of the shares between the date of death and disposition, the adjusted cost base of the shares should equal the proceeds.

[44] The paid-up capital of the shares of the new company held by the estate will be equal to the adjusted cost base of the shares of the operating company, subject to any reduction under section 84.1.

Tax Implications for the Survivor

Purchase by survivor holding company

The holding company owned by the survivor would receive the insurance proceeds on a tax-free basis which would be used to fund the purchase price to acquire the shares of the operating company from the deceased's holding company.[45] The surviving shareholder's holding company would realize a step-up in the adjusted cost base of the identical shares it owns in the operating company.

The proceeds would increase the capital dividend account of the surviving shareholder's holding company.[46] The surviving shareholder's holding company could elect to pay the maximum capital dividend in favour of its shareholders.[47] Such dividends would generally be received free of tax.

Because the survivor's holding company has used the proceeds to fund the purchase of the operating company's shares, the survivor's holding company may require funds from the operating company in order to be able to pay its capital dividend to the survivor(s).[48] Assuming that the companies are connected for tax purposes, an inter-corporate dividend may be paid free of income tax under the Act for this purpose. An alternative would be to amalgamate the survivor's holding company and the operating company in order to provide a source of funds for such tax-free dividends. The capital dividend account of the amalgamated company would include the balances in the predecessor companies' accounts.[49] The downside to such an amalgamation would be the loss of the adjusted cost base in the shares held by the survivor's holding company in the operating company as inter-company shareholdings disappear on an amalgamation.

---

[45] See note 13.

[46] Under subsection 89(1) the proceeds from the life insurance, net of the premiums paid on such policy, will be added to the corporation's capital dividend account. In order to maximize the amount of the life insurance added to the capital dividend account, consideration can be given to having each holding company own the life insurance on the life of their principal and pay the premiums thereon but with the death benefit payable to the other holding company. On the death of the deceased, the death benefit would be paid to the survivor's holding company. Since the survivor's holding company did not pay the premiums on the particular policy, on death, the full amount of the life insurance proceeds may, subject to challenge by the CRA, be added to the survivor holding company's capital dividend account. As the survivor's holding company has no adjusted cost basis in the life insurance policy, there is no reduction in the amount of the proceeds that can be added to the capital dividend account.

[47] Subsection 83(2).

[48] The operating company can fund the dividend to the holding company by borrowing funds. Provided that the amount of the dividend replaces the capital (accumulated profits and contributed capital) of the operating company used for the purpose of earning income from the business of the company, the interest on the borrowed funds should generally be deductible — see Interpretation Bulletin IT-533, Interest deductibility and related issues, dated October 31, 2003.

[49] Paragraph 87(2)(z.1) provides for the flow-through of the capital dividend account on an amalgamation.

¶409

Purchase by new holding company

The survivor may wish to form a new holding company to purchase the shares from the deceased's holding company. The old holding company of the survivor would own his shares in the operating company and would be the beneficiary of the life insurance policy. It would receive the insurance proceeds and would loan the funds to the new holding company to finance the purchase of shares by the new holding company from the deceased's holding company.

The old company, which would have the capital dividend account, could then be amalgamated with the operating company. This variation would facilitate the payment of capital dividends from the profits of the operating company while preserving the adjusted cost base of the shares purchased from the deceased's holding company.

Advantages

The survivor's holding company would be able to reflect the purchase price in the adjusted cost base of its shares in the operating company.[50] The life insurance proceeds would not be exposed to the creditors of the operating company. Life insurance premiums can be funded by tax-free inter-corporate dividends. The capital dividend account of a holding company would not be reduced as a result of any actual or deemed capital losses in the operating company and would be available to make tax-free distributions to the surviving shareholder.

Disadvantages

The main disadvantage of this structure is that it may result in the same gain being taxed twice. In terms of the deceased shareholder, the gain will either be taxed on the deemed disposition on death and/or the deceased shareholder's holding company will pay corporate tax on the disposition of the shares of the operating company to the survivor's holding company and the estate will pay personal tax on the distribution of the after-corporate tax proceeds as a dividend by the deceased holding company to the extent that such distribution is a taxable dividend. The surviving shareholder's holding company will not pay any additional tax to the extent of the higher adjusted cost base of its acquired shares when such shares are sold but the surviving shareholder will be taxable when the amount of the sale proceeds sheltered by such adjusted cost base is distributed as a taxable dividend.

A Combination Approach

A variation of the above structure would be to have criss-cross insurance at the holding company level followed by a purchase for cancellation by the operating company. This may be accomplished by having the holding company of the survivor contribute the life insurance proceeds as a loan or share subscription to the operating company. The operating company could then redeem or purchase for cancellation the shares of the deceased's company. The tax implications for the deceased's company in this situation are generally

---

[50] Section 47.

similar to an ordinary sale. While the redemption or purchase for cancellation would give rise to a deemed dividend under the general rules, subsection 55(2) would likely apply to convert the deemed dividend received by the deceased's holding company to be a capital gain to the extent that the purchase price exceeds the holding company's proportionate share of the post-1971 retained tax earnings of the operating company (commonly referred to as "safe income"). To the extent that there is "safe income" attaching to the deceased's holding company shares of the operating company, however, this alternative may provide a better result as the deemed dividend may be received by the holding company tax-free.[51] This approach should only be considered where the deceased's holding company's share of safe income of the operating company approximates the purchase price. Otherwise, the deceased's holding company may realize a capital gain and the survivor's holding company would not benefit from an increase in the adjusted cost base of the shares of the operating company.

Where the "safe income" is less than the purchase price, another alternative that would maximize the use of "safe income" and permit the survivor's holding company to acquire the shares of the operating company with full adjusted cost base is to reclassify the estate's holding company's shares of the operating company into a separate class (using either a section 51 or 86 reorganization) and have the operating company increase the stated capital of that class of shares by the amount of safe income attributable to such shares. The increase in stated capital should give rise to a tax-free inter-corporate dividend and an increase in the adjusted cost base of the shares by the amount of "safe income." The increase in the estate's holding company's adjusted cost base in its shares of the operating company will reduce the gain when such shares are sold to the survivor's holding company.

¶415
Deferred Sale Method

¶420 Deferred Sale — Individuals

Overview

The deferred sale method is a hybrid as it involves corporate-owned life insurance as well as a direct sale. The insurance policy or policies would be owned by the operating company. On the death of a shareholder, the estate would sell the shares to the survivors in exchange for a promissory note representing the purchase price. The survivors, who at that time would own all of the shares of the operating company, would receive a capital dividend arising and paid from the receipt of the life insurance proceeds by the operating company. The funds on account of the capital dividend received by the survivor would be used to discharge the promissory note.

---

[51] Section 186. See Interpretation Bulletin IT-269R3, Part IV Tax on taxable dividends received by a private corporation or a subject corporation, dated November 29, 1991.

Tax Implications for the Estate

If no rollover were available on death, the deceased would realize a capital gain, eligible for the capital gains exemption, as a result of the deemed disposition immediately prior to death.[52] The ownership or the receipt of the life insurance proceeds by the operating company, which are otherwise non-qualifying assets of the corporation for purposes of eligibility for the capital gains exemption, would not affect the capital gains exemption claim of the deceased taxpayer.[53] Although the fair market value of the life insurance and insurance proceeds may exceed 10 per cent of the fair market value of the corporation, the corporation would retain its status as a small business corporation.[54] The estate would acquire the shares for a cost equal to the fair market value of the shares immediately before death, with the result that there should be no additional tax payable on the actual sale.[55]

If a spousal rollover is available, then the spouse of the deceased or the spousal trust would acquire the shares for an adjusted cost base equal to the adjusted cost base of the deceased.[56] A capital gain would be realized by the spouse of the deceased on the actual sale to the survivor. If the shares qualify as shares of a qualified small business corporation, the $500,000 capital gains exemption may be available to shelter part of the gain. As the sale occurs after the death of the shareholder, the life insurance proceeds may disqualify the corporation where it represents more than 10 per cent of the value of the assets at the time of sale.[57]

---

[52] Paragraph 70(5)(a).

[53] See footnote 57 below.

[54] Defined generally under section 248 as a Canadian-controlled private corporation where all, or substantially all, of the assets are used principally in an active business carried on primarily in Canada. The CRA defines "all or substantially all" as a 90 per cent test (i.e., only 10 per cent can be passive assets).

[55] Paragraph 70(5)(b).

[56] Paragraph 70(6)(c).

[57] Subparagraph 110.6(15)(a)(ii) is intended to preserve the entitlement to the $500,000 capital gains exemption where a corporation owns life insurance by deeming the value of the insurance to be equal to the cash surrender value, if any, of the policy. However, this rule will only apply where the shares owned by the deceased are actually purchased or redeemed by the corporation within 24 months of the deceased's death using the life insurance proceeds. Therefore, as long as the life insurance proceeds are used by the corporation to redeem or purchase shares acquired by the survivor from the deceased's spouse (i.e., the shares that were owned by the deceased at the time of death), this rule should assist in allowing the corporation to meet the 90 per cent active business asset test. The survivor, however, will not wish to effect the purchase in this fashion since he or she will be left with no adjusted cost base in the acquired shares as they will have disappeared on the redemption. Instead the survivor will wish to transfer the acquired shares before redemption to a holding company for debt of the holding company. The acquired shares now owned by the holding company would be purchased by the corporation using the life insurance proceeds within the 24-month period thus satisfying the rule. The holding company would pay the debt owing to the survivor who would pay the debt owed to the deceased's spouse. Finally, in order to make use of the high adjusted cost base in the holding company, the survivor would transfer the remaining shares in the corporation to the holding corporation for shares of the holding corporation on a rollover basis elected under section 85. The holding corporation and the corporation would amalgamate. The high adjusted cost base in the shares formerly held in the holding company would now become high cost base shares in the amalgamated operating company.

¶420

Tax Implications for the Survivor

The survivor would receive the life insurance proceeds from the operating company as a tax-free capital dividend.[58] The survivor would thus be able to increase the aggregate adjusted cost base of all his shares to reflect the purchase price paid to the estate for the deceased's shares. If all of the shares owned by the survivor are identical shares then the adjusted cost base in the newly purchased shares would be averaged over all of the survivor's shares.[59]

Advantages

The advantage of the foregoing arrangement is that it enables the parties to use corporate-owned insurance while providing the survivor with a step-up in the adjusted cost base of his shares. As discussed, the adjusted cost base will reduce any gain on a subsequent sale, and can, in certain circumstances, be used to extract funds from the operating company tax-free[60].

Disadvantages

Where the operating company is the beneficiary of the insurance, the insurance proceeds would be exposed to the creditors of the operating company. The terms of the company's bank loan may require the lender's approval to the declaration of any dividends. If the operating company were insolvent, not only would the purchase price be jeopardized but there may be corporate law restrictions to declaring a dividend to the survivors. The shares of the operating company may be worthless. It may be necessary to have the parties to the shareholders' agreement agree to inject additional funds into the corporation for the purpose of making it solvent in that situation, or alternatively, the parties may rely on the personal covenant of the survivors that they would be obligated, in any event, to purchase the shares. The survivors would thus be required to use savings or to borrow funds in order to purchase the shares.

The ownership of the life insurance by the operating company also may raise valuation issues which may affect the status of the shares of the operating company as shares of a qualified small business corporation for purposes of determining whether the $500,000 capital gains exemption is available at the time shares of the corporation are sold. Subparagraph 110.6(15)(a)(i) deems the fair market value of the life insurance policy to be equal to its cash surrender value, but only if the life insured is a shareholder of the corporation, or of a "connected corporation" (generally requiring more than 10 per cent of votes and value). If someone other than a shareholder, such as an employee, is the life insured, then the value of the policy will be determined on general valuation principles.

On the death of a shareholder, subparagraph 110.6(15)(a)(ii) provides that the value of any life insurance owned by a corporation will be deemed to be equal to its cash surrender value, but only where the proceeds from the life insurance policy are used to repurchase the shares that were held by the

---

[58] Subsection 83(2).

[59] Section 47.

[60] See discussion at page 104 and Footnotes 41 and 42.

¶420

deceased shareholder immediately before death and such repurchase occurs within 24 months after death (or such extended time where written application has been made to, and given by, the CRA). Note that subparagraph 110.6(15)(a)(ii) only requires that the shares that were owned by the deceased be repurchased. There does not appear to be any requirement relating to the identity of the person who owns the shares at the time of actual repurchase.

Where the provisions of this paragraph are met, the receipt of the death benefit by the corporation should not affect the deceased's claim for the $500,000 capital gains exemption (unless the policy has a high cash surrender value that throws the company outside of the 90 per cent active business asset test). Where the requirements of that provision are not met (including on any sale of shares to a third party not followed by a repurchase within the prescribed time period), the receipt of the life insurance proceeds may cause the shares of the corporation to lose their status as shares of a qualified small business corporation.

If the deceased and the survivor did not deal at arm's length at the time the agreement was made, the CRA may apply paragraph 69(1)(b) to deem the estate to have sold the shares at fair market value (including the proceeds of insurance or the value of the insurance policy) which could be determined without reference to the provisions in the buy-sell agreement.[61] This may result in the estate realizing a greater capital gain on the actual sale without receiving increased proceeds. The cost of the shares to the survivor would not reflect the increased sale price as section 69 only applies to increase the purchase price for the vendor and does not provide for a corresponding adjustment to the cost of the shares to the purchasers. The parties may provide for a price adjustment clause in the buy-sell agreement so as to enable the survivor to make a cash adjustment to the estate and to increase the cost of his shares accordingly.[62]

Another valuation issue arises on the deemed disposition on death where the shares of a corporation (or subsidiary) owns life insurance. However, subsection 70(5.3) provides for a relieving rule for purposes of valuing the shares of a corporation that owns life insurance. This rule stipulates that the fair market value of any insurance policy on the life of the deceased shareholder will be deemed to be the cash surrender value. This provision will not only apply when the individual dies owning shares of the corporation insuring the individual's life, but also where the corporation owns insurance insuring a life of a person who does not deal at arm's length with the individual such as a spouse or a child. However, where a corporation owns insurance on an arm's length co-shareholder of the deceased shareholder or arm's length non-shareholder such as an employee of the corporation, general valuation principals will be applied in considering the valuation of the deceased's shares. It should be noted however that this provision should only be applicable if there was no buy-sell agreement in existence or if the buy-sell agreement did not provide for a comprehensive determination of the fair market value of the shares.

---

[61] See Interpretation Bulletin IT-405, Inadequate consideration — Acquisitions and dispositions, dated January 23, 1978 and Interpretation Bulletin IT-140R3, Buy-sell agreements, dated April 14, 1989.

[62] For more discussion on this issue see Chapter 3.

It should also be noted that these rules will also apply in determining the fair market value of any shares owned by a trust on the deemed disposition of capital property (including shares of a corporation which owns life insurance) that occurs (i) on the death of a spouse where the trust is a qualifying spousal trust and every 21 years thereafter, or (ii) on the 21st anniversary of the settlement of most other trusts and every 21 years thereafter.

Valuation issues may also impact the possible application of the penal corporate attribution rule in section 74.4. Generally speaking, these rules can apply to many income splitting or estate freeze type transactions. The rules will generally not apply where the corporation is a "small business corporation." In order to be a small business corporation, it is necessary that 90 per cent or more of the fair market value of the assets be used in an active business carried on primarily in Canada. It is possible that life insurance owned by a corporation may put the company offside in meeting the 90 per cent active business test. The relieving provisions described above in the context of the $500,000 capital gains exemption do not apply for the purposes of the corporate attribution rule contained in section 74.4.

Most provinces, with the current exception of Alberta, Prince Edward Island and Newfoundland, levy a provincial capital tax on corporations located in the jurisdiction. By definition, this tax focuses on the corporation's capital as reflected in its financial statements. Since corporate owned life insurance will be included on a corporation's financial statements, it may well attract capital tax liability depending on the particular jurisdiction's method of accounting adjustment or restatement policies in respect of such items.

Ontario's Corporate Minimum Tax (CMT) applies to a corporation's gross revenues in excess of $10,000,000 or total assets in excess of $5,000,000. CMT is based upon the income reported on the company's financial statements, subject to adjustment, and taxed at a rate of 4 per cent. Corporate owned life insurance policies may impact CMT liability in relation to any income or loss reported on the corporation's financial statements as a result of recording the policy's cash surrender value.

Because corporate owned life insurance policies may affect the corporation's balance sheet numbers, there may be consequences in relation to Large Corporations Tax. This federal capital tax applies on capital in excess of $10,000,000, but the tax now at .225 per cent is set to be phased out by 2008. Conversely, the small business tax deduction available to certain Canadian-controlled private corporations is currently reduced where a corporation's taxable capital exceeds $10,000,000. Where a corporation's ownership of life insurance will affect the corporation's taxable capital, Large Corporations Tax may be exigible as well as a reduced availability of the small business tax rate.

A Possible Solution

A variation which may solve the concerns about solvency, the potential valuation problem and the eligibility of the corporation as a small business corporation would be to have a new corporation formed during the lifetime of the shareholders. The operating company would annually subscribe for retractable preference shares in the new corporation in an amount sufficient to fund the insurance premiums. The new corporation would be the beneficiary of the insurance policy.

The common shares of the new corporation would be owned by an *inter vivos* trust. The trustees could be the shareholders and possibly a third party. The beneficiary would be the surviving shareholder(s). As a shareholder would cease to be a beneficiary on death, the trust interest should not be subject to a deemed disposition on death.[63] On the death of a shareholder, the new corporation would be wound-up and an amount equal to the premiums paid would be returned to the operating company as the redemption price of the preference shares. The CRA should not be able to include the mortality gain of the insurance in valuing the shares of the operating company for purposes of the deemed or actual disposition as the operating company is entitled only to the redemption of the preference shares in the new corporation. On the wind-up of the new corporation, the balance of the assets would be paid to the trust and the insurance proceeds (net of the adjusted cost basis of the policy) would be treated as a capital dividend and would not be taxable to the trust.[64] The trust would make a tax-free capital distribution to the survivor, who would use the funds to purchase the shares from the estate.[65] It would thus compliment the deferred sale arrangement described above.

Another alternative that may deal with just the valuation issue on the sale of the shares held by the deceased's holding company would be to have separate classes of preference shares of the operating company. Each shareholder would be issued a separate class of preference shares entitled exclusively to capital dividends on the death of the other shareholders. For example, if there were two shareholders, A and B, A may be issued a class of preference shares entitled to the capital dividend arising on the death of B. In this manner, the capital dividend may be paid to the survivor on a separate class of shares and may be used to fund the buy-out on death. As neither the common shares nor the preference shares owned by the deceased would be entitled to such insurance proceeds, it may be possible to rebut the argument by the CRA that the fair market value of such shares should be increased. This alternative

---

[63] Historically, the CRA took the position that the fair market value of a discretionary interest in a trust was indeterminate because the discretionary beneficiary could not be certain of receiving anything under the trust. Numerous commentators, wording of various provisions of the Act and the technical notes to various provisions of the Act all support the view that, as the fair market value of a discretionary interest in a trust is indeterminate, it must be assumed to have a value of nil. In a recent advance tax ruling, Ruling 2001-0111303 "Beneficiary added to a discretionary Trust," the CRA abandoned its earlier position and instead took the position that the fair market value at any time of a discretionary interest in a trust will approximate a proportionate share of the fair market value of the trust property at that time. In our view, the CRA's position is indefensible and if the CRA maintains that position (as they appear to be doing given similar comments in recent technical interpretation, Document 2003-0181465, "FMV of an Interest in a Discretionary Trust" — section 69(1)(b), dated April 3, 2003), it will cause extremely inappropriate results in some circumstances. Regard should obviously be given to the CRA's new position in structuring the terms of the trust perhaps by providing that any entitlement that a beneficiary may receive is only available upon 30 days' prior notice to the beneficiary provided that the beneficiary is alive at the end of such notice period.

[64] Subparagraph 88(2)(*b*)(i).

[65] Subsection 107(2).

would not assist in maintaining qualified small business corporation status if the relieving provisions of paragraph 110.6(15)(a) are otherwise not applicable.

Is the Arrangement Equitable?

Another problem with the deferred sale method is that the survivor may be in a substantially better after-tax position on an actual sale of the business than the deceased shareholder. Assuming that a company is worth $200,000 and that $100,000 of life insurance is obtained on the life of each of the two shareholders. The survivor would purchase the shares for a note and would receive $100,000 as a capital dividend which would be paid to the estate to discharge the note. Assume that the shares had an adjusted cost base of $100, a capital gain of $99,900 would be realized by the estate on the sale to the survivor (or on death if there were no spousal rollover) and the estate would receive net proceeds of approximately $76,823 after tax.[66] If the survivor subsequently sold all of the shares of the company for $200,000, the shares would have an adjusted cost base of $100,100 representing the aggregate of his subscription price of $100 and the price paid to the estate on the death of the first shareholder ($100,000). A capital gain of $99,900 would arise and the survivor would net approximately $176,823 assuming a fully taxable sale.

An alternative which may be more equitable for both parties would be for the company to obtain $200,000 of life insurance under a joint policy. On the death of a shareholder, a capital dividend of $100,000 would be paid to each of the estate and the survivor. The survivor would use his or her share of the capital dividend (i.e., $100,000) to buy the shares from the estate. There would be no deferred sale. The estate would realize a capital gain of $99,900 and would net approximately $176,823 after tax. If the survivor sold the business the next day for $200,000, he would realize a capital gain of $99,900 and would net approximately $176,823 after tax. The advantage of equalizing must be weighed against the increased cost of having the additional insurance coverage.

¶425 Deferred Sale — Holding Companies

Overview

This arrangement is the same as the foregoing except that it contemplates that the parties have formed holding companies to hold their shares in the operating company.[67] On the death of a shareholder of a holding company, the holding company of the survivor would purchase the shares of the operating company owned by the holding company of the deceased in exchange for a promissory note. The operating company would receive the life insurance death benefit and the maximum capital dividend would be paid to the holding company of the survivors and would be used to discharge the promissory note.

---

[66] Based generally on corporate and personal tax values applicable in the Province of Ontario in 2003.

[67] See Footnote 18.

Tax Implications for the Estate

If there is no rollover to a spouse available, there is a potential for double tax unless the company is wound up within the first taxation year of the deceased's estate.[68] There would be a deemed disposition on death of the shares of the holding company and the estate would be deemed to have acquired the shares for an amount equal to the deemed proceeds.[69] The holding company of the deceased may also realize a capital gain on the actual sale of shares. As discussed in a previous section, it may be possible to mitigate the problem by winding up the holding company within the first taxation year of the estate in order to enable the estate to incur a loss which may be carried back pursuant to the provisions of subsection 164(6).

If a rollover is available to a spouse or to a spouse trust, no double tax would result. No tax would arise on death with respect to the shares of the holding company owned by the deceased. On the actual sale of the shares, the deceased's holding company could realize a capital gain. The tax-free portion of the capital gain would be included in the capital dividend account of the corporation and would be eligible for distribution to the estate. The capital dividend would not be subject to tax. The taxable portion of the capital gain would be included in income and would be subject to tax. A portion of the corporate tax paid on the capital gain equal to $26^{2}/_{3}$ per cent of the taxable capital gain would be added to the RDTOH account of the holding company and would be eligible for a refund upon the distribution of sufficient taxable dividends.[70]

Tax Implications for the Survivor

The operating company would receive the insurance proceeds tax-free.[71] The insurance proceeds, net of the adjusted cost basis of the policy, would increase the capital dividend account of the operating company.[72]

After the survivor's holding company has acquired the shares of the operating company and issued a promissory note to the deceased's holding company, the operating company would pay the maximum capital dividend to the survivor's holding company. These funds would be used to repay the promissory note to the deceased's holding company.[73] The purchase price paid for the deceased's holding company's shares would increase the aggregate adjusted cost base of all of the shares of the operating company owned by the survivor's holding company.[74]

---

[68] The deceased will be subject to tax on the deemed disposition on death. The corporation may also be subject to a second level of tax on accrued gains at the time of the shareholder's death when its assets are sold or distributed.

[69] Paragraph 70(5)(a) and 70(5)(c).

[70] Section 129.

[71] Supra, footnote 13.

[72] Subsection 89(1).

[73] Subsection 83(2).

[74] Section 47.

¶425

The survivor's holding company could subsequently pay a capital dividend to its shareholders but there may be a cash flow problem as the survivor's holding company would have used the funds received from the operating company to pay the purchase price to the estate. Additional funds may not be available for the purpose of paying a tax-free dividend to the survivors. Taxable dividends may be paid to the survivor's holding company by the operating company[75]. Another alternative would be to amalgamate the survivor's holding company and the operating company in order that the profits of the operating company may be used for this purpose.[76]

Advantages

The advantages are that the parties may use corporate-owned insurance while providing the holding company of the survivors with a step-up in the adjusted cost base of their shares.

Disadvantages

The disadvantages are as outlined above for a deferred sale with individuals, namely that the insurance proceeds are exposed to the creditors of the company and the CRA may attempt to increase the sale price to reflect the mortality gain of the insurance.

¶430
Corporate Share Repurchase

¶435 Corporate Share Repurchase — Individuals

Overview

Under this structure, the terms of the shareholders' agreement would provide that the operating company redeem or purchase for cancellation the shares of a deceased shareholder. The operating company would maintain insurance for the purpose of funding the buy-out and would use the proceeds to purchase the shares from the deceased shareholder.

Tax Implications for the Estate

The tax implications for the estate may vary depending upon whether there is a spousal rollover on death. Other variables would be the adjusted cost base, paid-up capital of the shares and would occur when the structure for the corporate repurchase funded by life insurance was put in place.

---

[75] The operating company may borrow to fund the distribution to the holding company. The deductibility of interest on funds borrowed to pay a dividend was discussed in Footnote 49.

[76] Paragraph 87(2)(z.1) provides for the flow-through of the capital dividend account or life insurance capital dividend account on an amalgamation. The variation outlined above in the section Criss-Cross Insurance Holding Companies, Tax Implications for the Survivor would provide relief. By using a new holding company to purchase the shares from the deceased's holding company, part of the adjusted cost base of the shares of the operating company can be preserved while permitting the old holding company and the operating company to amalgamate.

On the death of the shareholder, the insurance proceeds would be received tax-free by the corporate beneficiary and the insurance proceeds, net of the adjusted cost base of the policy, would be added to the capital dividend account of the corporation. These funds would be used to fund the redemption of the purchase for cancellation.

On a redemption or purchase for cancellation of the shares of the operating company, a deemed dividend arises to the extent that the proceeds exceed the paid-up capital of the shares.[77] The operating company could elect to treat the deemed dividend as a capital dividend.[78] A capital dividend would be received on a tax-free basis by the estate.[79] The estate would be deemed to dispose of the shares for proceeds of disposition equal to the redemption proceeds minus the deemed dividend.[80] This would generally result in proceeds of disposition equal to the paid-up capital of the shares.

Assuming that there was no rollover on death, the estate would be deemed to have acquired the shares for a cost equal to the deemed proceeds to the deceased (i.e., equal to the fair market value of the shares immediately prior to death).[81] If a capital dividend were paid to the estate, it would not reduce the adjusted cost base of the shares owned by the estate. As a result, the difference between the fair market value of the shares immediately prior to death and the paid-up capital of the shares would generally be treated as a capital loss or business investment loss. The deduction of the loss by the estate or by the deceased on a carry back under subsection 164(6) may be limited by one or more stop loss rules which are applicable to losses arising on redemptions or purchases for cancellation where the estate is affiliated with the operating company or where the arrangement to acquire the shares of the operating company from the estate were not in place on April 26, 1995. Only the adjusted amount of the loss, after the application of the stop loss rules, may be carried back pursuant to subsection 164(6) to reduce or eliminate the capital gain arising on death if it is incurred within the first year of the estate.

¶440 Illustration

The following is intended to illustrate the tax consequences of a redemption of the shares of the operating company. This initial calculation does not take into account the application of stop loss rules.

The following assumptions are made:

The shares are not bequeathed to a spouse or to a spousal trust; both the fair market value at the time of death and the price of the shares determined in accordance with the buy-sell agreement is $100,000, the adjusted cost base of the shares is $100, the paid-up capital of the shares is $100, the insurance proceeds less the adjusted cost basis are $100,000 and are not included in the

---

[77] Subsection 84(3).

[78] Subsection 83(2).

[79] Ibid.

[80] The definition of "proceeds of disposition" in section 54 excludes the deemed dividend from proceeds of disposition.

[81] Paragraph 70(5)(b).

value of the shares on death; and a capital dividend election is made with respect to the full amount of the deemed dividend arising on redemption.

Deceased: Terminal Return
Death Of The Shareholder (Deemed Disposition)

Proceeds of disposition: paragraph 70(5)(a)	$100,000
Less adjusted cost base	100
Capital gain	$ 99,900
Taxable capital gain	$ 49,950

Estate
Corporate Share Repurchase

Proceeds on share purchase price	$100,000
Less paid-up capital	100
Deemed dividend: subsection 84(3)	$ 99,900
Capital dividend: subsection 83(2)	$ 99,900
Taxable dividend	NIL
Proceeds of Disposition	$100,000
Less deemed dividend	99,900
Proceeds	100
Less adjusted cost base: paragraph 70(5)(c)	100,000
Capital loss	($ 99,900)
Allowable capital loss carried back to offset taxable capital gain on death: subsection 164(6)	$ 49,950

Deceased Terminal Return
Death of shareholder — Net gain on deemed disposition

Taxable capital gain otherwise determined	$ 49,950
Allowable capital loss carried back to offset taxable capital gain on death: subsection 164(6)	$ 49,950
Net taxable capital gain after carryback	NIL

If the paid-up capital of the shares exceeded the adjusted cost base of the shares, then a capital gain could arise notwithstanding the fact that a capital dividend is declared. The reason is that the proceeds may be deemed to be equal to the paid-up capital (i.e., proceeds ordinarily determined minus the deemed dividend). A capital gain would arise as the proceeds would exceed the adjusted cost base.

If a spousal rollover were available on death, there would be no deemed disposition on death.[82] The spouse or spousal trust would acquire the shares for a cost equal to the adjusted cost base to the deceased.[83] A deemed dividend would result on the purchase for cancellation to the extent that the proceeds exceed the paid-up capital of the shares.[84] The operating company may elect to treat the deemed dividend as a capital dividend.

The proceeds of disposition of the shares would generally equal the paid-up capital of the shares. Depending on when the corporation was formed,

---
[82] Paragraph 70(6)(c), *supra* Footnote 2.
[83] Paragraph 70(6)(d).
[84] Subsection 84(3).

the adjusted cost base of the shares may equal the paid-up capital (e.g., if the corporation was formed after 1971 and shares were not purchased from third parties). In that case, no capital gain or loss would arise, and the stop loss rules would not be relevant. As a result, where a spousal rollover is available, neither the deceased nor the estate would be subject to tax as no tax would arise on death or on the purchase for cancellation.

¶442 Stop Loss Rules

Where no spousal rollover is available, the redemption or purchase for cancellation of the shares from the estate will generally give rise to a capital loss which may be denied: (i) if the arrangements to have the operating company purchase the shares from the estate using the life insurance proceeds were not in place on April 25, 1995, or (ii) if the estate was affiliated with the operating company immediately after the purchase.

Under the first stop loss rule, the loss arising from the disposition of a share by the estate to the operating company is generally reduced by 50 per cent of the amount of capital dividends, and life insurance capital dividends.[85] The effect of this stop loss rule is to prevent the tax-free buy-out of the deceased shareholder on death. The effective tax rate will generally now be one-half of the effective capital gains rate at the time. For example, in Ontario the effective tax rate in 2004 will be about 11.6 per cent of the gain realized by the deceased.

Where an estate disposes of shares acquired by it on death to the operating company, a capital loss arising from the disposition will also be reduced to the extent that any capital dividends received by the estate on the shares exceed one-half of the lesser of the individual's capital gain arising as a result of the deemed disposition on death and the estate's capital loss otherwise determined.[86] The reduction in the capital loss is offset to the extent that the taxpayer previously received taxable dividends.

The following table illustrates the tax consequences of a corporate repurchase where the first stop loss rule applies. For a side-by-side comparison we have also included again the illustration of general tax consequences of a corporate repurchase where the stop loss rules do not apply:

Deceased — Terminal Return
Death of a Shareholder

	No Stop Loss	Stop Loss
Proceeds of disposition: paragraph 70(5)(a)	$100,000	$100,000
Less adjusted cost base	$ 100	$ 100
Capital gain	$ 99,900	$ 99,900
Taxable capital gain	$ 49,950	$ 49,950

---

[85] Subsection 112.(3.2).
[86] Subsection 112(3.2).

Estate
Corporate Share Repurchase

	No Stop Loss	Stop Loss
Proceeds on share repurchase	$100,000	$100,000
Less paid-up capital	$ 100	$ 100
Deemed dividend (subsection 84(3))	$ 99,900	$ 99,900
Capital dividend (subsection 83(2))	$ 99,900	$ 99,900
Taxable Dividend	NIL	NIL
Proceeds of disposition	$100,000	$100,000
Less deemed dividend	$ 99,900	$ 99,900
Net proceeds of disposition	$ 100	$ 100
Less adjusted cost base	$100,000	$100,000
Capital loss	$ 99,900	$ 99,900

Capital loss is reduced by:
Lesser of:
- Capital dividend received by the estate — $99,900 .... $ 99,900
- Amount of loss otherwise determined (generally reduced by any taxable dividends received by the estate) — $99,900

Less 50% of lesser of:
- Amount of loss otherwise determined — $99,900 .... ($ 49,950)
- Capital gain from disposition of share on death — $99,900

	No Stop Loss	Stop Loss
Less loss reduction	NIL	($ 49,950)
Loss available for carryback	$ 99,900	$ 49,950

Summary
Deceased Terminal Return

	No Stop Loss	Stop Loss
Capital gain on death	$ 99,900	$ 99,900
Less loss carryback	($ 99,900)	($ 49,950)
Net capital gain	NIL	$ 49,950

Estate

	No Stop Loss	Stop Loss
Capital dividend	$ 99,900	$ 99,900
Net income	NIL	NIL
Total capital gain	NIL	$ 49,950
Taxable capital gain	NIL	$ 24,975

Where the first stop loss rule applies, the estate will receive the full proceeds as a tax-free capital dividend but the deceased will have a portion of the taxable capital gain remaining on the terminal return. In these circumstances, consideration can be given to the so-called "50 per cent solution" in order to avoid "wasting" a portion of the capital dividend account. Under this scenario, the operating company would only elect that one-half of the taxable dividend arising on the redemption be treated as a capital dividend. The tax consequences are illustrated below:

¶442

The 50% Solution
Terminal Return

Fair market value on death	$100,000
Adjusted cost base	$ 100
Capital gain	$ 99,900
Capital gains deduction	Nil
Net capital gain	$ 99,900
Taxable capital gain	$ 49,950
Section 164(6) loss capital loss	($ 49,950)
Net taxable capital gain	Nil

Estate

Proceeds on sale	$100,000
Less deemed dividend	$ 99,900
Proceeds	$ 100
Adjusted cost base	$100,000
Capital loss	($ 99,900)
Allowable capital loss	($ 49,950)
Section 164(6) loss carryback	($ 49,950)
Section 112(3.2) loss reduction	Nil
Loss otherwise determined	$ 99,900
Lesser of:	
• Capital divided received by estate — $49,950	$ 49,950
• Amount of loss otherwise determined — $99,900	
Less 50% of lesser of:	
• Amount of loss otherwise determined — $99,900	
• Capital gain from disposition of share on death — $99,900	($ 49,950)
Section 112(3.2) loss reduction	Nil

Deemed Dividend

Proceeds	$100,000
Less Paid-Up Capital	($ 100)
Deemed dividend	$ 99,900
Capital dividend	$ 49,950
Taxable dividend	$ 49,950

The 50 per cent solution plays off the fact that the first stop loss rules only "stop" the loss to the extent that such loss exceeds 50 per cent of the capital gain realized by the deceased on the deemed disposition on death. Under the 50 per cent solution, the estate will receive a portion of the proceeds as a taxable dividend rather than as a capital gain and 50 per cent of the capital dividend account will remain for the surviving shareholder. The deceased, however, will have no taxable capital gain on the terminal return. Under current tax rates, receipt of a taxable dividend will result in a slightly higher tax liability in the estate than if the full amount of the capital dividend account was distributed to the estate as a tax-free capital dividend and a portion of the taxable capital gain remained outstanding on the terminal return.[87]

Grandfathering and the first stop loss rule

The stop loss rule illustrated above was introduced in 1995. Prior to its introduction, it was possible to structure a corporate repurchase on the death of a shareholder funded by corporate owned life insurance so that no tax was payable by the deceased or by his or her estate. The tax was effectively deferred until the death of the surviving shareholder. Under the current regime, this tax-free result is only available in the case of a spousal rollover or in limited circumstances where arrangements for a life insurance funded buy-sell was in place prior to April 27, 1995, and was grandfathered under the old rule.

Grandfathering is available for individuals on a disposition of shares to a corporation on a redemption or a purchase for cancellation generally in two circumstances:

The first applies where the disposition occurred pursuant to an agreement in writing made before April 27, 1995. In the case where an agreement was in place before April 27, 1995, an amendment to the agreement may result in the loss of grandfathering if the amendment results in a "new" agreement.

In situations where it is necessary to make a change, consideration may be given to entering into a new agreement which deals only with the provisions necessary to be changed other than the life insurance funding provisions and providing that the new agreement supercedes the old but only with respect to those specific provisions. This may provide an additional argument that there has been no amendment of the old agreement at least as it relates to the insurance funding. If an individual holds shares in a holding company which in turn owns shares in an operating company that had life insurance on April 26,

---

[87] Based on the applicable tax rates for the year 2004 in the Province of Ontario, where an election is made to treat the full amount of the deemed divided as a capital dividend with the result that the stop loss rules apply, the total tax paid by the deceased in the terminal return is approximately $11,590. In the case of the 50 per cent solution, the total tax (paid by the estate) is approximately $15,634. However, the surviving shareholder is better off since 50 per cent of the capital dividend still remains within the operating company.

Because the stop loss rule in subsection 112(3.2) applies to each share separately and because the capital dividend election under subsection 83(2) must be made in respect of the entire dividend that is paid or deemed to be paid on the redemption or purchase of shares, consideration needs to be given to the mechanics of how the transaction should be structured. In our view, the best method is to pay out 50 per cent of the capital dividend acount as a capital dividend on the survivors shares. If sufficient funds are not available to the corporation, a daylight loan could be arranged. The shares of the deceased could then be purchased resulting in a deemed dividend. The election under 83(2) would then be made in respect of the entire deemed dividend notwithstanding that the capital dividend account is only 50 per cent of the deemed dividend. This excessive capital dividend payment will subject the paying corporation to a Part III tax equal to 75 per cent of the portion of the capital dividend that exceeds the actual capital dividend account at the time of the election. Finally, an excessive dividend election is made in accordance with the provisions of subsection 184(3). This election, required to be filed within 90 days of an assessment of tax under Part III, deems two dividends to have been paid - one as a capital dividend equal to the actual capital dividend account, and the second, as a taxable dividend in relation to the balance of the dividend deemed to arise on the redemption.

¶442

1995, it appears that shareholder agreements are required both at the operating company and the holding company levels for grandfathering to apply.

The second grandfathering circumstance is where life insurance was in place on April 26, 1995 to fund the acquisition of shares following death and the following requirements are met:

(i) the share was owned by the individual on April 26, 1995, or by a trust under which the individual was a beneficiary;

(ii) on April 26, 1995, the corporation or a partnership of which the corporation is a member was a beneficiary of the life insurance policy that insured the life of the individual or of the individual's spouse;

(iii) it was reasonable to conclude on April 26, 1995, the main purpose of the life insurance policy was to fund directly or indirectly the redemption or purchase for cancellation of the shares of the corporation.

In order to qualify for grandfathering under the owned life insurance requirement, the shares must be disposed of by the individual who owned the shares on April 26, 1995. Additional rules prevent the loss of grandfathering when the individual transfers shares to a spouse or to certain types of trusts. Specifically, the disposition can be made by the individual who owned the shares on April 26, 1995, or by such individual's spouse or common-law partner (or their estate); by a post 1971 spousal trust where such individual spouse or common-law partner is the beneficiary and the disposition occurs before the end of the third taxation year of the trust after the death of the spouse or common-law partner; or by an alter ego trust or joint partner trust, or a spousal trust created under the individual's will for the benefit of the individual spouse or common-law partner where the disposition occurs before the end of the third taxation year of such trust after the death of the individual (in the case of an alter ego trust) or the individual's spouse or common-law partner (in the case of a joint partner trust or spouse trust), as the case may be.

Where the shares of the corporation were held by the individual on April 26, 1995, and have been the subject of one or more tax-free reorganizations effected under one or more of sections 51, 85, 86, or 87, the substituted shares of the corporation or of another corporation received on such reorganization will also qualify for grandfathering.

In cases where corporate-owned insurance was in place on April 26, 1995, the insurance may subsequently be changed without jeopardizing the grandfathering.

Professionals should review the client's file to ensure whether a shareholder agreement was in place and whether it was adequate. In some cases, particularly in small businesses or family businesses, life insurance may have been in place without there being any shareholder agreement. A short agreement confirming that the insurance proceeds are to be used to purchase for cancellation the shares of the deceased should be prepared to support the claim for grandfathering.

¶442

Spousal rollover — effectively avoiding first stop loss rule

Even where no grandfathering is available, the shares of a company may be redeemed or purchased for cancellation without any tax to the deceased on the terminal return or to the estate on the redemption or purchase for cancellation if the deceased shareholder has a surviving spouse and the shares of the company held by the deceased are bequeathed to the surviving spouse or a trust for the spouse's benefit where the transfer qualifies for the spousal rollover under the Act. In this scenario, there will ordinarily be no deemed disposition of the shares on the death of the deceased shareholder. The spousal or spousal trust will realize a deemed dividend on the redemption or purchase for cancellation by the company, which can be received tax-free as a capital dividend from the life insurance proceeds provided the appropriate election is made. The redemption or purchase for cancellation will not give rise to a capital loss as the shares will have the original (usually nominal) adjusted cost base of the shares to the deceased as a result of the spousal rollover.

In order to achieve this result, the transfer of the shares of the company from the deceased to a spouse or a spousal trust must qualify for the spousal rollover. Generally, this requires that the shares vest with the spouse or the spousal trust within 36 months following the death of the deceased. Where the shares are subject to a mandatory buy-sell under a shareholders' agreement, the shares will not be considered to vest and the spousal rollover will not be available.[88] In order to avoid this problem, consideration can be given to structuring the buy-sell by providing the surviving spouse with a put and the corporation (triggered by the surviving shareholders) with a call to purchase the shares. The CRA has accepted that such a put and call arrangement in a shareholders' agreement will not disqualify a spousal rollover.

Family trusts and avoiding the first stop loss rule

Where shares of the company are held by a trust for the benefit of the members of the deceased principal's family, a tax-free redemption or purchase for cancellation of the shares is also available. In this scenario, there will be no deemed disposition of the shares on the death of the deceased shareholder as the shares are owned by the trust. The trust will realize a deemed dividend on the redemption or purchase for cancellation by the company, which can be received tax-free as a capital dividend from the life insurance proceeds provided the appropriate election is made. The redemption or purchase for cancellation will not give rise to a capital loss to the trust as the trust will have its original (usually nominal) adjusted cost base in the shares.

Second Stop Loss Rule

In the case where the estate is affiliated with the operating company immediately after the purchase, the capital loss (after any adjustment under the first stop loss rule) in the example may also be denied and the amount of such denied loss may be added to the adjusted cost base of shares held by a taxpayer in the operating company after the transfer. In the case of a purchase for cancellation, it is likely that the estate would not own any additional shares and

---

[88] See Interpretation Bulletin IT-449, Meaning of vested indefeasibly, September 25, 1987.

would not benefit from a step-up in the adjusted cost base to reflect the losses that were denied.

A corporation is affiliated with a person who controls the corporation or the spouse of that person. "Controlled" means "controlled, directly or indirectly in any manner whatever" which incorporates the concept of *de facto* control.[89] A corporation is affiliated with each member of an affiliated group of persons that controls the corporation or with a spouse of a member of such an affiliated group.

In the case where an estate is involved, the CRA has taken the position that the determination of whether the estate is affiliated with the corporation is based on the identity of the trustees of the estate. As a result, where the trustees of the estate are also the controlling shareholders of the corporation, the stop loss rules may apply to any loss arising on the redemption or purchase for cancellation of the shares held by the estate. Based on the foregoing, care must be taken to ensure that the selection of the trustees for the estate does not result in the application of the stop loss rules. Alternatively, where the stop loss rules may apply in such circumstances, consideration could be given to having the estate dispose of its shares on the winding-up of the corporation or of a new corporation inserted between the estate and the operating company.[90]

Note, however, that proposed amendments to the Act announced in the March 23, 2004 Federal Budget will add a specific provision to determine when a trust is affiliated with another person. Under the proposed amendments, a trust will be affiliated with any of its beneficiaries that hold a majority of the income or capital interests in the trust. Any person affiliated with such a beneficiary will also be considered affiliated with the trust. Two trusts will be affiliated if the contributors to both trusts are affiliated and the beneficiaries who hold a majority of the income or capital interest in the trust are affiliated.[91]

¶444 Tax Implications for the Survivor

The survivor increases his shareholdings by virtue of the elimination of the shares owned by the deceased. The survivor does not increase the adjusted cost base of his shares.

Advantages

As the insurance policy is owned by the operating company, the premiums are paid using corporate dollars. Assuming that the corporate tax rate is lower than the marginal tax rate of the individual shareholders, fewer after-tax dol-

---

[89] As a result, the stop loss rule may apply where the disposing shareholder exercises *de facto* control over the company after the redemption or purchase for cancellation. Query whether the shareholder would be considered to exercise *de facto* control of the company if the redemption or purchase for cancellation is funded in whole or part by a demand promissory note that exceeds the liquidity of the company. The CRA has taken this position in the past. See Appendix 2 for further discussion of these issues.

[90] The stop loss rule under subsection 40(3.6) does not apply where the loss arises on a disposition of the shares on a winding-up under subsection 69(5).

[91] See Appendix 2 for more details.

lars are used to discharge the insurance premiums. It is not necessary to have the company make a distribution by way of bonus or dividends in order to fund the insurance premiums.

If the corporation is required by its creditors to assign term insurance as collateral security for its loans, the premiums may be deductible.[92]

The survivors would increase their percentage interests in the company on a *pro rata* basis as a result of the purchase for cancellation of the shares owned by the deceased.

The insurance premiums, in essence, would be shared based on the proportionate shareholdings. This may be more equitable than a criss-cross arrangement at the shareholder level whereby a minority shareholder may be required to pay a disproportionate share of the premiums as the result of the age and health of the other shareholders. It is less complex to administer a corporate-owned insurance scheme as compared to criss-cross insurance. Fewer policies are involved and the corporation would undertake to discharge all of the premiums.

Where a spousal rollover is available or where the stop loss rules do not apply, a corporate share repurchase is the optimum structure for an estate as the estate would not be subject to any tax.

Disadvantages

A corporate share repurchase arrangement may not afford the shareholders flexibility to change the percentage shareholdings. For example, the parties may wish to allow a 20 per cent shareholder to become an equal shareholder in the event that one of the two 40 per cent shareholders dies. Under a corporate share repurchase arrangement, the interest of the 20 per cent shareholder would be automatically increased to 33 $1/3$ per cent rather than 50 per cent on the death of the shareholder. The remaining 40 per cent shareholder would increase his shareholdings to 66 $2/3$ per cent by virtue of the corporate share repurchase.

The capital gains exemption would not be available as a deemed dividend, rather than a capital gain, would be triggered.

For Ontario residents, there may be a valuation problem under the *Family Law Act* (FLA). The FLA allows a surviving spouse to elect within six months of death to opt under the Will or under the FLA. For purposes of computing the equalization payment under the FLA, there is a concern that insurance proceeds received by a company would increase the value of shares. However, as the valuation is made prior to death, the *Mastronardi* argument is available, that the insurance proceeds should not enter into the calculation. As the insurance proceeds would not be received by the survivor, the survivor would have no protection under the *Family Law Act*.

The relevant corporate statute may preclude the purchase for cancellation of shares.

---

[92] Paragraph 20(1)(e.2).

¶444

On a redemption or purchase for cancellation, the survivor does not increase the adjusted cost base of his shares. On the one hand the survivor may be viewed as being left holding the bag as his shares may have a nominal adjusted cost base with the result that a substantial capital gain may arise on his death or on the sale of the business. On the other hand, the survivor could be viewed as now owning 100 per cent of the company's assets with the only acquisition cost being 50 per cent of the premium cost of the insurance. If this is perceived to be a hardship, one way of mitigating this result would be not to exhaust the total capital dividend account on the purchase for cancellation. For example, the parties may obtain life insurance on each life equal to the total value of the business in order to ensure that one-half of the capital dividend of the corporation could be distributed to the survivor.

The stop loss rules may apply to preclude a capital loss.

If a capital dividend is available and it is desired that a capital loss be incurred within the first taxation year of the estate in order to offset the capital gain on death, problems may arise where the shares were owned prior to 1971 and either the taxpayer elected V-day value pursuant to subsection 26(7) of the Income Tax Application Rules or the taxpayer was eligible for the median rule but subsection 26(5) of the Income Tax Application Rules was not applicable.[93]

Notwithstanding the fact that the dividend is a capital dividend, a capital gain could be realized by the estate on a purchase for cancellation where the paid-up capital of the shares exceeds the adjusted cost base of the shares. As indicated above, generally the shares of the operating company would be deemed to be disposed of for proceeds equal to the paid-up capital (as the proceeds of disposition would be computed as the proceeds otherwise determined minus the deemed dividend).

Corporate-owned insurance may be exposed to the creditors of the corporation. The operating company may be unable to redeem the shares if it is insolvent. It may be possible to have the agreement provide that the surviving shareholders would personally purchase the shares in the event that the company is insolvent or alternatively would undertake to put adequate funds in the corporation so as to render it solvent. The survivors would thus personally guarantee the purchase of the shares. If the company is insolvent at the time of death, there may be some question as to the value of the company. If the agreement provides that the sale shall be at fair market value, the purchase price may be less than the insurance proceeds. Alternatively, the agreement may provide that the purchase price is the greater of the fair market value (i.e., the value otherwise determined by the formula in the agreement) and the life insurance proceeds payable on the death of the shareholder.

---

[93] See Howard J. Kellough and Peter E. McQuillan, *Taxation of Private Corporations and their Shareholders* (Canadian Tax Foundation, 1999), at p. 11:54 to 58.

¶444

¶445 Corporate Share Repurchase — Holding Companies

Overview

Under this alternative, the insurance is owned by the operating company and the shares of the operating company are owned by holding companies. On the death of an individual, the operating company would use the insurance proceeds to purchase for cancellation the shares owned by the holding company of the deceased.

Tax Implications for the Estate

Assuming that there was no spousal rollover, the shares of the holding company would be subject to a deemed disposition immediately prior to death and a capital gain would be realized. The capital gain may be sheltered by the capital gains exemption of $500,000 depending on whether the shares of the holding company are of a qualified small business corporation. The estate would be deemed to re-acquire the shares of the holding company for a cost equal to the deemed proceeds to the deceased.

The insurance proceeds would be received free of tax and would increase the capital dividend account of the operating company. On the purchase for cancellation of the shares of the deceased's holding company, the operating company would elect to treat the deemed dividend as a capital dividend. The deemed dividend would equal the difference between the proceeds and the paid-up capital of the shares.

The capital dividend would flow tax-free to the deceased's holding company.[94]

Subsection 55(2) would not apply to convert the deemed dividend to a capital gain provided that the dividend is a tax-free capital dividend.[95]

Assuming that the adjusted cost base of the shares equals the paid-up capital of the shares, no gain or loss would arise to the holding company on the deemed disposition of the shares. If the adjusted cost base exceeds the paid-up capital of the shares, it is possible that a capital loss or a business investment loss would be incurred. The capital loss, otherwise determined, would be reduced by taxable dividends, and capital dividends received by the holding company on the shares (see subsection 112(3)).

On the wind-up of the deceased's holding company, a deemed dividend would arise equal to the difference between the cash distributed and the paid-up capital of the shares. The holding company could elect to treat the deemed dividend as a capital dividend. The capital dividend account of the holding company would include capital dividends received from the operating company on the redemption of the shares. The proceeds of disposition would be equal to the actual cash distributed minus the deemed dividend.

---

[94] It would increase the capital dividend account or life insurance capital dividend account of the holding company. See subsection 89(1).

[95] Subsection 55(2) only applies to taxable dividends.

If the deemed dividend was a capital dividend, subject to the stop loss rules described above, it is possible that a capital loss would arise. A capital loss would be incurred if the proceeds of disposition are less than the adjusted cost base of the shares. If a loss is incurred within the year, it can be carried back pursuant to subsection 164(6) to reduce the capital gain arising on death.

If a spousal rollover were available on death, the tax consequences would be as outlined above with respect to the operating company and to the holding company. In summary, the insurance proceeds would be received by the operating company and would be used to purchase for cancellation the shares owned by the holding company of the deceased. The foregoing should not give rise to tax to the operating company or to the holding company.

On the wind-up of the holding company there would be no tax liability to the estate if the deemed dividend was a capital dividend, assuming that the proceeds of disposition (the proceeds less the deemed dividend) would equal the adjusted cost base of the shares.

In summary, assuming the purchase price was fully funded by life insurance, and assuming the holding company had no other assets, the effective tax rate would be nil where the spousal rollover applies or where grandfathering status renders the first stoploss rule inapplicable. In other situations the effective tax rate should be limited to one-half of the effective capital gains applicable to the deceased's gain on the shares of the holding company.

Tax Implications for the Survivor

On a purchase for cancellation of shares, the holding company of the survivor would realize an increase in its percentage interest in the corporation without obtaining an increase in the adjusted cost base of its shares in the operating company.

Advantages

A corporate share repurchase arrangement involving holding companies enables the proceeds of the insurance policy to be used to purchase for cancellation the shares of the deceased's holding company without incurring any tax to the operating company or to the holding company. There would be no Part IV tax with respect to either the premium payments (as the policy would be owned by the operating company) or the deemed dividend (assuming adequate insurance coverage to fund the purchase for cancellation). Similarly, there would be no deemed capital gain pursuant to subsection 55(2).

As the insurance is owned by the operating company, corporate dollars are used to discharge the insurance premiums.

Disadvantages

If the life insurance proceeds are insufficient to discharge the purchase price, then part of the deemed dividend would be a taxable dividend on the purchase for cancellation or redemption of the shares of the operating company owned by the deceased's holding company. This could give rise to a deemed capital gain pursuant to subsection 55(2) to the extent that the taxable dividend exceeds the deceased's holding company's share of the post-1971 retained tax earnings of the corporation. In addition, Part IV tax may arise with respect to the taxable dividend.

¶450 Combination Method

The optimum structure would be funded with corporate-owned insurance. It permits the estate to use its capital gains exemption and receive all of the proceeds on a tax-free base and permits the remaining shareholders to increase the adjusted cost basis of their shares. The shareholder agreement may contemplate a share sale by the estate to the extent of the unused capital gains exemption and a purchase for cancellation for the balance. Corporate owned insurance may be acquired by the operating company. On death, the estate would sell shares having an accrued gain equal to the unused capital gains exemption to the surviving shareholders for a promissory note. The balance of the shares would be purchased for cancellation and a capital dividend would be declared in respect of the deemed dividend. The balance of the capital dividend would be paid to the survivors who would discharge the promissory note. Under this scenario, the estate pays no tax and the survivors are able to increase the adjusted cost base of their shares in respect of portion of a the price.

This method could be refined further by permitting transfers to the spouse of the deceased followed by the sale triggered by a part-call arrangement.

¶455
Corporate Partnerships

The corporate partnership is becoming more popular given the flexibility which it affords corporate partners. Each company can have its own shareholders, its own investment policy and its own dividend policy. The corporations need not have the same year-end, and partnership rollovers are available for the admission or withdrawal of a partner. As the partnership may have a separate year-end, a further deferral of tax is available.

In terms of buy-sell arrangements on death, where the buy-out is structured at the corporate partner level, the consequences will be the same as those discussed above for buy-outs of shares of a corporation funded by insurance held either by the operating company, holding company, or individual shareholders. This section will review briefly the tax consequences where the buy-out is at the partnership level.

Where the partnership holds life insurance on the life of the deceased, the partnership will generally receive the proceeds of the life insurance tax-free.

Under the Act, the adjusted cost base of a partner's interest in a partnership is increased by that partner's share of the net life insurance received by the partnership in excess of the partnership's adjusted cost basis in the policy.

As a result, an allocation of life insurance to a corporate partner of a deceased principal will result in an increase in the corporate partner's adjusted cost base in the partnership in the year the partnership receives the insurance proceeds.[96] As a result, any distribution of the life insurance proceeds by the partnership to the corporate partner on a buy-out of its interest in the partnership will be a tax-free return of capital with a corresponding decrease in the corporate partner's adjusted cost base.

As well, the proceeds from the life insurance (less the cost of the policy) received from the partnership will be added to the corporate partner's capital dividend account[97] which can then be distributed tax-free as a capital dividend to the estate of the deceased principal. Where the distribution by the corporate partner to the estate is structured to give rise to a capital loss in order to avoid double tax, the stop loss rules may apply.

¶460

Conclusion

Recent legislative amendments have had a significant impact on the structuring of buy-sell agreements in closely held companies. While it is dangerous to generalize, the following are some guidelines.

A criss-cross insurance arrangement may be the most appropriate where the company and the shareholders are in roughly the same tax bracket. In that situation, the insurance policies should be owned outside of the operating company. It may be appropriate where the business is risky and the exposure to creditors is of concern. It would be attractive where the company is a small business corporation and the accrued gain of the shares to be sold does not exceed the unused capital gains exemption of the vendor. It may be viable for a corporate partnership.

Corporate share repurchases are attractive for an estate where the price is funded by corporate-owned insurance and the maximum capital dividend is declared. It may also be attractive where there is a holding company.

It may be worthwhile to form a side company if the operating company is engaged in a high-risk business. Consideration would be given to increased insurance coverage to increase the after-tax return to the estate. The deferred sale arrangement may be the optimum alternative for a company having both resident and non-resident shareholders where the survivor is a Canadian resident.

The combination approach may be the most attractive on death as it allows the estate to be bought out on a tax-free basis while affording the survivors an increase in the adjusted cost base of their shares.

Buy-sell agreements continue to be essential for closely held companies. A properly structured agreement can protect and benefit both the survivors and the estate.

---

[96] See Interpretation Bulletin IT-430R2.

[97] See Technical Interpretation 9119795.

Appendix 1

¶1000
Shareholders' Agreement

THIS SHAREHOLDERS' AGREEMENT made the ● day of ●, ●.

AMONG:

●, a corporation incorporated under the laws of the Province of Ontario

(hereinafter called "**Holdco 1**")

–and–

●, of the Province of Ontario

(hereinafter called "**Principal 1**")

–and–

●, a corporation incorporated under the laws of the Province of Ontario

(hereinafter called "**Holdco 2**")

–and–

●, of the Province of Ontario

(hereinafter called "**Principal 2**")

–and–

●, of the Province of Ontario

(hereinafter called "**Individual**")

–and–

●, a corporation incorporated under the laws of the Province of Ontario

(hereinafter called the "**Corporation**")

WHEREAS the parties wish to enter into this agreement in order to make arrangements regarding the organization and affairs of the Corporation and the sale of their shares of the Corporation under certain circumstances;

NOW THEREFORE THIS AGREEMENT WITNESSETH that in consideration of the mutual covenants herein contained and the sum of $1.00 of lawful money of Canada and other good and valuable consideration (the receipt and sufficiency of which is hereby acknowledged), the parties covenant and agree as follows:

Article 1 — Definitions and Interpretation

1.1 As used in this agreement, the following words and phrases shall have the following meanings, respectively:

(a) "**Affiliate**" and "**Subsidiary**" have the respective meanings ascribed thereto in the *Business Corporations Act* (Ontario);

(b) "**arm's length**" has the same meaning as that term is given in the *Income Tax Act* (Canada);

(c) "**Board of Directors**" means the board of directors of the Corporation from time to time;

(d) "**business day**" means any day other than a Saturday, Sunday or a civic or statutory holiday in Toronto, Ontario;

(e) "**Confidential Information**" means in this agreement, all information (including the terms and provisions hereof) concerning the business and affairs of the Corporation or any of its Affiliates or Subsidiaries of a confidential, non-public or proprietary nature (which information shall include, without limitation, trade secrets, know-how, intellectual property, marketing plans, cost figures, client lists, names and addresses of suppliers and customers, business contracts, software and operating systems, source codes and information relating to employees and other persons in a contractual relationship with the Corporation or any of its Affiliates and Subsidiaries), obtained, made available or disclosed in circumstances where the recipient (the "**Recipient**") ought reasonably to know that such information obtained directly or indirectly from, made available or disclosed by or on behalf of the Corporation or any Affiliate or Subsidiary thereof (the "**Disclosing Party**"), was obtained directly or indirectly from, made available or disclosed with an expectation on the part of the Corporation and/or the Disclosing Party that such information would be held in confidence by the Recipient and its employees, officers, agents or advisors. Confidential Information does not include any such information which: (i) at the time of its disclosure is publicly available though no fault of any person owing a duty of confidentiality to the Corporation or its Affiliate or Subsidiary; (ii) after disclosure, is released to the public by the Disclosing Party without restriction or otherwise properly becomes part of the public domain through no fault or action of the Recipient (but only after it is released or otherwise becomes part of the public domain); (iii) the Recipient can demonstrate was known to the Recipient or was in its possession at the time of

¶1000

disclosure and which was not acquired by such party directly or indirectly under any obligation of confidence to the Corporation or its Affiliates or Subsidiaries or from a person who, to the knowledge of the Recipient after exercising due diligence, owed an obligation of confidentiality to the Corporation or its Affiliates or Subsidiaries with regard to such information (for the purposes of this subsection (iii) information shall also be treated as confidential after the Disclosing Party shall have demonstrated to the Recipient that, notwithstanding its due diligence at the time of disclosure, the source of the information was in fact under a duty of confidentiality to the Corporation or its Affiliates or Subsidiaries with regard to such information); or (iv) the Recipient can demonstrate was independently developed by such Party without reference to or any use of the Confidential Information of the Disclosing Party;

(f) "**Date of Closing**" has the meaning ascribed to such term in section 7.5 hereof;

(g) "**Event of Default**" means, when used in relation to a Shareholder, that a Shareholder or its Principal has defaulted in the performance of its obligations pursuant to this Agreement or pursuant to any agreement entered into between such person and the Corporation and shall have failed to cure such default within 15 days after receipt by him of a notice from the Board of Directors or any other Shareholder asking him to cure such default;

(h) "**Event of Insolvency**" means, when used in relation to a Shareholder, that without the prior written consent of all of the Shareholders:

(i) the Shareholder or its Principal, as the case may be, makes an assignment for the benefit of its or his creditors; or

(ii) the Shareholder or its Principal, as the case may be, becomes bankrupt or, as an insolvent debtor, takes the benefit of any act now or hereafter in force for bankrupt or insolvent debtors; or

(iii) a receiver or other officer with like powers is appointed for the Shareholder or its Principal, as the case may be, for a substantial part of the assets of the Shareholder or its Principal, as the case may be, unless the appointment of such receiver or other officer with like powers is being disputed in good faith and such proceedings effectively postpone enforcement of such appointment; or

(iv) if the Shareholder is a corporation, a resolution is passed or an order is made or a petition is filed for the winding-up, liquidation, revocation or cancellation of incorporation of the Shareholder, unless such action is being disputed in good faith by appropriate proceedings and such proceedings effectively postpone enforcement of the position;

(i) "**Fair Market Value**" means the price determined in an open and unrestricted market between informed and prudent parties, acting at arm's length and under no compulsion to act, expressed in terms of money or money's worth;

¶1000

(j) "**fully-participating share**" means a security which participates to an unlimited amount in the earnings of the Corporation or upon the liquidation or winding-up of or other similar distribution of assets by the Corporation;

(k) "**Governmental Authority**" means any governmental or quasi-governmental authority including any federal, state, provincial, territorial, county, municipal or other governmental or quasi-governmental agency, board, parliament, legislature, regulatory authority, agency, tribunal, commission, branch, bureau, court, department or other law, regulation or rule-making entity (including a Minister of the Crown) or other instrumentality or political unit or subdivision having or purporting to have jurisdiction on behalf of any nation, state, province, municipality, district or any subdivision thereof;

(l) "**Immediate Family**" means, with respect to a Shareholder:

(i) if the Shareholder is an individual, the spouse or issue of that Shareholder provided such spouse or issue, as the case may be, is then *sui juris* and is not then a non-Canadian within the meaning of the *Investment Canada Act;*

(ii) if the Shareholder is a corporation, the Principal or the spouse or issue of the Principal of that Shareholder provided such spouse or issue, as the case may be, is then *sui juris* and is not then a non-Canadian within the meaning of the *Investment Canada Act;*

(iii) a corporation which is not then a non-Canadian within the meaning of the *Investment Canada Act* and which has no registered or beneficial shareholders other than the following (a "**Permitted Shareholder**"): (A) the Shareholder or the Principal of that Shareholder; or (B) the spouse and/or issue of the Principal or the Shareholder, as applicable, if then *sui juris;* or (C) any trust or trusts described in paragraph (iv) hereof, provided that the issued and outstanding shares of such corporation are free and clear of all claims, liens and encumbrances whatsoever and no person, other than a Permitted Shareholder, has any agreement or option or any right capable of becoming an agreement for the purchase of any of such shares and provided that the registered and beneficial shareholders of such corporation shall have agreed in writing with the parties hereto not to enter into an agreement or option to sell, transfer, assign, pledge, mortgage, charge, create a security interest in, hypothecate or otherwise dispose of, encumber or deal with, whether by will or otherwise, the shares of such corporation or permit such corporation to issue shares or grant options or rights in respect to the shares of such corporation except to the Immediate Family of that Shareholder, without the prior written consent of the other Shareholders first had and obtained, and all share certificates of such corporation shall have the legend set out in section 17.1 hereof endorsed thereon; or

(iv) a trust which has no trustees or beneficiaries (vested, contingent or otherwise) other than a Principal of that Shareholder (if such Shareholder is a corporation) or the spouse and/or issue of such Principal, or of a Shareholder, as applicable, provided that such trust is not then a non-Canadian within the meaning of the *Investment Canada Act;*

(m) "**Place of Closing**" means the offices of the solicitors for the purchaser in the subject transaction or such other place as may be agreed to in writing by the vendor and the purchaser in the subject transaction;

(n) "**Prime Bank Rate**" means the commercial lending rate of interest, expressed as an annual rate, which the Corporation's principal bankers quote in Toronto, Ontario as the reference rate of interest from time to time (commonly known as "prime") for the purpose of determining the rate of interest that it charges to its commercial customers for loans in Canadian funds;

(o) "**Principal**" means, with respect to Holdco 1 and Holdco 2, the persons listed below:

Shareholder	**Principal**
Holdco 1	Principal 1
Holdco 2	Principal 2

(p) "**Principals**" means each Principal;

(q) "**Sale**" means the sale of all or substantially all of the assets or a controlling interest in the business carried on by the Corporation (including such a Sale accomplished by a sale of shares, merger, amalgamation or arrangement if, immediately following such sale of shares, merger, amalgamation or arrangement, neither the then remaining Shareholders nor members of their respective Immediate Families (or any combination of such persons) owns a controlling interest, directly or indirectly, in such business) to a third party that is at arm's length from the vendor(s);

(r) "**Shareholder**" means each of Holdco 1, Holdco 2 and Individual and any other person who is a shareholder of the Corporation and whose holding is permitted in accordance with the terms hereof and who agrees to be bound by the provisions hereof, in each case so long as they are shareholders of the Corporation;

(s) "**Shareholders**" means every Shareholder; and

(t) "**Time of Closing**" means 2:00 p.m. (Toronto time) or such other time on the relevant closing date as may be agreed to in writing by the vendor and the purchaser in the subject transaction.

1.2 Unless otherwise provided for herein, all payments contemplated herein shall be paid in Canadian funds, in cash or by certified cheque.

1.3 This agreement shall be governed by and construed in accordance with the laws of the Province of Ontario and the federal laws of Canada applicable therein.

1.4 In this agreement, the use of the singular number shall include the plural and vice versa, the use of gender shall include the masculine, feminine and neuter genders and the word "person" shall include an individual, a trust, a partnership, a body corporate or public, an association or other incorporated or unincorporated organization or entity.

1.5 When calculating the period of time within which or following which any act is to be done or step taken pursuant to this agreement, the date which is the reference date in calculating such period shall be excluded. If the last day of such period is not a business day, the period in question shall end on the next business day.

1.6 Any references herein to any law, by-law, rule, regulation, order or act of any government, governmental body or other regulatory body shall be construed as a reference thereto as amended or re-enacted from time to time or as a reference to any successor thereto.

1.7 To the extent that this agreement specifies that any matters may only be or shall be dealt with or approved by or shall require action by the Shareholders, the discretion and powers of the directors of the Corporation to manage and to supervise the management of the business and affairs of the Corporation with respect to such matters are correspondingly restricted.

1.8 If shares of the Corporation are transferred by a Shareholder to one or more members of his or its Immediate Family, it shall be a condition of any such transfer that the applicable Shareholder remain entitled to and actually exercise all rights of such Shareholder hereunder. For greater certainty, any provision of this Agreement referring to or contemplating shares held by, or the number of shares held by, a Shareholder shall (without duplication) be deemed to include a reference to shares held by, or the aggregate number of shares held by, the particular Shareholder and the members of his or its Immediate Family in each case who are Shareholders, and, for further certainty, such aggregation shall apply for purposes of matters dealing with rights and obligations to vote, purchase or sell shares (including, without limitation, as a result of the occurrence of a Sale Event (as that term is defined in Article 7 below)) as contemplated herein so that a Shareholder and the members of its Immediate Family required to purchase or sell shares hereunder shall do so at the same time.

1.9 Any reference to shares of the Corporation means shares in the capital of the Corporation, as such shares exist at the close of business on the date of execution and delivery of this agreement; provided, that in the event of a subdivision, redivision, reduction, combination or consolidation, then a reference to shares of the Corporation shall thereafter mean the shares resulting from such subdivision, redivision, reduction, combination or consolidation.

1.10 If any Article, section or any portion of any section of this agreement is determined to be unenforceable or invalid for any reason whatsoever, that unenforceability or invalidity shall not affect the enforceability or validity of the remaining portions of this agreement and such unenforceable or invalid Article, section or portion thereof shall be severed from the remainder of this agreement.

Article 2 — Termination of Prior Agreements

2.1 All prior agreements among some or all of the parties hereto regarding the organization and affairs of the Corporation and/or the sale of any Share-

¶1000

holder's shares of the Corporation under certain circumstances, whether written or oral, are hereby terminated.

Article 3 — Warranties and Covenants

3.1 Each Shareholder warrants that:

(a) it is the registered and beneficial owner of that number and class of the issued and outstanding shares or securities convertible into shares of the Corporation set out opposite his name below:

Name	Number and Class of Shares or Securities Convertible into Shares
Holdco 1	100 Common Shares
Holdco 2	100 Common Shares
Individual	100 Common Shares

(b) the shares set out opposite each such person's name above are free and clear of all claims, liens, security interests and encumbrances whatsoever and, except as provided in this agreement, no person has any agreement or option or right capable of becoming an agreement for the purchase of any such shares and/or securities; and

(c) it is not a non-Canadian within the meaning of the *Investment Canada Act*.

3.2 Each of Holdco 1 and Holdco 2 warrants that it is a resident Canadian within the meaning of the *Business Corporations Act* (Ontario).

3.3 Principal 1 warrants that:

(a) he is the registered and beneficial owner of all of the issued and outstanding shares in the capital of Holdco 1; and

(b) such shares are free and clear of all claims, liens and encumbrances whatsoever and no person has any agreement or option or any right capable of becoming an agreement for the purchase of any of such shares and no person has any agreement or option or any right capable of becoming an agreement for the issuance or subscription of any unissued shares of Holdco 1.

3.4 Principal 2 warrants that:

(a) he is the registered and beneficial owner of all of the issued and outstanding shares in the capital of Holdco 2; and

(b) such shares are free and clear of all claims, liens and encumbrances whatsoever and no person has any agreement or option or any right capable of becoming an agreement for the purchase of any of such shares and no person has any agreement or option or any right capable of becoming an agreement for the issuance or subscription of any unissued shares of Holdco 2.

3.5 The Corporation warrants that:

¶1000

(a) the shares and securities listed in subsection 3.1 hereof are the only issued and outstanding shares or securities convertible into shares of the Corporation; and

(b) except as provided in this agreement, no person has any agreement or option or right capable of becoming an agreement for the purchase, subscription or issuance of any of the unissued shares of the Corporation or any securities convertible into shares of the Corporation.

3.6 Each Shareholder represents and warrants that the Corporation is not "associated" (as that term is defined in the *Income Tax Act* (Canada)) with any other corporation and hereby covenants that if the Corporation becomes so associated, all appropriate forms and elections will be filed to ensure that, to the maximum extent possible, the Corporation has allocated to it, in each taxation year, the amounts necessary with respect to its business limit to enable the Corporation to take the maximum small business deduction available in such taxation year, as those terms are used in the *Income Tax Act* (Canada).

Article 4 — Provisions for Control of the Corporation

4.1 The Shareholders shall each vote their shares of the Corporation and the parties hereto shall act in all other respects in connection with the corporate proceedings of the Corporation so as to ensure that the provisions of this agreement are complied with. Without limiting the generality of the foregoing, the Shareholders shall cause such meetings of the Corporation to be held, votes cast, resolutions passed, by-laws enacted, documents executed and all things and acts done to ensure the following continuing arrangements with respect to the operation and control of the Corporation:

(a) The affairs of the Corporation shall be managed by a Board of Directors which shall at all times consist of three directors, being one nominee of Holdco 1, so long as Holdco 1 (or a member of its Immediate Family) is a shareholder of the Corporation, one nominee of Holdco 2, so long as Holdco 2 (or a member of its Immediate Family) is a shareholder of the Corporation and one nominee of Individual so long as Individual (or a member of his Immediate Family) is a shareholder of the Corporation, of which the initial nominees are Principal 1, Principal 2 and Individual.

(b) Should any vacancy occur on the Board of Directors, such vacancy shall be filled forthwith by the appointment of a nominee or nominees by the Shareholder who is not then represented by the nominee or nominees to which he is entitled hereunder.

(c) (i) Notwithstanding anything herein contained, if an Event of Insolvency occurs with respect to a Shareholder (the "**Defaulter**"), such Defaulter shall not be entitled to be a director or to any nominees on the Board of Directors and the Shareholders shall cause such nominee director or directors of the Defaulter to forthwith resign or be removed and shall replace such nominee director or directors with such person or persons as may be designated by the other Shareholders.

(ii) Notwithstanding anything to the contrary herein contained, from and after the occurrence of such an Event of Insolvency, the Defaulter shall not be entitled to vote his or its shares or to receive notice of meetings of shareholders of the Corporation and, for the purposes of voting, for all purposes of this agreement, the other Shareholders will be deemed to own all of the shares of the Corporation. In addition, the Defaulter hereby irrevocably gives its proxy to the President of the Corporation (or if the Defaulter is the President, the Secretary of the Corporation) to vote its shares in any matter that such person determines and hereby appoints such person as its attorney (which appointment shall be continuing and shall survive incapacity of the donor of such power) to execute all necessary documents on behalf of the Defaulter to give effect to such proxy.

(iii) For the purposes of this agreement, if an Event of Insolvency occurs with respect to any member of the Immediate Family of a Shareholder, the Shareholder and all other members of the Immediate Family of such Shareholder shall be deemed to be Defaulters.

(d) The officers of the Corporation shall be such officers as the Board of Directors may determine from time to time.

(e) A quorum for a meeting of the shareholders of the Corporation shall be all of such shareholders, present in person or represented by proxy. A quorum for a meeting of the directors of the Corporation shall be a majority of the directors as long as there are three or more directors, provided that a quorum shall be all directors in the event that there are fewer than three directors. If proper notice of a meeting of the Board of Directors or shareholders of the Corporation, as the case may be, specifying the business to be transacted at the meeting, is given and a quorum of directors or shareholders, as the case may be is not present, then a meeting may thereafter be held on 48 hours' written notice of the second meeting to transact the business set forth in the original notice and, subject to the provisions of applicable law and notwithstanding any other provisions of this agreement, any directors or shareholders, as the case may be, present at that meeting shall constitute a quorum for the transaction of the business set out in the original notice in respect of that meeting and such business may be transacted by majority vote of those directors or shareholders, as the case may be, in attendance at the meeting.

(f) Except as otherwise provided in subsection 4.1(h) of this agreement and except as may be otherwise provided in this agreement, all decisions of the Board of Directors and of the shareholders of the Corporation shall require a simple majority of votes cast. Notwithstanding any statutory rule or rule of procedure to the contrary, the chairman of the meeting of the Board of Directors or at any meeting of the shareholders of the Corporation shall not be entitled to a second, extra or casting vote in the case of a tie vote at any such meeting.

(g) Subject to the terms hereof, all contracts and documents binding the Corporation which (1) are made out of the ordinary course of business

¶1000

and which are not terminable by the Corporation without liability upon giving no more than 30 days' notice, (2) have a term in excess of one year, or (3) involve a liability on the part of the Corporation in excess of $• in respect of any such contract or document, shall require the signatures of any two Shareholders, or such other individual(s) as may be determined by the Board of Directors from time to time.

(h) Notwithstanding anything to the contrary contained in this agreement, without the prior unanimous consent of the Shareholders, none of the following shall be effected:

(i) the issuance or sale by the Corporation or any Subsidiary of the Corporation of any of its shares or securities convertible into its shares or any subscription rights or warrants in respect of its shares or securities convertible into its shares;

(ii) the redemption or purchase by the Corporation or any Subsidiary of the Corporation of its issued shares or securities convertible into shares;

(iii) the filing of Articles (within the meaning of the *Business Corporations Act* (Ontario)) in respect of the Corporation or any Subsidiary of the Corporation;

(iv) the taking or instituting of proceedings for the winding-up, reorganization or dissolution of the Corporation or any Subsidiary of the Corporation;

(v) the enactment, revocation or amendment or any by-laws of the Corporation or any Subsidiary of the Corporation;

(vi) the sale, lease, exchange or other disposition of all or substantially all of the assets or undertaking of the Corporation or any Subsidiary of the Corporation;

(vii) any material change in the business of the Corporation or any Subsidiary of the Corporation;

(viii) the declaration of any dividend or the distribution of capital by the Corporation or any Subsidiary of the Corporation;

(ix) the repayment of any loans owing by the Corporation or any Subsidiary of the Corporation to any of the Shareholders or Principals, except for loans made in accordance with the terms of this agreement and the terms of which provide for repayment at specified times;

(x) the fixing, paying or changing of any salary, bonus, fee or other compensation paid or payable to any Principal or Shareholder, or to any director, officer or employee of the Corporation or any Subsidiary of the Corporation who does not deal at arm's length with the Shareholders or Principals except as provided herein;

(xi) the provision of financial assistance by the Corporation or any Subsidiary of the Corporation, whether by loan, guarantee or otherwise, to any Shareholder, Principal or any person not dealing at arm's length with a Shareholder or Principal;

(xii) the making of any contract or other arrangement between the Corporation or any Subsidiary of the Corporation and a Shareholder or Principal, or any person not dealing at arm's length with a Shareholder or Principal or the making of any payment to any such person, except as provided herein;

(xiii) the hypothecating, mortgaging, pledging, charging or otherwise encumbering of any of the assets of the Corporation or any Subsidiary of the Corporation;

(xiv) the creation of any Subsidiary; and

(xv) the hiring or firing of any employee of the Corporation or any Subsidiary of the Corporation who at the time in question is earning an annual remuneration (including all benefits) in excess of $● or the fixing or changing of any salary, bonus or other compensation paid or payable to any such employee or increasing the annual remuneration (including all benefits) of any employee of the Corporation or any Subsidiary of the Corporation to an amount in excess of such amount.

Article 5 — Operation and Financing of the Corporation

5.1 Proper books of account shall be kept by the Corporation and entries shall be made therein of all matters, terms, transactions and things as are usually written and entered into books of account in accordance with generally accepted accounting principles and each of the Shareholders shall at all times furnish to the others correct information, accounts and statements of and concerning all transactions pertaining to the Corporation without any concealment or suppression.

5.2 The external accountants of the Corporation shall be such firm of chartered accountants as the Shareholders shall appoint from time to time.

5.3 The Corporation shall maintain a bank account or bank accounts at such bank or trust company as the Board of Directors shall from time to time determine. All bank accounts shall be kept in the name of the Corporation and, subject to the terms hereof, all cheques, bills, notes, drafts or other instruments shall require the signatures of such individuals as the Board of Directors may from time to time determine. Until changed in accordance with the provisions hereof, any such instrument in excess of $● shall require the signature of any two Shareholders or Principals and any instrument of $● or less shall require the signature of any one Shareholder or Principal or such other individuals as may be determined by the Board of Directors from time to time. All monies received from time to time for the account of the Corporation shall be paid immediately into those bank accounts for the time being in operation, in the same drafts, cheques, bills or cash in which they are received and all disbursements on account of the Corporation shall be made by cheque on such bank or trust company.

5.4 The Shareholders agree that all further funds required for the purposes of the Corporation shall be obtained, to the greatest extent possible, by borrowing from a chartered bank or other lender. The decision whether such funds are required, from whom such funds will be borrowed and the terms and conditions of such borrowing shall be determined by the Shareholders from time to time. Each of the Shareholders covenants to use his reasonable best efforts to obtain such funds and covenants to execute and deliver all necessary documents, statements and assurances as may be required by such bank or other lender. Notwithstanding the foregoing, none of the Shareholders nor the respective Principals shall be required to advance funds to the Corporation or otherwise guarantee any of its obligations (whether on a several or joint and several basis), unless the Shareholders holding a majority of the issued and outstanding shares in the capital of the Corporation have agreed to. If the Shareholders holding a majority of the issued and outstanding shares in the capital of the Corporation determine that the Shareholders shall be required to advance funds to the Corporation or otherwise guarantee any of its obligations in accordance with this section 5.4, the Corporation shall give five business days notice (a "**Funding Notice**") to all Shareholders stating the amount of such advance of funds or guarantee, specifying the amount of and the date on which such funds or guarantee is required to be provided to the Corporation and the following provisions of this section 5.4 shall apply:

(a) on the date set out in the Funding Notice, each Shareholder shall contribute his or its proportionate percentage (based on the ratio that their respective holdings of fully participating shares of the Corporation then bear to each other) of the amount set forth in the Funding Notice and such amount shall be treated as a shareholder loan (a "**Shareholder Loan**");

(b) if a Shareholder (a "**Defaulting Shareholder**") fails to make any part or all of a contribution required by this section 5.4, the resulting deficiency shall be considered to be an amount (a "**Deficit Contribution**") owing by such Defaulting Shareholder to the Corporation, except as otherwise provided in subsection 5.4(c);

(c) any other Shareholder or combination of Shareholders (each, a "Contributing Shareholder") may contribute an additional amount equal to such Deficit Contribution to the Corporation on a proportionate basis (based on the ratio that their respective holdings of fully participating shares of the Corporation then bear to each other), unless otherwise agreed, and the amount of any such additional contribution shall be treated as a Deficit Contribution owing by such Defaulting Shareholder to the Contributing Shareholder or Contributing Shareholders, as the case may be;

(d) Deficit Contributions will bear interest at the Prime Bank Rate, plus 5%. Deficit Contributions owing by a Defaulting Shareholder to a Contributing Shareholder or Contributing Shareholders, as the case may be, shall be repayable on demand. Deficit Contributions owing by a Defaulting Shareholder to the Corporation shall be repayable on demand out of the funds of the Corporation available for such purpose; provided that all funds available from time to time for distribution to the Shareholders shall be applied and distributed *pro rata* in accordance with the amounts owing to each Shareholder as follows: (i) first, to the

¶1000

repayment of interest owing on Shareholder Loans; (ii) next, to the repayment of the principal amount of any Shareholder Loans; (iii) last, the balance, if any, will be distributed to the Shareholders by way of dividends or other distributions; and

(e) all surpluses distributable by the Corporation to a Defaulting Shareholder shall be paid to the Contributing Shareholder or Contributing Shareholders, as the case may be, *pro rata* in accordance with the amounts owing to such Contributing Shareholder or Contributing Shareholders, as follows: (i) first, in reduction of accrued interest outstanding on the Deficit Contribution owing to such Contributing Shareholder or Contributing Shareholders; and (ii) thereafter to such Contributing Shareholder or Contributing Shareholders in reduction of the principal portion of such Deficit Contribution owing to such Contributing Shareholder or Contributing Shareholders. Each Defaulting Shareholder hereby irrevocably authorizes and directs the Corporation to pay the Defaulting Shareholder's portion of any such distribution by the Corporation in accordance with the provisions of this section 5.4(e).

5.5 All Shareholder Loans made to the Corporation in accordance with the provisions of section 5.4 shall be treated as Shareholder's Loans and shall be upon the security and at the rate of interest (which shall be the same for all Shareholders), if any, as shall be determined by the Board of Directors, from time to time and, if required by the Corporation at the time of the making of the Shareholder Loan or at any time thereafter, shall be subordinated to any other arm's length secured indebtedness of the Corporation made in accordance with the terms hereof. None of such loans shall be called by the Shareholders or repaid to them, in whole or in part, except as is determined by the Board of Directors; provided, however, for greater certainty, that any amounts on account of such loans repaid to the Shareholders shall be repaid on a basis proportionate to their then total outstanding advances to the Corporation.

5.6 If a Shareholder or Principal (hereinafter in this Article sometimes called a "**Guarantor**") has guaranteed, with the unanimous consent of the other Shareholders (each, an "**Indemnifier**"), the obligations of the Corporation to any bank or other lender and the Guarantor makes payment to such bank or other lender under such guarantee, then the Indemnifier or Indemnifiers, as the case may be, shall pay to the Guarantor, forthwith upon demand, a fraction of such payment which is equal to the proportion of the Indemnifier's or Indemnifiers' fully participating shareholding or respective shareholdings in the Corporation. In addition, the Indemnifier or the Indemnifiers shall pay to the Guarantor, interest at the Prime Bank Rate, plus 5%, calculated and payable daily, not in advance, computed from the first day upon which such payment should have been made on the amount owing by it or by them to the Guarantor. For the purposes hereof, the Prime Bank Rate shall be determined daily to apply with respect to the monies owing at the end of the next succeeding day. The amount payable by the Indemnifier or Indemnifiers, as the case may be, hereunder together with interest thereon, calculated as aforesaid, shall be fully paid to the Guarantor before any dividend, salary, bonus, withdrawal or other distribution whatsoever from the Corporation is made to the defaulting

¶1000

Indemnifier or Indemnifiers, as the case may be, and the Corporation is hereby authorized and directed to pay the amount of any such dividend, salary, bonus, withdrawal or other distribution (to the extent of the amount owing by the Indemnifier or Indemnifiers to the Guarantor, as aforesaid) to the Guarantor in reduction of such amount.

Article 6 — Restrictions on Transfer of Shares

6.1 Each of the Shareholders covenants that it will not sell, assign, transfer, pledge, mortgage, charge, create a security interest in, hypothecate, enter into any agreement or option to or otherwise dispose of, encumber or deal with any of the shares of the Corporation or securities convertible into shares of the Corporation beneficially owned by him or it, except in accordance with the terms of this agreement, or except with the prior written consent of the other Shareholders. Notwithstanding anything herein contained, every transfer of all or a portion of the shares of the Corporation held by a Shareholder, and any issue of shares of the Corporation, in addition to the requirements of this Article 6, shall be subject to the condition that the proposed transferee, or holder, if not already bound by this agreement, shall first enter into an agreement with the other parties hereto, in a form satisfactory to them, to be bound by this agreement (as such agreement may be required to be amended in the circumstances). For greater certainty, but without limiting the foregoing, each of the Shareholders shall be bound by the provisions of this agreement in respect of any shares of the Corporation which may be acquired by such Shareholder after the date hereof.

6.2 Notwithstanding the provisions of section 6.1 hereof and any other provisions of this agreement which impose restrictions upon the disposition of any issued securities of the Corporation, each of the Shareholders shall have the right, without the approval of the other Shareholder, to dispose of all or any of his securities of the Corporation to any member of the Immediate Family of such Shareholder. No such disposition shall, however, be permitted or be valid or effective until written notice thereof shall have been given by such Shareholder to the other parties hereto and until the acquiror of the securities in question shall have entered into an agreement with (in a form satisfactory to) the other parties hereto consenting to the terms hereof and agreeing to assume and be bound by all of the obligations of the disposing Shareholder, as though such acquiror were the disposing Shareholder, in which event such acquiror shall, subject to the terms hereof, be entitled to all of the rights and be subject to all of the obligations on the part of the disposing Shareholder herein, *mutatis mutandis*. Notwithstanding such disposition, as between the disposing Shareholder and the other parties hereto, the disposing Shareholder shall remain liable as principal debtor under all covenants on this part contained herein and the disposing Shareholder agrees to unconditionally guarantee to the other parties hereto the due performance by the acquiror of all obligations imposed upon him or it hereunder. The guarantee of the disposing Shareholder is unconditional and may be enforced against him or it without requiring the other parties hereto first to proceed against the acquiror or proceed against or exhaust any security held or to pursue any other remedy whatsoever. The disposing Shareholder hereby authorizes the other parties hereto to renew, compromise, extend, accelerate or otherwise change the time for payment or any term relating to the performance of any such obligations and hereby waives presentment, protest, notice of protest, notice of dishonour, demand for performance and notice of acceptance of this guarantee by the other parties hereto.

6.3 Each of the Principals covenants that, so long as the Shareholder of which he is the Principal is a Shareholder, (i) no security of such Shareholder will be sold, assigned, transferred, pledged, mortgaged or charged, (ii) there will not be a security interest granted in respect of any such securities, and (iii) no agreement or option to dispose of or deal with any such securities will be entered into, except in accordance with the terms of this agreement, or except with the written consent of the other parties hereto.

6.4 Notwithstanding the provisions of section 6.3 hereof, subject to the terms hereof, each of the Principals shall have the right, without the approval of the other parties hereto, to dispose of all or any of his securities of the Shareholder of which he is the principal to any member of the Immediate Family of such Shareholder. No such disposition shall, however, be permitted or be valid or effective until written notice thereof shall have been given by the Principal of the applicable Shareholder to the other parties bound hereby and, to the extent necessary, until the acquiror of the securities shall have entered into a written agreement (in a form satisfactory to all concerned) with the parties bound hereby agreeing to be bound by all the obligations of the Principal in question as though the acquiror was such Principal and agreeing not to sell, assign, transfer, pledge, mortgage, charge, create a security interest in, hypothecate, enter into any agreement or option to or otherwise dispose of, encumber or deal with any of the said securities, except to the Principal or the Immediate Family of its Shareholder (provided that the provisions of this Article are complied with, *mutatis mutandis*, by the transferee thereof and by any transferor to whom the transferee shall have transferred his securities of the Shareholder and so on). Notwithstanding such disposition, to the extent necessary, as between the disposing Principal and the other parties bound hereby, the disposing Principal shall remain liable as principal debtor under all covenants on his part contained in this agreement and the disposing Principal agrees to unconditionally guarantee to the other parties bound hereby the due performance by the acquiror of all obligations imposed upon him hereunder. The guarantee of the disposing Principal is unconditional and may be enforced against him without requiring the other parties bound hereby first to proceed against the acquiror or to proceed against or exhaust any security held or to pursue any other remedy whatsoever. The disposing Principal hereby authorizes the other parties bound hereby to renew, compromise, extend, accelerate or otherwise change the time for payment or any term relating to the performance of any such obligations and hereby waives presentment, protest, notice of protest, notice of dishonour, demand for performance and notice of acceptance of this guarantee by the other parties bound hereby.

6.5 Each Principal and the Shareholder of which he is the Principal covenants that, so long as that Shareholder is a shareholder of the Corpora-

¶1000

tion, without the prior written approval of the other parties hereto no additional shares or securities convertible into shares or warrants or rights to acquire shares of such Shareholder will be issued, save and except to such Principal or to any member of the Immediate Family of its Shareholder. No such issuance shall, however, be permitted or be valid or effective until written notice thereof shall have been given by such Shareholder to the other parties bound hereby and, where shares are issued to any member of its Immediate Family, until the acquiror of those shares shall have entered into a written agreement with (in a form satisfactory to) the parties hereto agreeing not to sell, assign, transfer, pledge, mortgage, charge, create a security interest in, hypothecate, enter into any agreement or option to or otherwise dispose of or deal with any of the said shares except to the Principal or the Immediate Family of its Shareholder, provided that the provisions of this Article are complied with, *mutatis mutandis*, by the acquiror thereof. The Principal in question agrees to unconditionally guarantee to the other parties bound hereby the due performance by the acquiror of all of the obligations imposed upon him hereunder. The guarantee of such Principal is unconditional and may be enforced against him without requiring the other parties first to proceed against the acquiror or to proceed or exhaust any security held or to pursue any other remedy whatsoever. The Principal hereby authorizes the other parties bound hereby to renew, compromise, extend, accelerate or otherwise change the time for payment or any term relating to the performance of any such obligations and hereby waives presentment, protest, notice of protest, notice of dishonour, demand for performance and notice of acceptance of this guarantee by the other parties bound hereby.

6.6 Each Principal and the Shareholder of which he is a Principal covenants that, so long as the said Shareholder is a shareholder of the Corporation, neither of them shall cause or permit such Shareholder to take part in any amalgamation, merger, reorganization or similar proceeding, the effect of which would result in the Principal and/or members of the Immediate Family of its Shareholder owning less than 50% of the issued shares of each class of shares in the capital of the resulting body corporate from time to time outstanding. For purposes of this agreement, the Principal shall be considered to be the "Principal" of the resulting body corporate.

Article 7 — Sale Events

7.1 Upon the happening of any of the following events (a "**Sale Event**"):

(a) an Event of Insolvency occurs with respect to a Shareholder and the receipt by such insolvent Shareholder within 90 days of the date of the occurrence of such an Event of Insolvency of a written notice from the other Shareholders requiring the insolvent Shareholder to sell all of the shares of the Corporation beneficially owned by him or it;

(b) an Event of Default occurs with respect to a Shareholder and the receipt by such defaulting Shareholder within 90 days of the date of the occurrence of such and Event of Default of a written notice from the other Shareholders requiring the defaulting Shareholder to sell all of the shares of the Corporation beneficially owned by him or it;

¶1000

(c) a Principal (a "**Disabled Party**") of a Shareholder (the "**Disabled Shareholder**," which term shall include an individual Shareholder) through *bona fide* illness, physical or mental, shall be unable to devote the time and attention to the affairs of the Corporation required of such Principal or, if the Shareholder is a person other than a corporation, such Shareholder and such disability shall have continued for 12 months and the Shareholders which are not a Disabled Shareholder (the "**Healthy Shareholders**") having received a written notice (the "**Put Notice**") within 90 days following the expiration of such period (the "**Put Period**") from the Disabled Shareholder requiring the purchase of the shares of the Corporation owned by the Disabled Shareholder; or

(d) the Disabled Shareholder failing to deliver a Put Notice during the Put Period and the Disabled Shareholder having received a written notice (the "**Call Notice**") from the Healthy Shareholders within 90 days following the expiration of the Put Period requiring the sale of the shares of the Corporation owned by the Disabled Shareholder;

the Disabled Shareholder, the insolvent Shareholder or the defaulting Shareholder, as the case may be, (the "**Vendor**") shall sell all of the shares of the Corporation beneficially owned by the Vendor (the "**Purchased Shares**") to the other Shareholders (the "**Purchasers**") on a proportionate basis (based on the ratio that their respective holdings of fully participating shares of the Corporation then bear to each other), unless otherwise agreed by such Purchasers, and the Purchasers shall purchase from the Vendor the Purchased Shares, upon and subject to the terms and conditions hereinafter set forth.

7.2 The purchase price for the Purchased Shares shall be determined in accordance with the provisions of Article 13 hereof.

7.3 (a) If the transaction of purchase and sale is the result of the Sale Event referred to in subsection 7.1(a) or (b), the purchase price for the Purchased Shares shall be paid as follows:

(i) no less than 10% thereof at the Time of Closing; and

(ii) the balance of the purchase price, if any, shall be paid in equal, consecutive, quarterly instalments over a period of five years from the Date of Closing, with the first of such instalments to become due and payable one month after the Date of Closing, and the principal amount from time to time outstanding shall bear interest at a rate per annum, calculated monthly, not in advance, after default and before and after judgment and as well after as before maturity, which is equal to the Prime Bank Rate with interest on overdue interest at the same rate. Such interest shall be payable at the same times as payments of principal. The Prime Bank Rate shall be determined on the Date of Closing (as hereinafter defined) and on each payment date thereafter to apply with respect to the balance of the purchase price outstanding in the period until the next payment date.

(b) If the transaction of purchase and sale is the result of the Sale Event referred to in subsection 7.1(c) or 7.1(d), the purchase price for the Purchased Shares shall be paid as follows:

¶1000

(i) no less than 25% thereof at the Time of Closing; and

(ii) the balance of the purchase price, if any, shall be paid in equal, consecutive, quarterly instalments over a period of two years from the Date of Closing, with the first of such instalments to become due and payable one month after the Date of Closing, and the principal amount from time to time outstanding shall bear interest at a rate per annum, calculated monthly, not in advance, after default and before and after judgment and as well after as before maturity, which is equal to the Prime Bank Rate plus two percentage points with interest on overdue interest at the same rate. Such interest shall be payable at the same times as payments of principal. The Prime Bank Rate shall be determined on the Date of Closing (as hereinafter defined) and on each payment date thereafter to apply with respect to the balance of the purchase price outstanding in the period until the next payment date.

7.4 Notwithstanding the provisions of section 7.3 hereof, the unpaid balance of the purchase price for the Purchased Shares shall be accelerated and become immediately due and payable if, at any time while any amounts remain outstanding, the Purchasers cause, directly or indirectly, a Sale to take place.

7.5 The closing of the transaction of purchase and sale herein contemplated shall take place at the Place of Closing at the Time of Closing on the date (the "**Date of Closing**") which shall be the latest of:

(a) if the Sale Event is the event referred to in subsections 7.1(a), (b), (c) or (d) hereof, the date which is thirty days after receipt or deemed receipt by the addressee of such notice of the notice referred to in such subsection;

(b) the date which is seven days following receipt of all necessary governmental releases required to be obtained in order to effect a valid transfer of the Purchased Shares (and the parties hereto covenant and agree to use their best efforts to obtain such release); and

(c) the date which is 30 days after the purchase price for the Purchased Shares is finally determined in accordance with the provisions of Article 12 hereof.

7.6 (a) For the purposes of subsection 7.1(c) hereof, the period of disability for any Disabled Shareholder shall be deemed to commence on the first working day that the Disabled Party or Disabled Shareholder if the Shareholder is a person other than a corporation, does not attend to the affairs of the Corporation in the manner required of him as a result of such disability, statutory holidays and vacations excepted.

(b) In calculating the period of disability for the purposes of subsection 7.1(c), unless and until such Disabled Shareholder shall have returned to attending to the affairs of the Corporation in the manner required of him for thirty consecutive normal working days, the said period of disability shall be deemed to have continued without any interruption whatsoever.

¶1000

(c) The Disabled Shareholder shall, as long as the disability continues, be entitled to receive from the Corporation the then full compensation payable to him by the Corporation for a period of 90 days from the commencement of such disability. If such disability shall continue for more than 90 days, then, thereafter, as long as such disability continues, no further compensation shall be payable by the Corporation to the Disabled Shareholder. Notwithstanding the foregoing, the amount payable to the Disabled Shareholder shall be reduced by the amount of any payments received by the Disabled Shareholder, under any policy of disability insurance. For greater certainty, for so long as the Disabled Shareholder is a shareholder of the Corporation, such Disabled Shareholder shall be entitled to participate in any dividend or distribution made by the Corporation in accordance with his or its respective shareholdings.

Article 8 — Buy-Sell

8.1 One or more Shareholders (in this Article sometimes collectively called the "**Offeror(s)**" and individually an "**Offeror**") shall be entitled to give notice (in this Article called the "Buy-Sell Notice") to the other Shareholder(s) (in this Article sometimes individually called an "**Offeree**" and collectively called the "**Offerees**"), which Buy-Sell Notice shall be signed by the Offeror(s) and shall contain the following:

(a) the price at which the Offeror(s) will purchase or sell each issued share of the Corporation;

(b) an unconditional offer, irrevocable without the written consent of the Offeree(s), to purchase all of the shares of the Corporation beneficially owned by the Offeree(s) at the said price and upon and subject to the terms set forth in the Buy-Sell Notice; and

(c) an unconditional offer, irrevocable without the written consent of the Offeree(s), to sell all of the shares of the Corporation beneficially owned by the Offeror(s) at the said price and upon and subject to the terms and conditions set forth in the Buy-Sell Notice.

8.2 (a) Each of the Offerees shall be entitled to accept either of the offers contained in the Buy-Sell Notice by written notice delivered to each Offeror and each other Offeree within 20 days of receipt of the Buy-Sell Notice by the last of the Offerees to receive the Buy-Sell Notice.

(b) If one or more of the Offerees accepts the offer referred to in subsection 8.1(c) above within the above-noted period, then such Offeree(s) (in this Article sometimes called the "**Purchaser(s)**") shall purchase from the other Offeree(s) and from the Offeror(s) contemplated in subsection 8.1(b) (in this Article sometimes collectively called the "**Vendor(s)**") and the Vendor(s) shall sell to the Purchaser(s) all of the shares of the Corporation beneficially owned by the Vendor(s) (in this Article the "**Purchased Shares**") at the prices set forth in the Buy-Sell Notice.

(c) If none of the Offerees accepts the offer referred to in subsection 8.1(c) above within the above-noted period then the Offeree(s) (in this Article sometimes collectively called the "**Vendor(s)**") shall be deemed to have accepted the offer referred to in subsection 8.1(b) above and shall sell to the Offeror(s) referred to in subsection 8.1 all of the shares of the Corporation beneficially owned by each such Vendor on the earlier of:

(i) the last day of the period for acceptance of the offer contained in the Buy-Sell Notice; or

(ii) the date on which the last of the Offerees to have accepted such offer shall have delivered his notice of acceptance.

In such event, the Offeree(s) shall sell to the Offeror(s) (in this Article sometimes called the "**Purchaser(s)**") and the Purchaser(s) shall purchase from the Vendor(s) all of the shares of the Corporation beneficially owned by the Vendor(s) (in this Article the "**Purchased Shares**") at the prices set forth in the Buy-Sell Notice. In the event that there is more than one Purchaser, the Purchasers shall acquire the shares of the Vendor(s) in the ratio that their respective holdings of fully-participating shares of the Corporation then bear to each other.

8.3 The closing of a transaction of purchase and sale contemplated in this Article shall take place at the Place of Closing, at the Time of Closing, on the date (in this Article, the "**Date of Closing**") which is 15 days following the expiry of the 20-day period for acceptance.

8.4 Notwithstanding anything in the Buy-Sell Notice to the contrary, the aggregate price for the shares of the Corporation being purchased and sold hereunder shall be paid as follows:

(a) not less than 5% thereof shall be paid at the Time of Closing; and

(b) the balance shall be paid in equal consecutive monthly instalments over a period of two years from the Date of Closing, together with interest on the principal balance from time to time outstanding at a rate per annum, calculated monthly, not in advance, both before and after default or judgment and as well after as before maturity, which is equal to the Prime Bank Rate, with interest on overdue interest at the same rate. Such interest shall be payable at the same times as payments of principal, the first of such instalments of principal and interest to become due and payable one month after the Date of Closing, with interest at the aforesaid rate computed from the Date of Closing. The Prime Bank Rate shall be determined on the Date of Closing and on each payment date thereafter to apply with respect to the balance of the purchase price outstanding in the period until the next payment date.

8.5 Notwithstanding the provisions of section 8.4 hereof, the unpaid balance of the purchase price for the Purchased Shares shall be accelerated and become immediately due and payable if, at any time while any amounts remain outstanding, the Purchasers cause, directly or indirectly, a Sale to take place.

Article 9 — Right of First Refusal

9.1 If any Shareholder (hereinafter referred to as the "**Offeror**") receives a *bona fide* written offer (the "**Offer**") from any person, firm or corporation

¶1000

dealing at arm's length with the Offeror to purchase all of the shares of the Corporation owned by him, which is acceptable to him, he shall, by notice in writing (the "**Second Offer**"), offer to sell such shares (the "**Purchased Shares**") to the other Shareholders (hereinafter referred to as the "**Offerees**") in the ratio that their respective beneficial ownership of fully-participating shares of the Corporation bear to one other on the date of closing specified in the Offer at the same price and upon the same terms and conditions as are contained in the Offer. Such notice shall be accompanied by a true copy of the Offer. The Second Offer shall not be revocable except with the written consent of the Offerees and shall be open for acceptance by any one or more of the Offerees by delivery of a written notice of acceptance for a period of 30 days from the date upon which the Second Offer was received by the last of the Offerees to have received the same.

9.2 Notwithstanding anything to the contrary herein contained, the terms and conditions of the Second Offer shall be amended so that it shall state that any Offeree who desires to accept the Second Offer for more of the Purchased Shares than his proportion shall, in his acceptance, state the additional number of Purchased Shares he wishes to purchase.

9.3 In the event that the Offeree(s) do not specify that they desire to purchase, in the aggregate, all of the Purchased Shares, the Offeror shall be entitled to sell the Purchased Shares in accordance with the Offer. In the event that the Offeree(s) specify that they wish to purchase, in the aggregate, such number of shares equal to or in excess of the number of Purchased Shares, each Purchaser shall purchase that number of the Purchased Shares calculated as follows:

(a) each Purchaser shall be entitled to purchase, as an initial allocation, that number of Purchased Shares indicated in his acceptance of the Second Offer, up to his "**Proportionate Amount**" (which for these purposes is the proportion which the number of fully-participating shares of the Corporation beneficially owned by him bears to the number of fully-participating shares of the Corporation owned by all of the Offerees who shall have accepted the Second Offer); and

(b) in the event that the determination of the entitlement of the Offeree(s) in accordance with paragraph (a) above shall have resulted in an allocation of the Purchased Shares which is less than the aggregate number of shares the Offeror wishes to sell (the "**Initial Allocation**"), each Offeree who shall have specified the desire to purchase a number of such shares which is greater than his Proportionate Amount (hereinafter referred to as the "**Excess Purchasers**") shall purchase, as an additional allocation, that number of the Purchased Shares calculated as follows:

$$\frac{\text{Number of the Purchased Shares that such Excess Purchaser specified he would purchase}}{\text{Aggregate number of Purchased Shares of the Corporation that all Excess Purchasers specified they would purchase}} \times \text{Number of Purchased Shares minus number of Purchased Shares in Initial Allocation}$$

¶1000

9.4 Each Offeree who accepts the Offer shall be bound to purchase and the Offeror shall be bound to sell the Purchased Shares in accordance with the foregoing provisions hereof and upon the terms and conditions contained in the Second Offer.

9.5 Before consenting to the transfer of the Purchased Shares the Board of Directors shall be entitled to require proof that the sale took place in accordance with the Offer (except as to the date of closing which, subject to the provisions of section 9.7 hereof, may be varied) and that the third party Offeror under the Offer has agreed to be bound by the terms of this agreement as if he was the Offeror. The directors of the Corporation shall refuse to permit the recording of the transfer of the Purchased Shares which may have been sold otherwise than in accordance with the provisions of this agreement.

9.6 If a sale of the Purchased Shares pursuant to the Offer is not completed within 90 days from the giving of the Second Offer to the Offerees as aforementioned, no sale of the Purchased Shares to the third party shall be made without complying with the terms of this Article and so on from time to time.

9.7 The closing of the transaction of purchase and sale pursuant to the Second Offer contemplated in this Article 9 shall take place on the closing date specified in the Offer referred to in section 9.1 above.

Article 10 — Matching Bid

10.1 In the event that any Shareholder or Shareholders receives a *bona fide* cash offer (a "**Third Party Offer**") from a person acting at arm's length to each of the Shareholders and the Principals (a "**Third Party**") for all, but not less than all, of the outstanding shares of the Corporation which Shareholders holding not less than $66^2/_3\%$ of the issued and outstanding fully-participating shares of the Corporation wish to accept, then the following provisions shall apply.

10.2 The Shareholder(s), if any, who does not wish to accept the Third Party Offer (the "**Declining Shareholder**") shall be provided with a complete and true copy of the Third Party Offer and, within 15 days following receipt of the Third Party Offer, shall be entitled by written notice (the "**Notice**") to the Shareholder(s) who wishes to accept the Third Party Offer (the "**Accepting Shareholder**") to purchase all of the issued and outstanding shares of the Corporation owned by the Accepting Shareholder at the same price per share and upon the balance of the terms and conditions as set forth in the Third Party Offer. Any Declining Shareholder who does not deliver a Notice within such 15-day period shall be deemed to irrevocably indicate that they do not wish to purchase the shares of the Corporation owned by the Accepting Shareholder in accordance with the terms and conditions contained in the Third Party Offer. In the event that no Declining Shareholder delivers a Notice then the Declining Shareholder(s) shall be required to sell their shares of the Corporation to the Third Party in accordance with the Third Party Offer and shall be deemed to have accepted the Third Party Offer. If one or more of the Declining Shareholders delivers a Notice, then they shall be required to purchase all of the shares of the Corporation (the "**Purchased Shares**") owned or controlled by the Accepting Shareholder(s) (the "**Vendor**") at the same price per share and in accordance with the terms and conditions, except that the transaction of purchase and sale in question shall take place at the Place of Closing and at the Time of Closing on the date which is 20 days following receipt by the Accepting Shareholder of the Notice. For greater certainty, if there is only one Declining Shareholder who delivers a Notice, such Declining Shareholder shall be required to purchase all of the Purchased Shares and if there are two or more Declining Shareholders who have delivered a Notice then they shall be required to purchase in such proportions as they may agree or, failing agreement, *pro rata* in accordance with their respective fully-participating shareholdings.

10.3 If a Shareholder does not fulfil his obligation to sell or purchase as provided for herein, such Shareholder hereby irrevocably appoints the other Shareholder as his attorney (which appointment shall be continuing and shall survive incapacity of the donor of such power) to execute all such documents and to do all such things as may be necessary to either sell such Shareholder's shares of the Corporation to the Third Party in accordance with the Third Party Offer or to purchase the Purchased Shares from the Vendor pursuant to the Notice.

Article 11 — Death of Principal or Individual

11.1 Upon the death of either a Principal or Individual (the "**Deceased**"), the Shareholder of which the Deceased was the Principal, or the Individual, as the case may be (the "**Vendor**") shall sell all of the shares of the Corporation owned by the Vendor (the "**Purchased Shares**") to the Corporation and the Corporation shall purchase for cancellation from the Vendor the Purchased Shares, upon and subject to the terms and conditions hereinafter set out.

11.2 The purchase price for the Purchased Shares (the "**Purchase Price**") shall be determined in accordance with the provisions of Article 13.

11.3 If the proceeds of all insurance policies on the life of the Deceased with the Corporation named as beneficiary equals or exceeds the Purchase Price, then the Purchase Price shall be paid in full by the Corporation to the Vendor by certified cheque at the Time of Closing.

11.4 If the proceeds of all insurance policies on the life of the Deceased with the Corporation named as beneficiary is less than the Purchase Price or there are no such proceeds, then the Purchase Price shall be paid as follows:

(a) the greater of:
  (i) the amount of the proceeds of all such insurance policies (up to, for greater certainty, the amount of the Purchase Price); and
  (ii) 50% of the Purchase Price shall be paid by the Corporation to the Vendor by certified cheque at the Time of Closing; and

(b) the balance shall be paid in equal consecutive quarterly instalments over a period of two years from the Date of Closing, together with interest on the principal balance from time to time outstanding at a rate

¶1000

per annum, calculated monthly, not in advance, both before and after default and judgment and as well after as before maturity, which is equal to the Prime Bank Rate plus two percentage points, with interest on overdue interest at the same rate. Such interest shall be payable at the same times as payments of principal, the first of such instalments of principal and interest to become due and payable one month after the Date of Closing, with interest at the aforesaid rate computed from the Date of Closing. The Prime Bank Rate shall be determined on the Date of Closing and on each payment date thereafter to apply with respect to the balance of the Purchase Price outstanding in the period until the next payment date.

11.5 The purchase of the Purchased Shares shall take place at the Time of Closing at which time the Vendor shall tender the certificate or certificates representing the Purchased Shares to the Corporation. The purchase for cancellation of the Purchased Shares shall be staged as follows:

(a) the Corporation shall purchase for cancellation at the first closing (the "**First Closing**") that number of the Purchased Shares (the "**First Tranche**") the disposition of which results in a deemed dividend for income tax purposes to the Vendor in an amount equal to the increase in the Corporation's capital dividend account (as that term is defined in the *Income Tax Act* (Canada)) resulting from its receipt of the proceeds of life insurance arising upon the death of the Deceased, if any, and as applicable, but in no event to exceed the Purchase Price for the Purchased Shares; and

(b) after the First Closing, the balance of the Purchased Shares (the "**Second Tranche**") shall be purchased for cancellation by the Corporation at the second closing (the "**Second Closing**").

11.6 The First Closing and the Second Closing shall take place at the Place of Closing at the Time of Closing on the date (the "**Date of Closing**") which is the latest of:

(a) the date which is 60 days after the date of death of the Deceased;

(b) the date which is seven days following receipt of all necessary governmental releases or approvals required to be obtained in order to effect a valid transfer of the Purchased Shares;

(c) the date upon which the Corporation receives the proceeds of insurance referred to in Article 12 and payable on the death of the Deceased or, if applicable, the date on which it is finally determined that no proceeds of Insurance are payable; and

(d) the date which is 30 days after the Purchase Price is finally determined in accordance with the provisions of Article 13.

11.7 The Corporation shall take all corporate actions and effect all prescribed elections and filings as may be required under the Act so as to reflect the acquisition of the First Tranche equal to the amount by which the capital dividend account has been increased as a result of the insurance proceeds obtained from the death of the Deceased, but in no event to exceed the

Purchase Price. The Shareholders acknowledge that the transaction described in this Article 11 hereof contemplates the Corporation making an unequal distribution of a capital dividend to the Vendor and the remaining Shareholders (the "**Surviving Shareholders**") covenant and agree to execute such waivers and releases with respect to the *pro rata* share of such capital dividend as may be required to give effect to the foregoing.

11.8 Notwithstanding the provisions currently contained in this Article 11, the parties hereto acknowledge and agree that it is the intent that at the time a purchase is required by the Corporation of the Purchased Shares pursuant to this Article 11, that the same be conducted in the most tax effective manner for the benefit of the Vendor at such time. Accordingly, the parties hereto covenant and agree that, if the purchase and sale of the Purchased Shares at the time of death of a Deceased can be reasonably undertaken in a more effective manner for the benefit of the Vendor for tax purposes than is currently provided in the agreement, the parties will do so, so long as the same does not result in a material financial detriment to the Corporation or the other Shareholder.

Article 12 — Insurance

12.1 The parties hereby acknowledge and agree that on or before the execution of this agreement, they presently have or they shall procure insurance on the life of each of the Principal or Individual naming the Corporation as beneficiary thereunder. The parties hereby further acknowledge that, in order to ensure that sufficient funds will be available for the purposes of Article 11, the Corporation has obtained and shall obtain such additional policy or policies of insurance particulars of which shall be endorsed on Schedule "A" hereto and initialled by the owner and life insured under each such policy.

12.2 The Corporation shall pay, as they become due, all premiums in connection with the insurance policy or policies referred to in section 12.1 hereof, and shall maintain it or them in good standing at all times and shall not deal in any manner with such policy or policies and, without limiting the generality of the foregoing, shall not dispose of, surrender, borrow upon or in any way encumber such policy or policies. Upon the death of either a Principal or Individual under any of the said policies during the term of this agreement, the Corporation shall collect the proceeds thereof as soon as possible and shall pay and apply such proceeds as required by this Article 12.

12.3 Except as otherwise provided in this section 12.3, the Corporation shall not deal with such policies (except to make application for, collect and apply the insurance proceeds in accordance with this Article 12) nor modify or impair any rights or values of such policies. On the closing date of any transaction of purchase and sale wherein a particular life insured (the "**Departing Insured**") is the vendor or the Principal of the vendor (except upon the death or disability of such individual) or if this agreement should be cancelled with the consent of the parties or if the Corporation should be wound-up or dissolved, thereupon the ownership of the insurance policies then set out in Schedule "A" hereto shall be transferred to the life insured thereunder who is the Departing Insured or to all of the life insured thereunder, as the case may be, in consideration for the payment of the cash surrender value thereof, if any, together, with the full amount of any unexpired prepaid premiums for such policy and the owner(s) shall convey, assign, transfer or make over such policies of insurance of the person whose life is insured thereunder.

12.4 Each Principal and Individual shall use his best efforts to permit the Corporation to obtain and maintain such life insurance as is contemplated by this Article 12, including without limitation, attending for physical examinations and answering such questions as may be reasonably necessary and executing such applicable consents and authorizations as may be reasonably necessary for the placing of such insurance coverage.

12.5 The amounts and the coverage of such policies shall be reviewed and adjusted from time to time as the circumstances require annually so as to reasonably reflect the estimated Fair Market Value of the shares owned by the Shareholders, respectively.

12.6 If the Corporation shall default in the payment of the premiums or other charges payable in connection with the procurement and maintenance of such policies, any Shareholder may pay such premium or charge on behalf of the Corporation for so long as such default continues, such payments to constitute a Shareholders' loan, repayable upon demand together with interest calculated monthly from the date of each payment and based upon the Prime Bank Rate as of the date of each applicable payment plus one percentage point, notwithstanding anything to the contrary herein contained.

12.7 The parties hereto acknowledge and agree that the proceeds of any insurance policies placed on the life of each Principal and Individual may exceed the Fair Market Value of the shares owned by the Shareholders respectively. Accordingly, it is acknowledged and agreed that any proceeds of insurance received by the Corporation in excess of the amount which it is required to pay to the Vendor pursuant to Article 11 hereof shall be retained by the Corporation and neither the Vendor nor the estate of the Deceased shall be entitled to any portion of such proceeds in excess of the amount payable pursuant to Article 11 hereof.

Article 13 — Valuation

13.1 If the Shareholders are unable to agree unanimously on the Fair Market Value of the goodwill of the Corporation within 20 days following the occurrence of the event giving rise to the transaction of purchase and sale in question pursuant to Article 7 or Article 11, as the case may be, then an independent business valuator, to be unanimously agreed upon by the Shareholders, shall determine the Fair Market Value of the goodwill of the Corporation as at the last day of the month preceding that in which the applicable event occurs (the "**Valuation Date**").

If the Shareholders fail to choose an independent business valuator within 30 days following the said event, then such independent business valuator shall be chosen by a Judge having appropriate jurisdiction, sitting in the City of Toronto, upon the application of any of the Shareholders. In valuing goodwill, the valuator shall take into account and apply generally accepted accounting and valuation principles. However, if the event in question is the death or disability of a Principal, the valuator shall not have regard to the occurrence of his disability or death or the imminent possibility thereof. In addition, the valuator shall not apply any minority discount with respect to the value of any Shareholder's shares of the Corporation. Further, the valuator shall not consider the value of any life insurance policies owned by the Corporation insuring the lives of any Principal, including any death benefits payable under such policies, any cash surrender value thereof nor any other benefit available in respect thereof and shall not take into account any proceeds of insurance which may be received by the Corporation pursuant to Article 12. The valuation arrived at by the valuator, made as an expert and not as umpire or arbitrator, shall, in the absence of fraud, be final and binding, clerical errors excepted, and no appeal shall lie therefrom.

13.2 Upon the provisions of Article 7 or Article 11, as the case may be, becoming applicable, the Corporation shall cause its auditors or accountants, as the case may be, to prepare financial statements for the Corporation as at and for the fiscal period ending on the Valuation Date. In preparing such statements, the auditors or accountants, as the case may be, shall use generally accepted accounting principles (except as otherwise provided for herein) applied on a basis consistent with those used in the preceding fiscal year as if the statement date was the fiscal year-end of the Corporation, with the exception that only the book value of the assets, after deducting accumulated depreciation to the date of such statements as well as any other reserves established in accordance with generally accepted accounting principles, consistently applied, shall be reflected.

13.3 If there is any disagreement among the Shareholders as to the book value of any assets or liabilities of the Corporation, other than goodwill, the decision of the auditor or accountant, as the case may be, of the Corporation, made as an expert and not as an umpire or arbitrator, as set out in a written certificate signed by him, shall, in the absence of fraud, be final and binding, clerical errors excepted, and no appeal shall lie therefrom. The said auditor or accountant, as the case may be, may retain such experts as he may deem necessary in order to assist him in making any valuation and the costs thereof shall be paid by the Corporation.

13.4 The balance sheet forming part of the financial statements referred to in this Article shall hereinafter be referred to as the "**Adjusted Balance Sheet.**"

13.5 The net book value for each share (the "**Net Book Value**") of the Corporation shall be determined as follows:

(a) with respect to the shares of the Corporation which are not fully-participating shares and which are then issued and outstanding, the value of each such share shall be the lesser of: (i) the amount payable in accordance with the Articles on the redemption of such share; and (ii) the amount which the holder of such share would be entitled to receive upon the winding-up or dissolution of the Corporation on the Valuation Date assuming that upon such winding-up or dissolution, the assets of the Corporation are disposed of for proceeds

¶1000

of disposition equal to the values thereof set out in the Adjusted Balance Sheet;

(b) with respect to the shares of the Corporation which are full-participating shares, the value of each such share shall be determined by subtracting the aggregate of: (i) all liabilities shown on the Adjusted Balance Sheet; and (ii) the value of the issued and outstanding shares of the Corporation referred to in subsection 13.5(a) hereof, from the total assets of the Corporation as shown on the Adjusted Balance Sheet, and by dividing the resulting amount by the total number of issued and outstanding fully-participating shares.

13.6 The Fair Market Value for each share of the Corporation shall be the following:

(a) with respect to the shares of the Corporation which are not fully-participating shares, the Net Book Value thereof;

(b) with respect to the shares of the Corporation which are fully-participating shares the aggregate of: (i) the Net Book Value thereof; and (ii) the quotient obtained when the fair market value of the goodwill is divided by the total number of issued and outstanding fully-participating shares. If the liabilities shown on the Adjusted Balance Sheet exceed the assets shown on the Adjusted Balance Sheet, the amount of the deficiency shall be deducted from the agreed upon value of goodwill. In the event that the result obtained by deducting such deficiency is an amount which is less than $1.00, the Purchase Price for all of the Purchased Shares shall be an aggregate amount of $1.00.

13.7 The purchase price for the shares being purchased and sold pursuant to the provisions of Article 7 or Article 11, as the case may be, shall be the Fair Market Value of each such share determined pursuant to section 13.6 hereof multiplied by the number of such shares being purchased and sold.

Article 14 — General Sale Provisions

14.1 Except as may otherwise be provided in this agreement, the provisions of this Article shall apply to any sale of shares of the Corporation pursuant to Article 7, Article 8 and Article 11 hereof. For the purposes of this Article, a defined term used in Article 7, Article 8 or Article 11, as the case may be, shall have the meaning ascribed thereto in the applicable Article, unless otherwise defined in this Article 14.

14.2 At the Time of Closing, the Vendor shall:

(a) deliver to the Corporation signed resignations of the Vendor, its Principal, and his nominees, if any, as directors, officers and employees of the Corporation, as the case may be (for greater certainty, each Principal acknowledges and agrees that he shall not be entitled to notice or pay in lieu of notice as a result of the termination of his employment with the Corporation in these circumstances);

(b) assign and transfer to the Purchaser or the Corporation, as the case may be, the Purchased Shares and, subject to the provisions of section

14.9 hereof, shall deliver the required share certificate(s) duly endorsed for transfer into the Purchaser's or Corporation's name, as the case may be;

(c) do all other things required in order to deliver good and marketable title to the Purchased Shares to the Purchaser or the Corporation, as the case may be (subject to the provisions of section 14.9 hereof, if applicable), free and clear of any claims, liens and encumbrances whatsoever including, without limitation, the delivery of any governmental releases and declarations of transmission;

(d) deliver to the Corporation a release by each of the Vendor, its Principal and his nominees, if any, of all his claims against the Corporation with respect to any matter or thing arising up to and including the Time of Closing which the Vendor, its Principal or any such nominee knew or ought to have known in his capacity as a director, officer, shareholder, employee or creditor of the Corporation, or as a party to this agreement, as the case may be, provided however, that such release shall not relate to any indebtedness of the Corporation to the Vendor being purchased by the Purchaser hereunder or any indebtedness of the Corporation on account of accrued and unpaid salary, expenses, pension or other employee benefits or any claims which might arise out of the transactions of purchase and sale herein contemplated;

(e) provide the Purchaser or the Corporation, as the case may be, with evidence reasonably satisfactory to the Purchaser or the Corporation, as the case may be, that the Vendor is not then a "non-resident" of Canada within the meaning of the *Income Tax Act* (Canada), failing which the Purchaser shall be entitled to withhold a portion of the purchase price and to remit such amount to Canada Customs and Revenue Agency on account of non-resident withholding taxes; and

(f) deliver to the Purchaser or the Surviving Shareholders (if the sale is pursuant to Article 11), all directors of the Corporation and all other parties to this agreement (other than the Corporation), a release by the Vendor, its Principal and each of his nominees, if any, of all of his claims against such parties relating to matters the Vendor, its Principal or any such nominee knew or ought to have known in his capacity as a shareholder, director or officer of the Corporation or as a party to this agreement, except for any claims which might arise out of the transactions of purchase and sale herein contemplated.

14.3 If, at the Time of Closing, the Vendor, or any person for or on behalf of the Vendor, shall have any guarantees, securities or covenants lodged with any person to secure any indebtedness, liability or obligation of the Corporation, the Purchaser or the Surviving Shareholder (if the sale is pursuant to Article 11) and, if applicable, its Principal, or any of the parties hereto, then the Purchaser or the Surviving Shareholder (if the sale is pursuant to Article 11) shall deliver up or cause to be delivered up to the Vendor or cancel or cause to be cancelled such guarantees, securities and covenants at the Time of Closing.

¶1000

14.4 At the Time of Closing, the Purchaser or the Surviving Shareholder (if the sale is pursuant to Article 11) shall:

(a) deliver to the Vendor and his nominees, if any, a release by the Purchaser or the Surviving Shareholder and his nominees, if any, with respect to those matters which any of the Purchaser or the Surviving Shareholder or his nominees knew or ought to have known in his capacity as a director, officer or shareholder of the Corporation, or as a party to this agreement, of all his claims against each of the Vendor and his nominees, if any, in his capacity as a shareholder, director or officer of the Corporation, except for any claims which may arise out of the transactions of purchase and sale herein contemplated; and

(b) cause the Corporation to deliver to the Vendor and his nominees, if any, a release by the Corporation of all its claims against the Vendor and his nominees, if any, with respect to any matter or thing which the books and records of the Corporation reflect or which was done in the ordinary course of the Corporation's business and arising as a result of the Vendor or any such nominee being a shareholder, director, officer or employee of the Corporation, as the case may be.

14.5 If, at the Time of Closing pursuant to a transaction contemplated in Article 7, Article 8 or Article 11, the Corporation is indebted to the Vendor or its Principal or any member of its Immediate Family in an amount (the "**Indebtedness**") recorded on the books of the Corporation and verified by the external accountants of the Corporation, the Corporation shall, subject to any rights of set-off, repay such amount to such person at the Time of Closing.

14.6 If, at the Time of Closing pursuant to a transaction contemplated in Article 7, Article 8 or Article 11, the Vendor or its Principal or any member of the Immediate Family is indebted to the Corporation in an amount recorded on the books of the Corporation and verified by the external accountants of the Corporation, the Vendor or its Principal, as the case may be, shall, subject to any rights of set-off, repay such amounts to the Corporation at the Time of Closing.

14.7 If, at the Time of Closing, the Vendor fails to complete the subject transaction of purchase and sale, the Purchaser or the Surviving Shareholder, as the case may be, shall have the right, if not in default under this agreement, without prejudice to any other rights which it may have, upon payment of that part of the purchase price payable to the Vendor at the Time of Closing (for greater certainty, after deducting the amount of any adjustments or set-offs contemplated hereunder) to the credit of the Vendor in the main branch of the Corporation's bankers in the City of Toronto, to execute and deliver, on behalf of and in the name of the Vendor, such deeds, transfers, share certificates, resignations or other documents that may be necessary or desirable to complete the subject transaction and the Vendor hereby irrevocably appoints the Purchaser or the Surviving Shareholder, as the case may be, its attorney in that behalf (which appointment shall be continuing and shall survive incapacity of the donor of such power).

¶1000

14.8 At the Time of Closing, the Purchaser or the Corporation, as the case may be, shall deliver to the Vendor a non-negotiable promissory note as evidence of the unpaid balance of the purchase price for the Purchased Shares and any Indebtedness being purchased and the terms of payment thereof, in a form reasonably satisfactory to the Vendor. If not in default hereunder, the Purchaser or the Corporation, as the case may be, shall have the privilege of prepaying the whole or any part of the unpaid balance of the purchase price for the Purchased Shares or any Indebtedness being purchased, at any time or times, without notice or bonus, upon paying accrued interest to the date of prepayment. Any and all prepayments shall be applied against instalments of the unpaid balance of the said purchase price in reverse order of maturity. If the Purchaser or the Corporation, as the case may be, defaults in any payment of the unpaid balance of the purchase price for the Purchased Shares and any Indebtedness being purchased, or in the performance of any applicable covenant contained in section 14.10, without prejudice to any other rights which the Vendor may have, the whole unpaid balance of such purchase price shall, at the option of the Vendor exercised by the giving of written notice to that effect to the Purchaser or the Corporation, as the case may be, immediately be accelerated and become due and payable in full.

14.9 As security for any Indebtedness and any unpaid balance of the purchase price for the Purchased Shares payable pursuant to the transaction contemplated in Article 11, the Vendor shall have the benefit of the guarantee referred to in section 15.2. As security for any unpaid balance of the purchase price for the Purchased Shares payable pursuant to the transactions contemplated in Article 7 or Article 8 and, if applicable, the Indebtedness being purchased by the Purchaser hereunder, interest thereon and for the performance by the Purchaser of the applicable covenants contained in section 14.10 hereof, the Purchaser hereby grants to the Vendor a first ranking security interest in the Purchased Shares (the "**Pledged Shares**") pursuant to the provisions of the *Personal Property Security Act* (Ontario) (the "**Act**"). In order to perfect that security interest, the Purchaser shall, at the Time of Closing, deliver to the Vendor a share certificate registered in the name of the Vendor representing the Pledged Shares, to be held and dealt with by the Vendor in accordance with the provisions hereof:

(a) Subject to the terms hereof and notwithstanding the registration of the Pledged Shares in the name of the Vendor, so long as the Purchaser is not in default hereunder: (i) the Purchaser shall be entitled to vote the Pledged Shares; and (ii) all distributions, whether by way of dividend or otherwise, paid by the Corporation in respect of the Pledged Shares shall be paid to the Purchaser. The Vendor covenants to do whatever is necessary to give effect to the foregoing including, without limitation, delivering to the Purchaser proxies for the Pledged Shares and directions with respect to any payments with respect to the Pledged Shares, forthwith upon request in writing for same.

(b) Upon payment in full by the Purchaser of the unpaid balance of the Purchase Price for the Purchased Shares or, if applicable, the Indebtedness, the Vendor covenants to deliver to the Purchaser the share certifi-

¶1000

cate(s) representing the Pledged Shares, duly endorsed in blank for transfer.

(c) If the Purchaser defaults in any payment of principal or interest due on account of the unpaid balance of the Purchase Price for the Purchased Shares or, if applicable, the Indebtedness or if the Purchaser defaults in the performance of any applicable covenant by it contained in section 14.10 hereof, then the provisions of the Act shall govern the rights, remedies and obligations of the Vendor in respect of such default. To the maximum extent permitted under the Act, the legal fees and expenses (on a solicitor and his client basis) incurred by the Vendor in enforcing its security shall be recoverable by the Vendor.

(d) Subject to the Vendor's right to foreclose on the Pledged Shares, in the event that the disposition of the Pledged Shares (or any part thereof) by the Vendor results in a deficiency, the Purchaser shall remain liable to the Vendor for the immediate payment of such deficiency balance owing, together with accrued interest thereon.

14.10 The Purchaser or the Surviving Shareholder, as the case may be, and the Corporation covenant that, as long as any unpaid balance of the purchase price for the Purchased Shares and, if applicable, the Indebtedness, is outstanding in connection with a transaction of purchase and sale pursuant to the provisions of Article 7, Article 8 and Article 11 (other than as a result of a Sale Event referred to in subsection 7.1(a) or (b)):

(a) neither the Corporation nor any Subsidiary of the Corporation will repay any loans owing to the Purchaser or the Surviving Shareholder, as the case may be, its Principal, any member of their Immediate Family or any person not dealing at arm's length with any of them nor pay any interest thereon;

(b) neither the Corporation nor any Subsidiary of the Corporation will redeem or purchase any of its shares or effect a reduction of capital;

(c) neither the Corporation nor any Subsidiary of the Corporation will encumber, dispose of or in any way deal with any of its assets except in the normal course of its business; provided, however, that the Corporation or any Subsidiary of the Corporation may only grant security on any of its assets to a chartered bank or other financial institution for the *bona fide* purpose of securing borrowings required by the Corporation or any Subsidiary of the Corporation for the conduct of its business in the ordinary course;

(d) neither the Corporation, the Purchaser nor the Surviving Shareholder, as the case may be, shall take any action to wind-up or otherwise terminate the corporate existence of the Corporation or any Subsidiary of the Corporation;

(e) there shall be no material change in the nature of the business of the Corporation or any Subsidiary of the Corporation as conducted on the Date of Closing;

(f) except to the extent section 7.4 is complied with, neither the Corporation nor any Subsidiary of the Corporation shall take any action with a view to its amalgamation, consolidation or merger with any other corporation or the amendment of its Articles or sell, lease, exchange, transfer or dispose of its undertaking or any material part thereof as an entirety or substantially as an entirety;

(g) the Purchaser or the Surviving Shareholder, as the case may be, will deliver to the Vendor, forthwith after their preparation, all financial statements, whether audited or unaudited, of the Corporation or any Subsidiary of the Corporation which are, or are required to be, reviewed by the Board of Directors;

(h) no additional shares or securities convertible into shares of the Corporation or any Subsidiary of the Corporation or rights to subscribe for such shares or securities will be issued or sold, unless the proceeds from the issue and sale of such shares or securities are applied to reduce any Indebtedness and any unpaid balance of the purchase price for the Purchased Shares; and

(i) the aggregate amount of any and all withdrawals and distributions (the "**Withdrawals**") in any fiscal year of the Corporation from the Corporation to the Purchaser or the Surviving Shareholder, as the case may be, or its Principal or any member of its Immediate Family or any persons not dealing at arm's length with any of them, (collectively, the "**Subject Persons**") including, without limitation, salary, allowance, dividends, bonuses, repayment of loans, interest thereon, or any amounts on the redemption or purchase of shares or reduction of capital by the Corporation shall not exceed the aggregate of 110% of the amount of the Withdrawals received by the Subject Persons in the immediately preceding fiscal year.

For greater certainty, none of the Purchaser, the Surviving Shareholder or the Corporation will be subject to any of the foregoing covenants in respect of a transaction of purchase and sale as a result of a Sale Event referred to in subsection 7.1(a) or (b).

14.11 From and after the occurrence of an event giving rise to a transaction of purchase and sale to which this Article applies until the Time of Closing, the Shareholders shall not do, nor cause, nor permit to be done anything except that which is in the ordinary course of business of the Corporation or any Subsidiary of the Corporation. Further, the parties hereto covenant and agree that from and after the occurrence of an event giving rise to a transaction of purchase and sale to which this Article applies, they shall do all things necessary or desirable to cause the transaction of purchase and sale to be completed as soon as possible.

Article 15 — Guarantee

15.1 Each Principal hereby unconditionally guarantees that the Shareholder of which he is the Principal will duly and punctually observe and perform all of the covenants and obligations on its part to be observed and

¶1000

performed pursuant to the provisions of this agreement or pursuant to any instrument or agreement delivered pursuant to or contemplated by this agreement and hereby undertakes and agrees to indemnify and save harmless the other Shareholders and Principals from and against all liability, harm, loss, costs, charges, damages and expenses of any nature whatsoever (including legal fees on a solicitor and client basis) occasioned by any act or default of the Shareholder of which he is the Principal contrary to such covenants and obligations or which may be incurred, suffered or sustained by reason of any failure to observe and perform all or any of such covenants and obligations.

15.2 The Principal of the Surviving Shareholder (as that term is defined in Article 11) hereby unconditionally guarantees that the Corporation will duly and punctually observe and perform all of the covenants and obligations on its part to be observed and performed pursuant to the provisions of Article 11 and Article 14 or pursuant to any instrument or agreement delivered pursuant to or contemplated by such provisions and hereby undertakes and agrees to indemnify and save harmless the Vendor (as that term is defined in Article 11) from and against all liability, harm, loss, costs, charges, damages and expenses of any nature whatsoever (including legal fees on a solicitor and client basis) occasioned by any act or default of the Corporation contrary to such covenants and obligations or which may be incurred, suffered or sustained by reason of any failure to observe and perform all or any such covenants and obligations.

15.3 Any guarantee provided for under this Article 15 shall be continuing, unconditional and irrevocable and a fresh cause of action shall be deemed to arise in respect of each such default. Without limiting the generality of the foregoing, the obligations of each Principal hereunder shall not be released, discharged, impaired or in any way affected by any extensions of time, indulgences or modifications granted by any party in favour of another, to enforce any of the terms of provisions of this agreement or by the bankruptcy, insolvency, dissolution, amalgamation, winding-up or reorganization of the Corporation, or the Shareholder of which he is the Principal or by any other act or proceeding in relation to the Corporation, the Shareholder of which he is the Principal or this agreement whereby the Principal might otherwise be released or exonerated, and each Principal hereby waives any right to require the Shareholders and Principals to exercise or exhaust any action or recourse against any other party before requiring performance by such Principal pursuant to this guarantee.

Article 16 — Restrictive Covenants

16.1 (a) Each Shareholder and each Principal shall not, while it or any member of its Immediate Family (collectively, the "**Departing Shareholder**") is a shareholder of the Corporation and for a period of 12 months thereafter, directly or indirectly, either individually or in partnership or in conjunction in any way with any person or persons, whether as principal, agent, consultant, shareholder, guarantor, creditor or in any other manner whatsoever:

(i) solicit, interfere with or endeavour to entice away from the Corporation or its Affiliates or Subsidiaries, or accept any business from or the

¶1000

patronage of or render any service to, sell to or contract or attempt to contract with any person, firm or corporation who was a client, customer or supplier of the Corporation, its Affiliates, or Subsidiaries, or a prospective client, customer or supplier of the Corporation, its Affiliates or Subsidiaries with whom the Corporation, its Affiliates or Subsidiaries have or have had any dealing during the 12-month period immediately preceding the date upon which the Departing Shareholder ceases to be a Shareholder of the Corporation (to the extent but only to the extent that such business, patronage, service, or contract is substantially similar to and competitive with the business of the Corporation or the business of any of its Affiliates or Subsidiaries or any additional businesses from time to time carried on by the Corporation or any of its Affiliates or Subsidiaries (collectively, a "**Competitive Business**"));

(ii) offer employment to or endeavour to entice away from the Corporation or its Subsidiaries or Affiliates, any person employed (or retained as a consultant) by the Corporation or its Subsidiaries or Affiliates at the date of such Shareholder ceasing to be a shareholder of the Corporation, or who was so employed or retained at any time during the previous one-year period or interfere in any way with the relationship between any such employee (or consultant) and the Corporation, its Affiliates or Subsidiaries; or

(iii) engage in anywhere in North America, carry on or otherwise be concerned with or have any interest in, or advise, lend money to, guarantee the debts or obligations of, permit his name, or any part thereof, to be used or employed by any person, firm, association, syndicate or corporation engaged in or concerned with or having any interest in a business (in any form) which is a Competitive Business.

(b) The Shareholders and Principals have or will have specific knowledge of the affairs of the Corporation, its Affiliates and Subsidiaries and their business. Therefore, the Shareholders and Principals hereby acknowledge and agree that all covenants, provisions and restrictions contained in this section 16.1 are reasonable and valid in the circumstances of this agreement, and all defences to the strict enforcement thereof by the Corporation (and its Affiliates and Subsidiaries, in respect of which the Corporation is contracting herein as agent) are hereby waived.

16.2 (a) The Shareholders and Principals acknowledge that in the course of being, or being associated with, a Shareholder, the Shareholders and Principals will have access to and will be entrusted with Confidential Information.

(b) The Shareholders and Principals acknowledge and agree that the Confidential Information is the exclusive property of the Corporation and its Affiliates and Subsidiaries. Except as may be required by applicable laws, and except as permitted hereunder, each Shareholder and Principal covenants and agrees that it will not disclose (directly or indirectly) at any time any of the Confidential Information to any person, other than to its directors, officers, employees, agents or professional advisors that have a need to know such information, nor shall the Shareholder or Principal use or exploit (directly or indirectly), such information for any purpose other than for the benefit of the Corporation, nor will it disclose for any purpose other than for the benefit of the Corporation the private affairs of the Corporation and its Affiliates and Subsidiaries or any other information which it may acquire during its tenure as a Shareholder or Principal with respect to the business and affairs of the Corporation and its Affiliates and Subsidiaries.

(c) Notwithstanding the foregoing, a Shareholder or Principal shall be entitled to disclose such Confidential Information if such disclosure is required pursuant to applicable laws or pursuant to a subpoena, order, recommendation or direction issued by a court, arbitrator or any Governmental Authority, provided that the Shareholder or Principal shall first have:

(i) properly notified the Corporation;

(ii) consulted with the Corporation, at the Corporation's sole expense, on the advisability of taking steps to resist such requirements; and

(iii) if the disclosure is required or deemed advisable, co-operated with the Corporation, at the Corporation's sole expense, in an attempt to obtain an order or other assurance that such information will be accorded confidential treatment.

(d) Nothing in this section 16.2 or in section 16.3 shall be construed as limiting or impairing in any way any of the rights of the Corporation, its Affiliates and Subsidiaries whether at law, in equity or otherwise against the Shareholder or Principal with respect to the disclosure, use or exploitation in any manner whatsoever to any person or for any purpose, as the case may be, of any of the Confidential Information.

16.3 The covenants in sections 16.1 and 16.2 are given by the Shareholders and each Principal acknowledging that the Corporation and its Affiliates and Subsidiaries carry on, or will carry on, business initially throughout North America, that it or he will have significant responsibilities in connection with such corporations and their respective businesses and affairs, and that it or he either has or will have specific knowledge of the private affairs and business of the Corporation and its Affiliates and Subsidiaries. Therefore, the parties hereby agree that all restrictions contained in sections 16.1 and 16.2 are reasonable, necessary and fundamental to the protection of the Corporation, its Affiliates and Subsidiaries and their businesses and that a breach by a Shareholder or Principal would result in immediate and irreparable damages to the Corporation that could not adequately be compensated for by monetary award. Accordingly, it is expressly agreed by each Shareholder and its respective Principal, that, in addition to all other remedies available to it, the Corporation shall be entitled to the immediate remedy of an interim, interlocutory and permanent injunction as well as an accounting of all profits arising out of any breach by the Shareholder or the Principal or nominees thereof.

¶1000

16.4 The provisions of this Article 16 shall survive the termination of this agreement.

Article 17 — General Contract Provisions

17.1 All share certificates of the Corporation shall have the following legend endorsed thereon forthwith after the execution of this agreement and from time to time thereafter:

> "The transfer of shares represented by this certificate is subject to a shareholders' agreement."

17.2 All notices, requests, demands or other communications (collectively, "Notices") by the terms hereof required or permitted to be given by one party to any other party, or to any other persons shall be given in writing by personal delivery or by registered mail, postage prepaid, or by facsimile transmission to such other party as follows:

(a) to Principal 1 and Holdco 1 at:

•

(b) to Principal 2 and Holdco 2 at:

•

(c) to Individual at:

•

(d) to the Corporation at:

•

Telecopier Number: •

or at such other address as may be given by such person to the other parties hereto in writing from time to time. If any party bound hereby or any permitted transferee of shares hereunder shall not have given the parties hereto notice setting forth an address for the giving of Notices, the Notice for such person shall be deemed to have been properly given if given in accordance with the terms hereof as if given to the transferor(s) of such shares. All such Notices shall be deemed to have been received when delivered or transmitted, or, if mailed, 48 hours after 12:01 a.m. on the day following the day of the mailing thereof. If any Notice shall have been mailed and if regular mail service shall be interrupted by strikes or other irregularities, such Notice shall be deemed to have been received 48 hours after 12:01 a.m. on the day following the resumption of normal mail service, provided that during the period that regular mail service shall be interrupted all Notices shall be given by personal delivery or by facsimile transmission.

17.3 The parties shall sign such further and other documents, cause such meetings to be held, resolutions passed and by-laws enacted, exercise their vote and influence, do and perform and cause to be done and performed such further and other acts and things as may be necessary or desirable in order to give full effect to this agreement and every part hereof. This agreement may be executed in several counterparts, each of which so executed shall be deemed to

¶1000

be an original and such counterparts together shall be but one and the same instrument. Time shall be of the essence of this agreement and of every part hereof and no extension or variation of this agreement shall operate as a waiver of this provision. This agreement constitutes the entire agreement between the parties with respect to all of the matters herein and its execution has not been induced by, nor do any of the parties rely upon or regard as material, any representations or writings whatever not incorporated herein and made a part hereof and may not be amended or modified in any respect except by written instrument signed by the parties hereto. The Schedules referred to herein are incorporated herein by reference and form part of the agreement. This agreement shall enure to the benefit of and be binding upon the parties and their respective heirs, executors, administrators, successors, legal representatives and permitted assigns.

17.4 Notwithstanding anything to the contrary contained herein, the following provisions shall govern:

(a) If either Principal dies at any time before the Time of Closing of a transaction of purchase and sale pursuant to the provisions of Article 7 or Article 8, the provisions of Article 11 shall apply and with respect to the transaction of purchase and sale not yet completed, the applicable provisions in respect of such transaction of purchase and sale shall be suspended pending completion of the transaction contemplated in Article 11.

(b) At any time following (i) the occurrence of a Sale Event (as that term is defined in Article 7) and until the transaction of purchase and sale pursuant to the provisions of Article 7 is completed or it is clear no such transaction will be completed; or (ii) the death of a Principal, no Shareholder may give a Buy-Sell Notice pursuant to Article 8.

(c) If either Principal becomes a Disabled Party at any time after the giving of a Buy-Sell Notice but before the date (the "**Acceptance Date**") on which an Offeree shall have accepted an offer (the "**Accepted Offer**") contained in the Buy-Sell Notice, then the provisions of Article 7 shall apply and the provisions of Article 8 shall be suspended during the period of disability or until the completion of the transaction of purchase and sale pursuant to the provisions of Article 7. Once revived, the Date of Closing in respect of a transaction of purchase and sale contemplated by the Accepted Offer shall be extended for a period equal to the period of suspension.

17.5 The parties hereto covenant and agree, as soon as reasonably practicable following the date hereof, to execute such further and other documents, instruments, deeds and appointments as are reasonably necessary in order to give effect to the grant of powers of attorney (which powers shall be continuing and shall survive the incapacity of the donor thereof) herein provided, including the powers of attorney set forth in subsection 4.1(c)(ii), section 10.3 and section 14.7 of this Agreement, in accordance with applicable laws.

DATED as of the date first above written.

¶1000

[HOLDCO 1]

Per: _____
•

Witness: _____

[Principal 1]

[HOLDCO 2]

Per: _____
•

Witness: _____

[Principal 2]

Witness: _____

[Individual]

[CORPORATION]

Per: _____
•

Per: _____
•

Per: _____
•

¶1000

SCHEDULE "A"
LIFE INSURANCE

Life Insured	Owner	Amount	Insured and Policy Number

Appendix 2

¶2000

Overview

This Appendix will focus on some of the provisions of federal taxation legislation referred to in chapter 2 that affect corporations.

It is useful to provide a discussion of the distinctions drawn in Canadian taxing legislation between various types of corporations: public and private corporations, Canadian corporations, and Canadian-controlled corporations. Since many Canadian businesses are owned and operated by family members or groups, a discussion of the rules pertaining to the significance of the term "arm's length" in business dealing will be followed by a review of the rules governing related, affiliated and associated persons and corporations under the Act.

¶2005

Classification of Corporations for Tax Purposes

The Act provides interlocking definitions that determine how corporations are treated for income tax purposes. The core definitions take their meaning from the fundamental concepts of residence and control of a corporation, which are both tools used by the CRA when considering the tax consequences of actions undertaken by corporations and their shareholders. The final determination of a corporation's tax status under the Act is the result of layering the various defined terms and concepts. Thus, a "Canadian-controlled private corporation";[1] is defined by reference to several under-

---

[1] See subsections 125(7) and 248(1) for the full definition, which will be considered in more detail later in this Appendix. See also Interpretation Bulletin IT-458R2, Canadian-controlled private corporation, dated May 31, 2000.

lying defined terms: "private corporation;"[2] "Canadian corporation,"[3] which is rooted in a finding of being resident in Canada; and the notion of control.

Since Canada's tax rules apply to individuals, corporations, and trusts that are resident in Canada, we begin with a look at the concept of residence. Under the common law, a corporation is considered to be resident in the jurisdiction where its central management and control take place — in short, the place where the board of directors holds its meeting and makes its decisions.[4]

The statutory test is set out in subsection 250(4) of the Act which provides that a corporation will be resident in Canada — and therefore be a "Canadian corporation" — throughout a taxation year under certain circumstances. Under paragraph 250(4)(*a*), a corporation incorporated in Canada after April 26, 1965 is deemed to be resident irrespective of where its central management and control actually take place. Under paragraph 250(4)(*c*), a corporation incorporated in Canada before April 27, 1965 is deemed to be resident in Canada if it was resident in Canada under the common law rules in any taxation year ending after April 26, 1965 or carried on business in Canada during any taxation year ending after that date. Once a corporation is deemed to be resident in Canada for that taxation year, it will be deemed to be resident in Canada for all subsequent taxation years.

There are two exceptions to the general deeming rules in subsection 250(4). The first exception is found in subsection 250(5), whereby a corporation (which is included in the definition of "person" in 248(1)) is deemed not to be a resident of Canada if the corporation is treated as a resident of another country under the terms of the relevant tax treaty[5] between Canada and that other country. The second exception is found in subsection 250(5.1) and applies when a corporation has been continued under the laws of another taxing jurisdiction outside of Canada. Accordingly, a corporation that was incorporated in Canada and which would otherwise be resident in Canada will cease to be resident if it is continued under the corporate statutes of another country. It must be noted that a corporation that is issued articles of continuance into a Canadian jurisdiction under Canadian corporate rules is deemed to be a Canadian corporation as a result of that continuance.

The Act uses the concept of control in many different instances. For example, control is used to assist in determining whether a corporation is "related," "affiliated" or "associated" with another person or whether a corpo-

---

[2] See subsections 89(1) and 248(1) for the full definition, which will be considered in more detail later in this Appendix.

[3] See subsection 89(1) for the full definition, which will be considered in more detail later in this Appendix.

[4] See the decision of the House of Lords in *De Beers Consolidated Mines Ltd. v. Howe*, [1906] A.C. 455, 95 LT. 221, 13 Mans. 394, 5 Tax Cas at 21 (H.L.), which has been cited with approval by the Canadian courts in *Pete v. Minister of National Revenue* (1990) 91 DTC 204 (T.C.C.), [1991] 1 C.T.C. 2001; *Placrefid Ltd. v. Minister of National Revenue*, 86 DTC 1327 (T.C.C.), [1986] 1 C.T.C. 2449 and *Gurd's Products Co. v. The Queen* (sub nom. R. v. Gurd's Products Co.), 85 DTC 5315 (Fed. C.A), [1985] 2 C.T.C. 85, 60 N.R. 184. Note, it is important that the members of the board of directors are not regarded as mere puppets or nominees of the controlling shareholders. If that occurs, the tax residence of the shareholders may become the tax residence of the corporation.

[5] See subsection 248(1) for a definition of "tax treaty."

¶2005

ration is a Canadian-controlled private corporation. The two approaches to determining control are based on the application of the concepts of *de jure* and *de facto* control to a corporation. The former refers to who has the legal right to elect the board of directors, while the latter refers to the individual or group who, directly or indirectly, may influence the election of the board of directors and the daily management of the corporation.

In essence, *de jure* control is found to exist when an individual shareholder or group of shareholders owns enough shares to be able to elect the majority of the board of directors of the corporation. In a series of cases, beginning with *Buckersfield's Ltd. v. the Minister of National Revenue*[6] and culminating in the decision of the Supreme Court of Canada in *Duha Printers (Western) Ltd. v. The Queen*,[7] *de jure* control has been held to be the Canadian benchmark. It should be noted that some of the leading jurisprudence dealing with control was decided in the context of determining whether a corporation was a Canadian-controlled private corporation. There are one or two decisions made in this context that represent a departure from the strict application of the *de jure* control test largely due to the Canadian tax court's reaction to creative tax planning efforts.[8]

In 1988, subsection 256(5.1) was added to the Act which effectively added a *de facto* control definition applicable to any provision which uses the phrase controlled "directly or indirectly in any manner whatever." Thus, under subsection 256(5.1), whenever a person, who may or may not be a shareholder, has a sufficient degree of influence, whether direct or indirect, over the corporation and its actions, the Act deems that person to be the "controller" of the corporation. Clearly, the application of subsection 256(5.1) is a matter of fact and the result will vary accordingly.

The concept of *de facto* control is relevant for many purposes including determining when corporations are controlled by the same person or group of persons for purposes of the association rules, whether a corporation is controlled by a taxpayer in determining the availability of the five-year capital gains reserve on sales to a corporation,[9] in determining control for purposes of applying the capital loss denial rules on dispositions by a corporation of shares of certain controlled corporations,[10] for purposes of the replacement property

---

[6] (1964) 64 D.T.C. 5301 (Can. Ex. Ct), [1965] 1 Ex. C. R. 299, [1964] C.T.C. 504.

[7] (*Sub nom. Minister of National Revenue v. Duha Printers (Western) Ltd.*) 225 N.R. 241, (sub nom. *Duha Printers (Western) Ltd. v. Canada*) 159 D.L.R. (4th) 457, 98 D.T.C. 6334, [1998] S.C.R. 795, 39 B.L.R.

[8] For example, in *Oakfield Developments (Toronto) Ltd. v. Minister of National Revenue* 71 DTC 5175 (S.C.C.), it was determined that non-residents had control of a Canadian corporation where all of the common shares were held by the non-residents giving the non-residents 50 per cent of the votes while preferred shares the other 50 per cent of the votes and limited rights were owned by a key employee. The Articles of the Corporation provided that the Corporation could be wound-up on the vote of 50 per cent of the shareholders and the bulk of the Corporation's assets would pass to the common shareholders. In these circumstances the Court held that the corporation was controlled by the non-residents.

[9] Subparagraph 40(2)(a)(ii).

[10] Subparagraph 40(2)(b).

¶2005

rules,[11] the application of superficial loss rules and whether a corporation meets the definition of Canadian-controlled private corporation in subsection 125(7), and for certain aspects of the provisions dealing with the capital dividend account in subsections 83(2.2), 83(2.4), 89(1) and 89(1.1).

In Interpretation Bulletin IT-64R4, Corporations: association and control, dated August 14, 2001, the CRA provides a discussion of *de facto* control within the context of the association rules of section 256. Of particular assistance are paragraphs 17 and 19 of IT-64R4, which state as follows:

> 17. *De facto* control consists of all forms, other than *de jure* control, by which a person may exercise control over a corporation. *De facto* control may even exist without the ownership of any shares. It can take many forms, e.g., the ability of a person to change the board of directors or reverse its decisions, to make alternative decisions concerning the actions of the corporation in the short, medium or long term, to directly or indirectly terminate the corporation or its business, or to appropriate its profits and property. A potential influence, even if it is not actually exercised, would be sufficient to result in *de facto* control.
>
> 19. Whether a person or group of persons can be said to have *de facto* control of a corporation, notwithstanding that they do not legally control more than 50 per cent of its voting shares, will depend on each factual situation. The following are some general factors that may be used in determining whether *de facto* control exists:
>
> (a) the percentage of ownership of voting shares (when such ownership is not more than 50 per cent) in relation to the holdings of other shareholders;
>
> (b) ownership of a large debt of a corporation which may become payable on demand (unless exempted by subsection 256(3) or (6)) or a substantial investment in retractable preferred shares;
>
> (c) shareholder agreements including the holding of a casting vote;
>
> (d) commercial or contractual relationships of the corporation — for example, economic dependence on a single supplier or customer;
>
> (e) possession of a unique expertise that is required to operate the business; and
>
> (f) the influence that a family member, who is a shareholder, creditor, supplier, etc., of a corporation, may have over another family member who is a shareholder of the corporation.
>
> Although the degree of influence is always a question of fact, close family ties (between parents and children or between spouses) especially lend themselves to the development of significant influences. Generally, these persons must demonstrate their economic independence and autonomy before escaping presumptions of fact which apply naturally to related persons.

Finally, in 2001, new subsection 256(6.1) was added "for greater certainty" but effectively overruling the tax decision of *Parthenon Investments Ltd. v. The Queen*,[12] providing that a corporation may be controlled simultaneously by

---

[11] Subsection 44(7).

[12] 97 DTC 5343; [1997] 3 C.T.C. 152 (F.C.A.).

persons or groups of more than one level above it in a corporate chain.[13] Subsection 256(6.2) specifies that the rule regarding simultaneous control in subsection 256(6.1) also applies to the concept of *de facto* control in subsection 256(5.1).

The effect of this rule is to ensure that in situations where an operating corporation has a direct 100 per cent parent which is a Canadian corporation but where the Canadian corporation itself is 100 per cent owned by a non-resident, the non-resident will be considered to control the operating company as well as the Canadian corporation. Since one of the controllers will be non-resident, the operating company will not be a Canadian controlled private corporation.

Once a corporation has been found to be resident in Canada under the provisions of subsection 250(1), the next step is to determine if it is a "Canadian corporation" within the meaning of subsections 89(1) and 248(1). A Canadian corporation is a corporation that is resident in Canada and was either incorporated in Canada or resident in Canada throughout the period that began on June 19, 1971 and ends at the time that the corporation's status is determined.

It must then be determined whether the corporation is a private corporation. Under subsection 89(1), a private corporation is defined as being a corporation that is resident in Canada, is not a "public corporation" and is not "controlled" by one or more public corporations. It should be noted that the definition is tied to legal control of the corporation as the phrase "directly or indirectly in any manner whatever" is not included in the definition.

According to subsection 89(1), a "public corporation" is either:

- a corporation that is resident in Canada with shares that are listed on a prescribed stock exchange in Canada;[14] or

- a corporation (other than a prescribed labour-sponsored venture capital corporation) that is resident in Canada at the date in question if, at any time after June 18, 1971 and the date in question, the corporation elected in the prescribed manner to be treated as a public corporation and was designated by the Minister to be a public corporation.[15]

The final level of classification of a corporation for tax purposes lies in determining whether the corporation in question is a "Canadian-controlled

---

[13] Paragraph 256(6.1)(a) specifies that, where a subsidiary would be controlled by its parent if the parent were not itself controlled by any other person or group, the subsidiary is considered to be controlled both by the parent and by the person or group that controls the parent. Paragraph 256(6.1)(b) is a rule of similar effect that applies where the subject corporation would be controlled by a group (the "first-tier group") if no member of the first-tier group were itself controlled by a third party. In that case, the subject corporation is considered to be controlled both by the first-tier group and by any higher tier group which includes, in respect of each member of the first-tier group, either the member or a person or group by whom the member is controlled. If one person controls all members of the first-tier group, that person would constitute a higher tier group.

While the concepts set out in this provision deal directly only with the corporation and persons in the two levels of ownership immediately above it, application of the provisions sequentially from the top of the chain makes it applicable to corporate chains with three or more levels.

[14] See subsection 89(1) definition of "public corporation" at sub-clause (a).

[15] See subsection 89(1) definition of "public corporation" at sub-clause (b).

¶2005

private corporation" (hereafter "CCPC") within the meaning of subsection 125(7):

> "*Canadian-controlled private corporation*" means a private corporation that is a Canadian corporation other than
>
> (a) a corporation controlled, directly or indirectly in any manner whatever, by one or more non-resident persons, by one or more public corporations (other than a prescribed venture capital corporation), by one or more corporations described in paragraph (c), or by any combination of them,
>
> (b) a corporation that would, if each share of the capital stock of a corporation that is owned by a non-resident person, by a public corporation (other than a prescribed venture capital corporation), or by a corporation described in paragraph (c), were owned by a particular person, be controlled by the particular person, or
>
> (c) a corporation a class of the shares of the capital stock of which is listed on a prescribed stock exchange.[16]

Paragraph (b) of the CCPC definition states that the shares held by any number of non-resident persons, one or more public corporations or one or more corporations described in paragraph (c) will be treated as if they were held by a single non-qualified person. This refinement was introduced to preclude the CCPC definition from applying to private corporations resident in Canada where shares are widely held by non-residents and public corporations. Paragraph (c) of the CCPC definition is written to preclude CCPC status for a Canadian-resident private corporation whose shares are traded on a foreign stock exchange.

The key characteristic that distinguishes CCPCs from other private corporations that are also Canadian corporations is that a CCPC is one that is not legally or factually controlled by anyone, whether an individual or a corporation, that generally falls within the public company or non-resident categories set out in the section. The inclusion of the phrase "directly or indirectly in any manner whatever" in paragraph (a) of the CCPC definition requires consideration of the *de facto* control rules contained in subsection 256(5.1).

The definition of a "Canadian-controlled private corporation" is a misnomer since a Canadian corporation with 50 per cent of the votes held by a non-resident or public corporation and the other 50 per cent held by Canadian resident individuals will still be a CCPC even though not controlled by Canadian residents.

A corporation that qualifies as a CCPC is eligible for the small business deduction as set out in subsection 125(1), which serves to reduce the tax that would otherwise be payable on the corporation's income from an "active business"[17] that is carried on primarily in Canada. This can result in a signifi-

---

[16] See Reg. 3200 for a list of prescribed Canadian stock exchanges and Reg. 3201 for a list of prescribed foreign exchanges.

[17] "Active business" is defined in subsection 248(1). It does not include income generated or derived from a specified investment business or a personal service business. For a discussion of these types of business activities, see section 125 and Interpretation Bulletin IT-73R6, The small business deduction, dated March 25, 2002.

cant tax saving for a corporation and tax deferral for its shareholders. The shareholders of a CCPC may also be eligible for the $500,000 capital gains deduction under the provisions of section 110.6, which allows each shareholder to shelter lifetime cumulative capital gains of up to $500,000 on the sale, transfer or other disposition of qualified small business corporation shares. This lifetime exemption may also be available on the disposition of qualified farm property, including an interest in a family farm partnership and shares of a family farm corporation. A discussion of the capital gains exemption under section 110.6 can be found in Chapter 2.

In summary, the classification or characterization of a corporation for income tax purposes may confer significant benefits on the corporation and the shareholders, both while the shares are held and on disposition, whether by way of a lifetime transfer or sale, an estate freeze or corporate reorganization, or deemed disposition of the death of a shareholder. This is especially true if the corporation is a CCPC.

¶2010

Arm's Length, Related Persons, Affiliated Persons and Associated Corporations Rules

As noted, the majority of Canadian businesses that are operated as corporations are owned by people who are related to one another, whether by blood, adoption, marriage or common-law partnership. It is widely assumed that, when family members deal with one another — even in a business context — they do so on a preferential basis. In short, they are presumed to not deal with one another as if they were at arm's length. This notion has been incorporated into the Canadian tax rules.

A clear understanding of the meaning of "arm's length," as set out in subsection 251(1), is therefore crucial as this is an essential element in determining how certain transactions among shareholders and their corporations are treated for tax purposes.[18] The arm's length rules lay out the foundation for the consequential determination of when individuals and corporations are considered to be affiliated[19] or associated.[20] Each category (related, affiliated and associated) determines the nature of the relationship between individuals and corporations for tax purposes. These categories apply to both *inter vivos* and *post-mortem* transfers of shares between corporations and shareholders or their estates.

Related persons, as defined in paragraph 251(2)(*a*), are those individuals who are related to one another by blood, adoption or marriage or common-law partnership. As such, they are automatically considered to deal with one

---

[18] See Interpretation Bulletin IT-419R, Meaning of arm's length, dated August 24, 1995.

[19] See section 251.1.

[20] See section 256.

another at non-arm's length for income tax purposes.[21] Under section 251(1) it is a question of fact whether persons who are not related to one another deal at arm's length, so the insights of the Tax Court of Canada into this issue in *RMM Canadian Enterprises Inc. v. The Queen*[22] are worth noting:

> It is true that a determination whether persons are at arm's length requires that the court make findings of fact, but whether, on the facts, there is in law an arm's length relationship is necessarily a question of law. Even Parliament which, subject to constitutional limitations, is supreme and has the power to deem cows to be chickens, cannot turn a question of law into a question of fact. All that paragraph 251(1)(*b*) means is that in determining whether, as a matter of law, unrelated persons are at arm's length, the factual underpinning of their relationship must be ascertained. The meaning of "arm's length" within the *Income Tax Act* is obviously a question of law.[23]

The Courts have, therefore, developed criteria that should be considered when trying to assess whether a factual non-arm's length relationship exists. Three criteria or tests are commonly used to determine whether the parties to a transaction are dealing at arm's length. They are:

(a) the existence of a common mind which directs the bargaining for both parties to the transaction,

(b) parties to a transaction acting in concert without separate interests, and

(c) "*de facto*" control.

The common mind test emerges from two cases. The Supreme Court of Canada dealt first with the matter in *Minister of National Revenue v. Sheldon's Engineering Ltd.*, 55 DTC 1110, [1955] C.T.C. 174. At pages 1113-14, Locke J. speaking for the Court, said the following:

> Where corporations are controlled directly or indirectly by the same person, whether that person be an individual or a corporation, they are not by virtue of that section deemed to be dealing with each other at arm's length. Apart altogether from the provisions of that section, it could not, in my opinion, be fairly contended that, where depreciable assets were sold by a taxpayer to an entity wholly controlled by him or by a corporation controlled by the taxpayer to another corporation controlled by him, the taxpayer as the controlling shareholder dictating the terms of the bargain, the parties were dealing with each other at arm's length and that subsection 20(2) was inapplicable.

The decision of Cattanach, J. in *Minister of National Revenue v. T.R. Merritt Estate*, 69 DTC 5159 is also helpful. At pages 5165-66 he said:

> In my view, the basic premise on which this analysis is based is that, where the "mind" by which the bargaining is directed on behalf of one party to a contract is the same "mind" that directs the bargaining on behalf of the other party, it cannot be said that the parties were dealing at arm's length. In

---

[21] As noted in Chapter 1 — General Contents of Shareholders' Agreements, the definition of related persons will likely be amended to reflect recent court decisions that held that the federal definition of "marriage" was unconstitutional. See Note 8 in that Chapter for more details.

[22] 97 DTC 302, (T.C.C.). Hereinafter referred to as *RMM Canadian*.

[23] *Ibid* at p. 310.

¶2010

other words where the evidence reveals that the *same* person was "dictating" the "terms of the bargain" on behalf of *both* parties, it cannot be said that the parties were dealing at arm's length.

The acting in concert test illustrates the importance of bargaining between separate parties, each seeking to protect his own independent interest. It is described in the decision of the Exchequer Court in *Swiss Bank Corporation v. Minister of National Revenue* 71 DTC 5235, [1971] C.T.C. 427; aff'd [1972] 72 DTC 6470, C.T.C. 614.[24] At page 5241 Thurlow J. (as he then was) said:

> To this I would add that where several parties — whether natural persons or corporations or a combination of the two — act in concert, and in the same interest, to direct or dictate the conduct of another, in my opinion the "mind" that directs may be that of the combination as a whole acting in concert or that of any of them in carrying out particular parts or functions of what the common object involves. Moreover as I see it no distinction is to be made for this purpose between persons who act for themselves in exercising control over another and those who, however numerous, act through a representative. On the other hand if one of several parties involved in a transaction acts in or represents a different interest from the others the fact that the common purpose may be to so direct the acts of another as to achieve a particular result will not by itself serve to disqualify the transaction as one between parties dealing at arm's length. The *Sheldon's Engineering case* [*supra*], as I see it, is an instance of this.

Finally, it may be noted that the existence of an arm's length relationship is excluded when one of the parties to the transaction under review has *de facto* control of the other. In this regard reference may be made to the decision of the Federal Court of Appeal in *Robson Leather Company Ltd v. Minister of National Revenue*.[25]

In essence, then, the finding of a factual non-arm's length relationship hinges on the nature and scope of the interaction between the parties; whether one individual or entity is, in fact, making or directing the decisions on behalf of both parties in a given transaction; and the degree of control that one party has over the actions of the other. However, it does not automatically follow that every agent-principal relationship or every case where a person has been

---

[24] At issue in *Swiss Bank* was whether interest payments made by a Canadian company were made to an arm's length party. In the case, financing for a Canadian real estate company was provided by a Swiss fund for investment in Canada. Money was raised by issuing certificates, and from 1966 to 1968 the Canadian company paid interest to the certificate holders in Swiss francs, and the Minister assessed for non-resident withholding tax on the interest on the basis that the Swiss certificate holders did not deal at arm's length with the company.

[25] In this decision, the court held that the vendor and purchaser corporations were not dealing with each other at arm's length based on a number of circumstances from which the court concluded that Charles Robson was in *de facto* control of both corporations partly due to the large debt owing by the vendor company to the Robson interests. It was also held that the accountant, who was also the secretary of both the vendor and the purchaser in the transaction, had no separate interest from Mr. Robson and the various transactions and that the latter was the "directing mind" at the material time. Another factor was the opinion that Mr. Robson, although only one of three trustees of the family trust, controlled the trust because of his right to change the trustees. Since the family trust owned the majority of the shares of the purchaser and since Mr. Robson had a controlling interest in the vendor, the purchaser and vendor were viewed as not dealing at arm's length.

retained to perform a specific service for a fee is a non-arm's length relationship.[26]

Under paragraph 251(1)(b), a taxpayer and a trust do not deal at arm's length where the taxpayer is beneficially interested in the trust. The term beneficially interested, defined in subsection 248(25) is extremely widely framed including any person who is named as a beneficiary, a member of a named class of beneficiaries or any person not named or currently included within a class of beneficiaries but who could, by virtue of a power contained within the trust deed, be specifically added or included within an added class of beneficiaries where the trust has acquired property from such a person or a person not dealing at arm's length with such a person.

The deeming rule in paragraph 251(5)(b) also extends to the relationship between the trust and anyone who does not deal with the beneficiary at arm's length.

The cornerstone for determining whether persons are related within the meaning of the Act is subsection 251(2). Related persons are, firstly, those who share a blood relationship, such as parent and child or other descendants and siblings. The extended meaning of the terms "child," "parent," "brother" and "sister," "grandparent," "aunt" or "great aunt" and "uncle" or "great uncle," and "niece" and "nephew" are found in subsection 251(1) with respect to "child" and paragraph 252(2)(a)–(g) and must be considered by shareholders and their advisors when buy-sell structures and their tax implications are examined. It should be noted that uncles and aunts and their nieces or nephews are not related within the meaning of subsection 252(2) but may nevertheless not deal at arm's length as a factual matter.

Next, persons are related to one another by marriage if they are either married to each other or if one person is married to a person who is related by blood to the other.[27] In-law relationships are typically captured by this latter provision. Adoptive relationships arise when a person is the adopted child (in fact or in law) of the other or as the child of a person connected by blood (excepting siblings) to the other.[28] Under subsection 251(4), a "related group" is a group of persons each member of which is related to every other member of the group, while an "unrelated group" means a group of persons that is not a related group.

When subsection 251(2) is applied to the relationship between individuals and corporations, the existence of *de jure* control is at issue. Thus, under subparagraphs 251(2)(b)(i) (iii), a corporation is related to the person who controls it; the person who is a member of a related group that controls it; any person who is related to the individual who controls the corporation; or any person who is related to a person who is a member of the related group that controls the corporation. Similarly, if a person owns shares in two or more

---

[26] See *RMM Canadian*, above at Note 20, at pp. 311.

[27] See paragraph 251(6)(b).

[28] See paragraph 251(6)(c).

separate corporations, that person, in his, her or its capacity as shareholder, is considered to be related to himself, herself or itself.[29]

Finally, corporations can be related to one another as set out in paragraph 251(2)(c) based on the attribution of ownership rules set out in paragraph 251(5)(b). This provision deems a person to be regarded as the owner of shares which he or she has a contractual right to acquire or to cause the corporation to redeem or cancel otherwise than on death, permanent disability or bankruptcy. In addition, where a person has the right to cause a corporation to redeem or cancel shares otherwise than on death, permanent disability or bankruptcy, those shares are deemed to have been acquired by the corporation for the purpose of determining the relationship between the parties. Neither a right of first refusal nor shotgun buy-sell arrangement appear to fall within this rule.

Where two corporations are found to be related to the same corporation, the two corporations are also considered to be related to each other under subsection 251(3).

The category of "affiliated persons" is found in subsection 251.1(1) and was added to the Act when the stoploss rules were reformed under the 1995–1997 technical legislation.

The provisions of section 251.1 must be considered when a share redemption buy-sell agreement is used as the transfer mechanism to move ownership and control of a corporation between shareholders. A key distinction between the "related person" and "affiliated person" rules is that control is defined in subsection 251.1(3) as meaning "controlled, directly or indirectly in any manner whatever," thereby importing the wider *de facto* definition of control in subsection 256(5.1). Further, the affiliated rules are currently limited to individuals and their spouses or common-law partners rather than the far wider group of individuals who may be found to be related within the meaning of section 251. This may or may not be advantageous depending on the circumstances. It should be noted that the 2004 federal budget has proposed to extend the affiliated person rules to trusts.[30]

The final and most complex category is that of associated corporations as contained in subsection 256(1). The concept of association is used to determine whether or not a corporation is required to share the small business

---

[29] See paragraph 251(5)(c).

[30] The March 23, 2004 federal budget proposes to amend the definition of section 251.1 of the Act by providing that for purposes of determining whether a trust is affiliated with another person, the trustee is not regarded as the owner of the property. Instead, a person will be affiliated with the trust if the person is a "majority interest beneficiary" of the trust or would be otherwise affiliated with the majority interest beneficiary of the trust.

Two trusts will be affiliated with each other if (i) a contributor to one trust is affiliated with the contributor to the other trust and (ii) a majority interest beneficiary of one trust is or is affiliated with a majority interest beneficiary of the other trust, a majority interest beneficiary of one trust is affiliated with each member of a majority interest group of beneficiaries of the other trust, or each member of the majority interest group of beneficiaries of each trust is affiliated with at least one member of the majority interest group of beneficiaries of the other trust.

(continued on next page)

deduction with one or more "associated corporations."[31] Two or more corporations will generally be considered associated if one corporation controls the other or if two or more corporations are controlled by the same shareholder or group of shareholders. Both *de facto* and *de jure* control will be relevant in determining control. In addition, corporations will be associated where certain cross ownership tests are met.

Accordingly, two corporations each owned by a husband and a wife may still be regarded as associated if, as a factual matter, they are controlled by, say, the husband.

A corporation will be found to be associated with another corporation under the following circumstances:

- one of the corporations is controlled, directly or indirectly in any manner whatever, by the other;
- both corporations are controlled, directly or indirectly in any manner whatever, by the same person or group of persons;
- each of the corporations is controlled, directly or indirectly in any manner whatever, by a person, and the person who controlled one of the corporations is related to the person who controlled the other and either of those persons (but not both) owned not less than 25 per cent of the issued shares of any one class, other than a "specified class" of each corporation;
- two corporations are associated with each other if one of the corporations is controlled, directly or indirectly in any manner whatever, by a person and that person was related to each member of a group of persons that so controlled the other corporation and the person who alone controlled one of the corporations owned not less than 25 per cent of the issued shares of any class, other than a "specified class," of the other corporation; or
- two corporations are associated with each other if each of the corporations is controlled by a related group and each of the members of one of

---

(continued from previous page)

For these purposes, a contributor will be defined to include a person who has at any time made a loan or transfer of property in any manner whatever to the trusts other than where the person deals at arm's length with the trust and is not immediately after that time a majority interest beneficiary of the trust. Any loan made must carry commercial terms. A majority interest beneficiary of a trust will mean a person whose beneficial interest in the income of the trust at any time together with income interests in the trust of all persons with whom the person is affiliated is greater than 50 per cent of the fair market value of all income interests in the trust at that time or, the fair market value of whose beneficial interest, if any, in the capital of the trust at that time together with the capital interests of all affiliated persons, is greater than 50 per cent of the fair market value of all capital interests in the trust. Finally, where the right of the person under the trust depends on any discretionary rights provided by the trust terms, the power is deemed to have been fully exercised for the purposes of determining that person's interest or rights to receive income or capital under the trust. Accordingly, it would appear that any beneficiary of a fully discretionary trust could be viewed as a majority interest beneficiary by virtue of this rule.

This rule will have significant implications with respect to the application of the stop loss rules in the context of trusts.

[31] See section 125.

the related groups was related to all members of the other and one or more persons who are members of both related groups either alone or together, owned in respect of each corporation, not less than 25 per cent of the issued shares of any class, other than a "specified class."[32]

Further, subsection 256(1.2) contains a number of deeming provisions that ensure that the association rules are not avoided. For example, ownership of shares in the same corporations results in shareholders being found to be a related group of persons for the purposes of associated status under the Act. The CRA has stated that where there are two equal shareholders and the operation of the corporation is not deadlocked, the two shareholders are considered to be a controlling group.[33]

A corporation will be deemed to be controlled by another corporation, a person, or a group of persons if shares worth more than 50 per cent of the fair market value (and regardless of any voting entitlement)[34] of all classes of the corporation's issued and outstanding shares are owned by that other corporation, person or group of persons. Association is also deemed to exist if common shares with a fair market value of more than 50 per cent of the fair market value of all issued and outstanding common shares are owned by the other corporation, person or group of persons (and regardless of whether such common shares have any voting entitlement).[35]

In addition, subsection 256(1.2) contains a number of "look through" provisions that are used to ensure that associated status is deemed to exist. For example, the shares of a corporation that are owned by a holding corporation are deemed to be owned by the shareholder of the holding corporation under paragraph 256(1.2)(*d*) based on the fair market value of the share ownership in the holding company. There are similar "look through" provisions in paragraphs 256(1.2)(*e*) and (*f*) that, respectively, apply to shares of a corporation owned by a partnership or a trust.

Under subsection 256(1.3), shares owned by a minor child are deemed to be owned by a parent for the purpose of association unless it can be reasonably considered that the child manages the business of the corporation without a significant element of control by the parent. When taken in conjunction with the "look through" provisions of paragraph 256(1.2)(*g*), ownership of shares held by a trust for the benefit of minor children will be attributed to their parents. Accordingly, an estate freeze involving the establishment of a trust for minor children (or spouses) will result in the association of two corporations

---

[32] Shares of a specified class are defined in subsection 256(1.1) as being non-voting, non-convertible preference shares which pay a fixed dividend not to exceed a rate prescribed by the Act determined by reference to the fair market value of the shares and which shares may only be redeemed or retracted at an amount equal to the fair market value of such shares together with any declared but unpaid dividends.

[33] See the CRA Income Tax Technical News #7, Control by a Group — 50/50 Arrangement, dated February 21, 1996.

[34] For the purposes of the deeming provisions in paragraph 256(1.2)(*g*) of the Act, the FMV of shares is determined without reference to the voting attributes of the shares.

[35] See paragraph 256(1.2)(*c*).

formerly owned by, say, husband and wife respectively, where the trust acquires common shares in either one of such companies.

When two corporations that are otherwise not associated are each associated with the same corporation, subsection 256(2) provides that associated status applies.

The CRA also has the authority under subsection 256(2.1) to determine that a number of otherwise unassociated corporations exist for the sole purposes of gaining access to the small business deduction and that they are, as a consequence, each associated with one another if one of the main purposes of the separate existence of the corporations in question is to reduce taxes otherwise payable.

In the context of buy-sell agreements, under the related persons and associated corporations rules, a person will be regarded as the owner of shares which he or she has a contractual right to acquire or to cause the corporation to redeem or cancel otherwise than on death, permanent disability or bankruptcy. In addition, where a person has the right to cause a corporation to redeem or cancel shares otherwise than on death, permanent disability or bankruptcy, those shares are deemed to have been acquired by the corporation, with the result that a relationship or association is established between the parties. Neither a right of first refusal nor a shotgun buy-sell arrangement appear to be caught by this rule[36] but the impact on any other companies owned by the shareholders should be considered where the shareholders' agreement provides for a mandatory sale otherwise than by death, bankruptcy or permanent disability (e.g., on retirement or breach of the shareholders' agreement).

---

[36] See the CRA's Technical Interpretation 9214367, in which the CRA confirmed that paragraph 251(5)(b) does not apply to a "right of first refusal" and does not usually apply to a shotgun arrangement.

INDEX

A

	Paragraph
Adjusted cost base	
. life insurance policy	335
Adoption	
. connection	
. . control of corporation by persons	2010
. persons deemed connected	
. . buying-outs	178
. persons deemed connected by	2010
Affiliated persons	
. amalgamations	
. . buying/selling shares	225
. buying/selling shares	178
. stop-loss rule	
. . buying/selling shares	225
. test	2010
. . buying-outs	178
Allowances	
. retiring — see Retiring allowances	
Amalgamations	
. affiliated corporations	
. . buying/selling shares	225
. capital property	
. . bump in cost	225
Anti-avoidance rules	
. dividends deemed to be capital gain	
. . buy-outs	240
. intercorporate dividends deemed to be capital gain	
. . buy-outs	240
Arm's length	
. definition	2010
Associated corporations	
. anti-avoidance	2010
. association deemed	2010

	Paragraph
Associated corporations — continued	
. control by a person or group	
. . buying-outs	178
. . de facto control	2005
. . de jure control test	2005
. . definition	2010
. . third party association	2010
. corporation deemed associated	2010
. de jure control by a person or group	
. . buy-outs	178
. definition	2010
. . buying-outs	178
. ownership of shares	
. . buying-outs	178
. parent deemed to own shares held by minor	2010
. separate existence	
. . anti-avoidance	2010
. shares deemed owned by parent where held by minor	2010
Audit	
. annual requirement	150
Avoidance of tax — see Tax avoidance	

B

Bankruptcy — see Insolvency

Beneficially interested	
. definition	2010
Beneficiaries	
. trust	
. . beneficially interested defined	2010
Blood relationship	
. connection	2010
. . control of corporation by persons	2010
. definition	2010

	Paragraph
Blood relationship — continued	
. persons connected	
. . buying-outs	178
Board of directors — see **Directors**	
Books and records — see also **Documents; Financial statements**	
. audit	150
. inspection by shareholders	150
Butterfly transactions	
. capital gains exemption	
. . exception	210
Buying/selling shares	
. affiliation test	178
. breach of agreement	170
. call right	
. . definition	170
. . price determination	170
. capital gains exemption	178
. capital gains exemption for qualified small business corporation shares	210
. cash value of life insurance policy as funding	180
. closing deliveries	175
. disability	170
. disability insurance as funding	180
. funding alternatives	180
. holding companies as funding	180
. insolvency	170
. . sample clause in agreement	1000
. installment payments	180
. life insurance death benefits as funding	180; 325
. loss of professional certification	170
. mandatory sale event	
. . definition	170
. . price determination	170
. . sample clause in agreement	1000
. matching bid provisions	170
. . sample	1000
. matrimonial property claims	170
. payments based on production or use	180
. place of closing	175
. . sample clause in agreement	1000
. promissory note as mode of payment	175; 315
. put right	
. . definition	170
. . price determination	170
. retirement	170
. right of first refusal	
. . hard vs. soft	170
. . sample clause in agreement	1000

	Paragraph
Buying/selling shares — continued	
. security on deferred obligations	175
. shareholder loans to be settled on closing	175
. shotgun or Russian roulette clauses	170
. sinking fund financing	180; 315
. tag-along or piggyback clauses	170
. tax implications	178
. tax implications	205–265
. . bump in cost on amalgamations	225
. . cancellation or redemption of shares	235-250
. . capital dividend election by CCPC	220
. . capital gains exemption for small business corporation shares	210
. . capital gains reserve on future procccds	215
. . change of control on cancellation of shares by corporation	255
. . consulting fees	260
. . deemed dividends on non-arm's length sale	215
. . intercorporate dividends deemed to be capital gains	240
. . interest deduction on loss of income source	215
. . interest expense deduction for purchaser	225
. . non-arm's length purchaser	215
. . non-arm's length sale	225
. . non-compete payments	260
. . non-resident vendor	265
. . reduction of paid-up capital on non-arm's length sale	215
. . retiring allowances	260
. . roll-overs to spouse, spousal trust, etc.	215
. . sale by holding company	220
. . staggered redemption of shares	250
. . stop-loss rules	225
. termination of employment	170
. time of closing	175
. . sample clause in agreement	1000
. valuation methods	170
. . sample clause in agreement	1000
. whether corporation is related	178
Buy-outs — see **Buy-sell; Buying/selling shares**	
Buy-sell	
. bump in cost on amalgamations	
. . criss-cross insurance	409
. choice of funding based on tax implications	385
. criss-cross insurance	
. . holding company	409

Boa

Index

	Paragraph
Buy-sell — continued	
. deferred sale method	
. . holding company	425
. impact of shareholders' agreement	105
. insurance funded	
. . partnership	375
. *inter vivos*	
. . cash surrender value of life insurance as funding option	325
. . disability insurance as funding option	325
. *inter vivos* vs. *post mortem*	105; 175
. . bank loans to finance	315
. . capital reorganization to fund	315
. . cash on hand financing	315
. . disability buy-out insurance to fund	325
. . earn-out arrangement	315
. . financing outside the corporation	315
. . financing within the corporation	320
. . funding alternatives	310–325
. . holding companies to fund	320
. . installment payment arrangements	315
. . promissory notes to finance	315
. . retained earnings funding arrangement	320
. . sale of assets to finance	315
. . sinking fund to finance	315
. . stage purchase method	315
. interest expense deduction for purchaser	315
. life insurance most cost effective funding option	385
. non-resident shareholders	380
. notice requirement	1000
. *post mortem*	
. . business continuation tool	300–305
. . capital gains reserve on future proceeds	407
. . corporate partnerships	455
. . criss-cross insurance	407–409; 460
. . deferred sale method	415–425
. . funding options	300
. . identical property	407
. . life insurance as funding option	300
. . life insurance death benefits as funding option	325
. . optimum structure	450
. . redemption of shares	435–445
. . types of structures	400–460
. *post mortem* promissory note to defer sale	415
. redemption of shares	
. . attractiveness	460
. . holding company	445
. . individuals	435
. . roll-overs to spouse, spousal trust, etc.	440

	Paragraph
Buy-sell — continued	
. stop-loss rules	
. . redemption of shares	440
. tax planning issues	105
. trustees as parties to shareholders' agreement	125
By-laws	
. conflict with shareholders' agreement	
. . interpretation	145
. unanimous shareholders' agreement	150

C

Calls — see Buying/selling shares
Capital
. paid-up — see Capital, paid-up
Capital, paid-up
. reduction
. . non-arm's length sale of shares ... 215
Capital dividends — see Dividends, capital
Capital gains
. deemed
. . intercorporate dividends ... 240
. exemption
. . buy-outs ... 178
. . cumulative net investment loss deduction ... 210
. . exceptions ... 210
. . qualified farm property ... 2005
. . qualified small business corporation shares ... 210; 2005
. reserves for future proceeds
. . buy-outs ... 215; 315
. . *post mortem* buy-outs ... 407
. sale of shares by holding company
. . buy-outs ... 220
Capital tax
. deferred sale structure for buy-sell ... 415
Carry-along — see Buying/selling shares
Cases
. *Beament*, 70 DTC 6130 (S.C.C.) ... 355
. *Buckersfield's Ltd.*, 64 DTC 5301 (Can.Ex.Ct.) ... 2005
. *Cabezuelo*, 83 DTC 679 (T.C.C.) ... 235
. *Canadian Pacific Ltd.*, 2002 DTC 6742 (F.C.A.) ... 178
. *Duha Printers (Western) Ltd*, 98 DTC 6334 (S.C.C.) ... 2005
. *Emerson*, 88 DTC 6184 (F.C.A.) ... 215
. *Gurd's Products Co.*, 85 DTC 5135 (F.C.A.) ... 2005
. *Ludco*, 2001 DTC 5505 (S.C.C.) ... 225
. *Mastronardi*, 77 DTC 5217 (F.C.A.) ... 355

	Paragraph
Cases — continued	
. *McNichol*, 97 DTC 111 (T.C.C.)	320
. *Oakfield Developments (Toronto) Ltd.*, 71 DTC 5175 (S.C.C.)	2005
. *OSFC Holdings Ltd*, 2001 DTC 5471 (F.C.A.)	178
. *Parthenon Investments Ltd.*, 91 DTC 5343 (F.C.A.)	2005
. *Pete*, 91 DTC 204 (T.C.C.)	2005
. *Placrefid Ltd.*, 88 DTC 1327 (T.C.C.)	2005
. *RMM Canadian Enterprises Inc.*, 97 DTC 302 (T.C.C.)	2010
. *Stewart*, 2002 DTC 6369 (S.C.C.)	225
. *Swiss Bank Corporation*, 71 DTC 5235 (F.C.A.)	2010
. *T R Merritt Estate*, 69 DTC 5159 (F.C.A.)	2010
. *Wood*, 87 DTC 312 (T.C.C.)	210

Cash value — see Life insurance

CCPC — see Private corporations, Canadian-controlled

Certificates
. non-resident selling share
. . buy/sell agreement...................................265
. shares...165

Change of control
. corporations
. . cancellation of shares..............................255

Children
. rollover of interest in life insurance policy.......350
. shareholdings
. . deemed held by parents for associated corporations rules................2010

Collateral — see Guarantees

Common-law partners — see Spouses

Common-law partnership — see Marriage; Matrimonial regime

Conflict
. interpretative clause in shareholders' agreement...145

Consideration
. clause to make agreement enforceable.........135

Consulting fees
. buy-out
. . alternative payment to departing shareholder..260

Control
. acquisition — see Change of control
. change — see Change of control
. common mind test.......................................2010
. de jure
. . test...2005

	Paragraph
Control — continued	
. definition for associated corporations rules	2010
. effective date of acquisition	120
. . sample clause in agreement	1000
. test	
. . buy-outs	178

Controlled corporation
. common mind test.......................................2010

Controlled corporations
. acquisition of control
. . cancellation of shares..............................255
. change of control
. . cancellation of shares..............................255
. control by a person or group
. . definition...2010
. de jure control test......................................2005
. simultaneous control...................................2005

Corporations
. active business test.....................................2005
. affiliation test..2010
. . buying-outs..178
. Canadian
. . definition...2005
. classification for tax purposes....................2005
. controlled — see Controlled corporations
. deemed not resident...................................2005
. deemed resident in Canada......................2005
. individuals related
. . buying-outs..178
. paid-up capital — see Capital, paid-up
. private vs. CCPC..................................2000–2005
. public
. . definition..2005
. public vs. private..................................2000–2005
. related
. . buying-outs..178
. residence test..2005
. small business — see Small business corporations

Criss-cross insurance — see Life insurance

D

Death
. closely-held company.................................370
. deemed disposition
. . valuation of shares where life insurance proceeds...................................170
. deemed disposition of interest in life insurance policy.......................................355
. shareholder spouse.....................................165
. . cash value of life insurance policy...............170

Index

	Paragraph
Death	
. shareholder spouse — continued	
.. right to buy/sell shares	170
. sole shareholder	370
Deductions	
. interest on loan	
.. buy-outs	215; 225
.. buy-sell	315
. investment expenses	
.. capital gains exemption	210
. life insurance premiums used as collateral for loan to buy-sell	360
Definitions	
. adjusted cost base of life insurance policy	335
. affiliated persons	2010
.. buying-outs	178
. arm's length	2010
. associated corporations	2010
.. buying-outs	178
. avoidance transaction	
.. buying/selling shares	178
. beneficially interested	2010
. blood relationship	2010
. call right	170
. Canadian corporation	2005
. Canadian-controlled private corporation (CCPC)	2005
. control (of a corporation) for associated corporations rules	2010
. cumulative net investment loss	
.. capital gains exemption	210
. drag-along right	170
. fair market value	
.. agreement	1000
.. buying/selling shares	170
. index-linked life insurance policy	330
. investment expenses	
.. capital gains exemption	210
. investment income	
.. capital gains exemption	210
. joint life insurance	330
. matching bid provisions	170
.. sample clause in agreement	1000
. multiple lives insurance policy	330
. permanent life insurance policy	330
. private corporation	2005
. public corporation	2005
. put right	170
. related corporations	2010
. related persons	2010
.. connected by blood relationship	2010
. retiring allowance	260

	Paragraph
Definitions — continued	
. tag-along right	170
. tax avoidance transaction	
.. buying/selling shares	178
. term life insurance policy	330
. term-to-100 life insurance policy	330
. universal life insurance policy	330
. whole life insurance policy	330
Directors	
. board composition	150
. fiduciary duties	150
. meetings	150
.. sample clause in agreement	1000
. remuneration	
.. unanimous shareholders' agreement	150
. statutory liabilities	
.. alteration in agreement	150
Disability	
. right to buy/sell shares	170
Disability insurance	
. funding buy-sell method	325
Dividends	
. anti-avoidance rules	
.. deemed capital gains	240
. capital gain strips	240
.. buy-outs	240
. declaration	150
. deemed	
.. cancellation of shares in buy-out	235; 245
.. non-arm's length sale of shares	215
.. non-arm's length sale of shares by non-resident	265
.. non-arm's length sale of shares in buy-out	225
.. redemption of shares in buy-out	235; 245
.. redemption of shares in *post mortem* buy-sell	435–440
.. withholding of tax of non-residents	265
. non-residents	
.. withholding of tax	265
. private corporation's refundable tax	
.. buy-outs	220
. staggered redemption of shares in buy-out	250
. taxable preferred shares	
.. tax on corporations issuing	245
Dividends, capital	
. election by CCPC	
.. buy-outs	220
. life insurance corporations	
.. non-taxable to recipient	335

Div

Dividends, capital — continued
- withholding tax of non-residents 380
- - U.S. Canada tax treaty 380

Dividends, inter-corporate
- anti-avoidance rules
- - buy-outs 240
- *post mortem* buy-sell
- - safe income 409

Divorce — see also Marriage; Matrimonial regime
- matrimonial property claims 165
- - right to buy/sell shares 170

Documents — see also Books and records
- signing authorities 150
- - sample clause in agreement 1000

Drag-along — see Buying/selling shares

E

Elections
- capital dividend by CCPC
- - buy-outs 220
- CCPC to pay capital dividend
- - buy-outs 220
- rollover of shares to corporation 165

Emigration
- deemed disposition of interest in life insurance policy 355

Employees
- remuneration
- - unanimous shareholders' agreement 150
- sole proprietor's death
- - transfer of shares 370

Employment
- shareholders 150
- termination — see also Retiring allowances
- - right to buy/sell shares 170

Exemptions
- capital gains
- - butterfly transactions 210
- - buying/selling shares 178
- - cumulative net investment loss deduction 210
- - qualified farm property 2005
- - qualified small business corporation shares 210; 2005

Expenses
- investment
- - definition for capital gains exemptions 210

F

Fair market value
- buying/selling shares 170
- - definition in agreement 1000

Family trusts
- redemption of shares as *post mortem* buy-sell vehicle 440

Farmers and fishermen
- qualified farm property
- - capital gains exemption 2005

Financial statements — see also Books and records
- annual requirement 150

Financing — see also Loans
- buying/selling shares 180
- *inter vivos* and *post mortem* buy-sell
- - alternatives 310–325
- - capital reorganization 315
- - cash on hand 315
- - disability buy-out insurance 325
- - earn-out arrangements 315
- - holding companies 320
- - installment payment arrangements 315
- - loan from financial institution 315
- - outside the corporation 315
- - promissory note arrangements 315
- - retained earnings arrangement ... 320
- - sale of assets 315
- - sinking fund 315
- - stage purchase method 315
- - within the corporation 320
- *inter vivos* buy-sell
- - cash value of life insurance policy 325
- - disability insurance 325
- loans vs. share subscription 155
- *post mortem* buy-sell
- - alternatives 300
- - life insurance 300
- *post-morterm*
- - life insurance death benefits 325
- sinking fund
- - buying/selling shares 180; 315

Form
- shareholder's agreement 1000

Funding — see Financing; Loans

G

GAAR — see Tax avoidance

General anti-avoidance rule
- application
- - buying/selling shares 178

Index

	Paragraph
General anti-avoidance rule — continued	
. artificial transactions	
. . buying/selling shares	178
Group	
. related	
. . control of corporation	2010
Guarantees	
. loans to corporation	155

H

Holding company
. buy-outs
. . capital gains 220
. *post mortem* buy-outs
. . criss-cross insurance 409
. . deferred sale method 425
. . redemption of shares method 445

Husbands — see Marriage; Matrimonial regime; Spouses

I

Identical properties — see Property, identical

Income
. safe — see Safe income

Income, investment
. definition
. . capital gains exemption 210

Individuals
. affiliation test
. . buying-outs 178
. related
. . connected by blood relationship 2010

Information Circulars
. IC 88-2 .... 178; 225
. IC 89-3 .... 350; 355
. IC 72-17R4 .... 178; 265

Insolvency
. buying/selling shares 170
. . sample clause in agreement 1000

Instruments — see Documents

Insurance — see Disability insurance; Life insurance

Interest
. deduction
. . loss of income source on buy-outs 215
. . purchaser in buy-out 225
. . purchaser in buy-sell 315

Interpretation
. recitals in shareholders' agreement 130
. shareholders' agreement conflict with by-laws 145

Interpretation Bulletins
. IT-64R4 .... 178; 2005
. IT-66R6 .... 220; 409
. IT-73R6 2005
. IT-87R2 .... 335; 345
. IT-123R6 335
. IT-140R3 .... 355; 415
. IT-149R4 409
. IT-221R3 2005
. IT-236R4 .... 215; 315; 407
. IT-243R4 .... 220; 409
. IT-269R3 409
. IT-291R3 .... 46; 250
. IT-305R4 315
. IT-309R2 .... 325; 360
. IT-387R2 .... 225; 407
. IT-405 415
. IT-416R3 305
. IT-419R 178; 2010
. IT-430R3 .... 335; 360
. IT-449 440
. IT-458R2 .... 210; 2005
. IT-462 .... 180; 315
. IT-484R2 .... 210; 215
. IT-489R 180; 320
. IT-491R 178
. IT-498R 215
. IT-511R 408
. IT-533 .... 225; 315

Investment income — see Income, investment

Investments
. cumulative net loss
. . definition 210
. expenses
. . definition for capital gains exemption 210

L

Life insurance
. accrual taxation requirement 345
. adjusted cost base
. . definition 335
. capital dividend account
. . dividends out of non taxable 335
. . mortality gain 335
. cash value as collateral for loan to fund buy-sell 325
. . deductible portion of premium 360
. cash value as valuation of buying/selling share 170
. cash value to fund buy-outs 180; 325
. . sample clause in agreement 1000
. . tax treatment 335

	Paragraph
Life insurance — continued	
. cash value to fund buy-sell	325
. criss-cross	
. . *post mortem* buy-out	407–409; 460
. death	
. . deemed disposition of interest	355
. death benefits to fund buy-outs	180; 325
. deduction of premiums used as collateral for loan to buy-sell	360
. departure from Canada	
. . deemed disposition of interest	355
. disposition of an interest	
. . inclusions	335
. . proceeds determination	335
. . rollover to spouse, etc.	350
. . value	335
. exemption test policy	345
. funding buy-sell tool	300
. index-linked	
. . definition	330
. joint	
. . definition	330
. multiple lives	
. . definition	330
. net cost of pure insurance	
. . determination	335
. permanent	
. . definition	330
. . types	330
. term policy defined	330
. term-to-100	
. . definition	330
. transfer of policies	
. . tax treatment	350
. trust property	
. . 21-year deemed disposition	355
. types	330
. universal	
. . definition	330
. valuation of interest	355
. . planning strategies	350
. whole	
. . definition	330
. . types	330

Loans — see also Financing
. buy-sell financing tool 315
. . sample clause in agreement 1000
. guarantees from shareholders 155
. interest deduction
. . loss of income source on buy-outs 215
. shareholders
. . buy-out closing 175

Loa

	Paragraph
Loans — continued	
. unanimous shareholders' agreement	150
. . sample clause	1000
. vs. share subscription as method of financing	155

Losses
. cumulative net investment
. . definition 210

M

Marriage — see also Matrimonial regime
. connection
. . control of corporation by persons 2010
. persons connected 2010
. . buying-outs 178

Matching bid — see Buying/selling shares

Matrimonial regime — see also Divorce; Marriage
. dissolution on death or divorce 165
. . right to buy/sell shares 170

Meetings
. directors 150
. . sample clause in agreement 1000
. shareholders 150
. . sample clause in agreement 1000

Mergers — see Amalgamations

Minority shareholders
. importance of agreement 105

Minors — see Children

N

Non-compete covenant
. treatment to payor in buy-out 260

Non-residents
. buying/selling shares
. . certificate of compliance 265
. buy-sell
. . tax implications 265
. . tax planning 380
. corporations
. . deemed not resident 2005
. dividends
. . withholding of tax 265
. non-arm's length sale of shares
. . deemed dividend 265
. withholding tax — see also Withholding tax of non-residents
. . capital dividends 380
. . . U.S. Canada tax treaty 380
. . dividends and deemed dividends 265

Index

O

Officers
. appointment by unanimous agreement.......... 150
. remuneration
.. unanimous shareholders' agreement........... 150

P

Partnership
. corporate
.. *post mortem* buy-sell....................... 455
. insurance funded buy-sell................ 375

Pay — see Remuneration

Piggyback — see Buying/selling shares

Private corporations
. definition....................................... 2005
. dividend refund
.. buy-outs....................................... 220
. small business deductions — see Small business deduction
. vs. public corporations................ 2000–2005

Private corporations, Canadian-controlled
. definition................................ 2005; 2005
. election to pay capital dividend
.. buy-outs....................................... 220
. private corporations vs............... 2000–2005
. small business deduction.................... 2005

Property, identical
. *post mortem* buy-sell........................ 407

Provisions — see Reserves

Puts — see Buying/selling shares

R

Records — see Books and records

Related
. buying-out context............................. 178
. definition for control of corporations............. 2010

Related persons
. definition....................................... 2010
.. buying-out context........................... 178

Reserves
. future proceeds of disposition
.. buy-outs................................. 215; 315
.. *post mortem* buy-outs.................... 407
. instalment sales
.. buying/selling shares....................... 180

Residence
. corporations................................... 2005
.. continuation................................ 2005
. deemed
.. corporations................................. 2005

Retirement
. right to buy/sell shares..................... 170

Retiring allowance
. buy-out
.. alternative payment to departing shareholder....................... 260

Retiring allowances
. definition....................................... 260

Rollovers
. interest in life insurance policy to spouse, etc................. 350
. shares to *alter ego* trust
.. buy-outs................................ 215; 440
.. buy-sell funding method................... 315
. shares to joint-partner trust
.. buy-outs....................................... 215
.. buy-sell funding method................... 315
. shares to spousal trust
.. buy-outs....................................... 215
.. buy-sell funding method................... 315
.. *post mortem* buy-outs.................... 407
.. *post mortem* buy-outs via redemption of shares..................... 440
. shares to spouse
.. buy-outs....................................... 215
.. buy-sell funding method................... 315
.. *post mortem* buy-outs.................... 407
.. post-mortem buy-outs via redemption of shares..................... 440
. transfer of shares to corporation..................... 165

S

Safe income
. intercorporate dividends
.. *post mortem* buy-sell..................... 409

Salary — see Remuneration

Securities — see Shares

Security — see Guarantees

Separation — see Divorce; Matrimonial regime

Severance pay — see Retiring allowances

Shareholders
. death
.. cash value of life insurance policy................ 170
.. closely-held company....................... 370
. deemed dividend
.. redemption or cancellation of shares.......... 235; 245
. divorce... 165
. right to buy/sell shares..................... 170
. employment................................... 150
. guarantees of loans to corporation................. 155

	Paragraph
Shareholders — continued	
. inspection of books and records	150
. loans	
. . buy-out closing	175
. meetings	150
. . sample clause in agreement	1000
. non-resident	
. . buy-sell	380
. paid-up capital — see Capital, paid-up	
. pre-emptive rights	
. . unanimous shareholders' agreement	150
. protection	150
. redemption or cancellation of shares	
. . change of control	255
. rollover of shares to corporation	165
. sole	
. . death	370
. spouse's death	165
. . right to buy/sell shares	170
. staggered redemption of shares	
. . buy-out	250
Shareholders' agreement	
. audit	150
. board of directors composition	150
. books and records	150
. . sample clause	1000
. breach	
. . right to buy/sell shares	170
. business description	140
. conflict with by-laws	145
. consideration to ensure enforceability	135
. contents	110–180
. date of acquisition of control	120
. . sample clause in agreement	1000
. *de jure* control acquisition	
. . sample clause in agreement	1000
. *de jure* control acquisition	120
. default rule	105
. directors' statutory liabilities altered	150
. dividend declaration	150
. employment of shareholders	150
. exit clauses	170
. fiduciary duties of directors	150
. financial statements	150
. financing	155
. impact of buy-sell structure	105
. importance for minority shareholders'	105
. interpretative clauses	145
. . sample	1000
. loans	150
. . sample clause	1000
. loans vs. share subscription as method of financing	155

	Paragraph
Shareholders' agreement — continued	
. management of the company	150
. matching bid provisions	170
. . sample	1000
. model	1000
. modification	105
. parties	
. . buy-out provisions	125
. . buy-sell	125
. . choice	125
. . description	125
. . non-shareholders	125
. . spouses	125
. . unanimous vs. ordinary	125
. protection of shareholders	150
. recitals as interpretative tool	130
. salient provisions	105
. sample	1000
. share capital	165
. . changes	165
. share subscription	150
. share subscription vs. loans as method of financing	155
. shareholders' meetings	150
. . sample clause	1000
. signing authorities	150
. . sample clause	1000
. spouses as parties	125
. surplus distribution	160
. tag-along or piggyback clauses	170
. tax planning issues for buy-sell	105
. title mere formality	115
. trustees as parties	
. . buy-sell	125
. unanimous vs. ordinary	115
. . appointment of officers	150
. . by-laws	150
. . dissolution of corporation	150
. . management of company	150
. . parties	125
. . pre-emptive rights	150
. . remuneration of directors, officers and employees	150
. . supermajority approval	150
Shares	
. *alter ego* trust rollover	
. . buy-outs	215
. . buy-sell funding method	315
. amalgamation	
. . bump in cost	225
. authorized share capital	165
. . changes	165

Index

	Paragraph
Shares — continued	
. cancellation	
. . change of control	255
. . deemed dividend to shareholders	235
. certificates	165
. deemed owned by parent where held by minor	2010
. identical — see Property, identical	
. joint partner trust rollover	
. . buy-outs	215
. . buy-sell funding method	315
. non-arm's length sale	
. . deemed dividend	215
. non-arm's length sale in buy-out	
. . deemed dividend	225
. non-resident's	
. . non-arm's length sale, deemed dividend	265
. ownership by associated corporations	
. . buying-outs	178
. redemption	
. . deemed dividend to shareholders	235; 245
. . family trust to avoid stop-loss rule	440
. . post-mortem buy-sell	435–440
. redemption, etc. by corporation	
. . deemed dividend to shareholders	245
. small business corporations	
. . impact of buy-outs on capital gains exemption	210
. spousal rollover	
. . buy-outs	215
. . buy-sell funding method	315
. . post-mortem buy-outs via redemption of shares	440
. spousal trust rollover	
. . buy-outs	215
. . buy-sell funding method	315
. . post-mortem buy-outs via redemption of shares	440
. staggered redemption by corporation	
. . buy-out shareholders	250
. subscription	150
. . vs. loans as method of financing	155
. taxable preferred	
. . tax on corporations issuing dividends	245
. transfer	
. . key employees	370
. . will	370
. transfers	165
. . restrictions in agreement	1000
. valuation	
. . agreed-to value	170
. . book value	170
. . cash value of life insurance policy	170

	Paragraph
Shares	
. valuation — continued	
. . fair market value	170
. . formula-based approach	170
. . independent appraisal	170
. . sample clause in agreement	1000
Small business corporations	
. capital gains exemption	
. . active business test	210
. . 50% fair market value test	210
. shares of qualified	
. . capital gains exemption	2005
. . impact of buy-outs on capital gains exemption	210
Small business deduction	
. tax rate reduction	2005
Sole proprietor	
. death	
. . tax planning	370
Spouses — see also Divorce; Matrimonial regime	
. division of assets on death or divorce	165
. . right to buy/sell shares	170
. parties to shareholders' agreement	125
. persons deemed connected	2010
. rollover of interest in life insurance policy	350
. rollover of shares	
. . buy-outs	215
. . *post mortem* buy-outs	407
. . *post mortem* buy-outs via redemption of shares	440
Supermajority approval	
. unanimous shareholders' agreement	150
Surplus	
. priority of distribution	160

T

Tag-along — see Buying/selling shares

Tax avoidance
. avoidance transaction
. . buying/selling shares ... 178
. *bona fide* purpose
. . buying/selling shares ... 178
. definition
. . buying/selling shares ... 178
. GAAR application
. . buying/selling shares ... 178
. general anti-avoidance rule
. . buying/selling shares ... 178
. object and spirit test
. . buying/selling shares ... 178
. 2000-2002 case law ... 178

	Paragraph
Transfers	
. shares	165
. . restrictions in agreement	1000
. tax-free — see Rollovers	
Trustees	
. buy-sell	
. . parties to shareholders' agreement	125
Trusts	
. beneficiaries	
. . beneficially interested defined	2010
. family — see Family trusts	
. spousal — see Spouses	

U

	Paragraph
U.S. Canada tax treaty	
. direct intercorporate dividends	380

V

	Paragraph
Valuation	
. shares — see Shares	
Value — see Consideration; Fair market value	

W

Wages — see Remuneration

	Paragraph
Withholding tax of non-residents	
. capital dividends	380
. . U.S. Canada tax treaty	380
. dividends and deemed dividends	265

Wives — see Marriage; Matrimonial regime; Spouses